Programming Complex Systems 9

Edited by
Fevzi Belli and Hinrich E. G. Bonin

Alfried Pollmann

Logic/Object-Oriented Concurrent Robot Programming and Performance Aspects

Walter de Gruyter
Berlin · New York 1997

Dr.-Ing. Alfried Pollmann, Department of Electrical and Electronics Engineering, University of Paderborn, Germany

∞ Printed on acid-free paper which falls within the guidelines of the ANSI to ensure permanence and durability.

Library of Congress Cataloging-in-Publication Data

Pollmann, Alfried.
Logic/object-oriented concurrent robot programming and performance aspects / Alfried Pollmann.
(Programming complex systems ; 9)
Includes bibliographical references and index.
ISBN 3-11-015072-7 (cl.)
1. Robots–Programming. 2. Logic programming. 3. Object-oriented programming (Computer science)
I. Title. II. Series.
TJ211.45.P64 1996
670.42'72–dc20 96-31349
CIP

Die Deutsche Bibliothek – CIP-Einheitsaufnahme

Pollmann, Alfried:
Logic/object-oriented concurrent robot programming and performance aspects / Alfried Pollmann. – Berlin ; New York : de Gruyter, 1997
(Programming complex systems ; 9)
ISBN 3-11-015072-7
NE: Programmierung komplexer Systeme

Printing: WB-Druck, Rieden am Forggensee. – Binding: Mikolai GmbH, Berlin. – Cover Design: Johannes Rother, Berlin. – Printed in Germany

Friendship is unnecessary, like philosophy, like art, ... It has no survival value; rather it is one of those things that give value to survival.

Antoinne de Saint-Exupéry (1900-1944)

To all my friends
in Ireland, Freiburg, Trier, Neuenbeken,
and of the Globetrotter in Paderborn

Editorial Notes

After a period of rapid development in robotics, especially in techniques for industrial robots during the last decades, today the robot technique is settled to conventional development. There are known methods and tools for robot programming, simulation, control, and application. But development never stops, new techniques in robotics will come up by an interdisciplinary research and development. Concepts, tools, and methods of computer science, mathematics, or control theory are applied to the special conditions of robots. Their combination with robotics will improve and modernize industrial robot systems. The greater part of the present-day development takes place in the areas of robot programming, simulation, and control.

The work presented by Dr. Pollmann gives an important contribution to the development of modern robot control and programming tools. It is an example of the integration of concepts and methods into robotics, which are developed in computer science. They become more and more important in industrial applications, because only the use of powerful and sophisticated tools and procedures can help to increase the productivity.

The work is based on a systematic analysis of conventional robot programming methods and control. It enlarges the possibilities and introduces new capabilities by including the object-oriented programming method and a concept of concurrency. The work describes the theoretic foundation including such features like message passing, task scheduling and the description of robot control and environment. It gives a concept for the implementation of an advanced robot planning and programming tool. The content is clearly structured and gives a ground work to advanced robotics, which is needed for the implicit programming of industrial robots.

Christian Blume

Fachhochschule Köln, August 1996

Preface

Do it automatically. These days, this precept goes far beyond manufacturing machines and stored-program controller. Integrated in production environments, industrial robots with different construction and degrees of freedom extend the capabilities of automatization systems in manufacturing and assembly processes supplanting human work more and more in dangerous and precision tasks. Moreover, powerful and flexible robot programming methodologies support efficiently problem solving of these increasingly complex current and future robot tasks.

Bridging the gap between the conventional and the logic programming world by object-orientation and Prolog, the translation of robot tasks to elemental robot activations is further driven by advantages of enhanced programmability, support of concurrent processing and task allocation, as well as the simple integrability of additional (robot) hardware and extentability of the overall programming environment by the inheritance mechanism.

Declarative programming by Prolog incorporates a powerful and flexible technique to design planning systems facilitating the programming only by defining what to do rather than how to do.

Object-orientation and the object-oriented program design are having an impact on software development similar to the effect the microprocessor had on computing. Object-oriented data base design, technical and scientific computer applications as well as test and software development tools based on this paradigm are coming into vogue, and even software for learning and playing are commonplace. Furthermore, object-oriented concurrency supports processing of time-critical applications ensuring real-time criteria through job distribution and multi-processor networks. Especially considering robotics, all these advantages and characteristics are the most promising guarantor for materializing the requirements current and future robot jobs are associated with.

This book is for a technical audience that wants to understand and to deploy robotics with a special-purpose programming philosophy. Electrical engineers and scientists with robotics background are introduced into real-time robotics in order to learn how to design programs programs applying message passing without violating fundamental robot laws. Readers who have been deterred from robotics will find here an introduction to existing robot programming languages and an overview about programming environments actually being under development including a robot programming classification as well as a programming approach, with many illustrations based on familiar examples.

This work is based on my PhD thesis at the University of Paderborn. It introduces general techniques of robot programming and a new concept for concurrent robot control. Applying a hybrid object-oriented programming environment various concurrency models providing different granularity of parallelism support the robot task design and enable their efficient execution. The basic idea, the integration of concurrency into robot control, can also be furtherly developed and adopted into other robot programming systems. This work is useful for all who are concerned with robot programming and/or object-oriented applications for multi-processor systems. May it help to capture a better understanding of utilizing concurrency with a special emphasis on robot programming.

My view of concurrent robot programming including the performance assessment has been greatly enriched by discussions with many people over the last years. In this regard, I would particularly like to give my thanks to Professor Fevzi Belli for his support with my research work at the University of Paderborn, the editors Professor Belli and Hinrich Bonin for their promotion to publish this work, and Professor Erik Maehle and Professor Christian Blume for their valuable hints and remarks. I also thank two men who have influenced me in more ways than they know: Alireza Azem and Oliver Jack. Through the years of our common work at the university colleagues were to friends, and I'm not sure whether this work would ever be finished without their additional motivation in hard times. My special thanks are due to my colleagues Radu Crişan and Stefan Schurig for providing particular encouragement and a sympathetic ear on numerous occasions.

While any book is ultimatively the author's responsibility, this book also benefited greatly from a succession of technical support at all stages of its development; particularly from my students including Jens Nentwich, Andreas Krawinkel, Claudia Czirr, Martin Kaufmann, Than Binh Huynh, and Jörg Fitzke for their help and their hints to improve my work. Special credit is due to Jürgen Wille spending a lots of hours assisting special parts of my research through comments and suggestions.

I'd like to thank my parents Willi and Resi in particular for their patience, help and encouragement without this work could not be created and for their endless love and support all along my life.

Last, it has become a cliché in textbooks and monographs; after thanking one and all for their assistance, the author gallantly accepts blame for all remaining errors in the text. This is usually done with with no small amount of pomp and circumstance — a ritualistic incantation to ward off the evil spirits of error. I will forgo this exercise and close these acknowledgements by paraphrasing a piece of graffiti that I read anywhere at a wall: To err is human. To really foul up, use a computer. Unfortunately, in writing this book, I find myself subject to both of these sources of error, and no doubt many mistakes remain. I can only take comfort in knowing that error is the one inevitable side effect of our human past and the probable destiny of our artificially intelligent future.

Alfried Pollmann

Paderborn, August 1996

Contents

IV Appendices 201

List of Figures

List of Tables

Notations and Symbols

Object-Orientation

$\mathcal{L}$	object-oriented language based on logic programming
$\mathcal{O}$	object representation of $\mathcal{L}$
o_i	an element (object) of $\mathcal{O}$
$\mathcal{I}$	set of robot instructions
$\mathcal{H}$	set of all classes in a class hierarchy
$\mathcal{H}_{\mathcal{F}}$	set of fatherclasses
$h_{\mathcal{F},i}$	a fatherclass of $\mathcal{H}_{\mathcal{F}}$
$\mathcal{H}_S$	set of subclasses
$\mathcal{V}$	set of instance variables
v_i	an element of the set $\mathcal{V}$
$\mathcal{C}$	set of classes
c_i	element of $\mathcal{C}$
$\mathcal{M}$	set of methods
m_i	a method of the set $\mathcal{M}$
$\mathcal{M}_{n_i}$	the set of methods of the message n_i
$\mathcal{O}^{\mathcal{N}}$	set of object names
$\mathcal{O}^{\mathcal{A}}$	set of object names realized as a Prolog atom
$\mathcal{O}^{\mathcal{V}}$	set of object names realized as a Prolog variable
$\tilde{o}_i$	element of $\mathcal{O}^{\mathcal{N}}$

Concurrency

$\mathcal{N}$	set of messages
n_i	a message of $\mathcal{N}$
$\mathcal{K}$	set of channels
k_i	a channel of $\mathcal{K}$
Θ	set of message passing operators
:<>:	SEQ-operator
:<>	PAR_I-operator
:<<:	PAR_{II}-operator
:<<	PAR_{III}-operator
$\mathcal{R}$	set of results
r_i	a result of $\mathcal{R}$
Π	set of ports
π	an element (port) of Π
$A_\psi(\ldots)$	receiver determination function
$D_\sigma(\ldots)$	distribution process
o_s	sender object
o_e	receiver object
O_s	sender object presented as process
O_e	receiver object presented as process
$\sqsubset$	instantiation symbol (is an instance of)
$a \not\sqsubset b$	a is not an instance of b
$a \rightarrow P$	a then p
$(a \rightarrow P \mid b \rightarrow Q)$	a then P choice b then Q (provided $a \neq b$)

$P \| Q$	P in parallel with Q
$k.v$	communication of value v on channel k

Set Theory

$[\,]$	the empty list
ϕ	the empty set
$A \cap B$	A intersect B
$A \cup B$	A union B
$A \subseteq B$	A is contained in B
$\|\mathcal{M}\|$	cardinality of the set $\mathcal{M}$
$\bigcap_{n \geq 0} A_n$	intersection of family of sets
$\bigcup_{n \geq 0} A_n$	union of family of sets
$a \backslash b$	a without b
$\forall a \in A$	for all a in set A
$\exists a \in A$	there exists an a in set A

Sensing

$\mathcal{B}$	the set of barcodes
b_i	a barcode of $\mathcal{B}$
$\mathcal{F}$	union set of all error codes
$\mathcal{F}_S$	the set of system error codes
$f_{S i}$	a system error code of $\mathcal{F}_S$
$\mathcal{F}_{\mathcal{R}}$	the set of read error codes
$f_{\mathcal{R} i}$	a read error code of $\mathcal{F}_{\mathcal{R}}$
$\mathcal{E}_S$	the set of system error messages

$e_{\mathcal{S}i}$	a system error message of $\mathcal{E}_{\mathcal{S}}$
$\mathcal{E}_{\mathcal{R}}$	the set of read error messages
$e_{\mathcal{R}i}$	a read error message of $\mathcal{E}_{\mathcal{R}}$

Robot

W	working cell of a robot
Ω^W	overall robot operational space of a working cell W
Ω_{ρ_i}	local operational space of robot ρ_i
$\omega_{\rho_i,j}$	position j within the local operational space Ω_{ρ_i}
Ω^κ	a critical section
Ł_{Ω^κ}	list used to manage the queries of a critical section
Φ_w	rotation angle about the z-axis of a robot
Φ_s	shoulder rotation angle of a robot
Φ_e	elbow rotation angle of a robot
Φ_p	rotation angle of the wrist pitch of a robot
(r_e, z_e)	tool center point TCP
O	coordinate basic origin
O_n	transformed coordinate basic origin

Scheduling

$\mathcal{A}$	set of scheduling constraints
$\mathcal{P}$	set of processors (transputers)
p_i	a processor (transputer) of $\mathcal{P}$
$\langle\alpha\|\beta\|\gamma\rangle$	specification of a scheduling problem
α	processor (transputer) characteristics

β	robot task characteristics
γ	optimality criterion (e.g. schedule length minimization)
$\mathcal{T}$	set of robot tasks
t_i	a task t_i of $\mathcal{T}$
$\mathcal{T}_\mathcal{A}$	the task-dependent subset of $\mathcal{T}$
$t_a \prec_\mathcal{A} t_b$	task t_b is task-dependent from task t_a
$\mathcal{T}_\mathcal{D}$	the data-dependent subset of $\mathcal{T}$
$t_a \prec_\mathcal{D} t_b$	task t_b is data-dependent from task t_a
$\tilde{\mathcal{T}}$	the independent subset of $\mathcal{T}$
$t_a \not\prec_{\mathcal{A},\mathcal{D}} t_b$	task t_b is independent from task t_a
$t' \prec t''$	t' is the predecessor of t'' and t'' is the successor of t'
$[\![p_i]\!]$	load of processor p_i
$t_k \leadsto p_j$	task t_k is assigned to transputer p_j
L	list symbol
L_{n_i}	message n_i in terms of a list
$\mathrm{L}_\mathcal{D}$	a list of data-dependent tasks
L_σ	list of robot tasks to be scheduled
L_{Si}	a sublist of $\mathrm{L}_\mathcal{D}$
τ_i	processing time of task t_i
τ_{idle}	idle time of a processor
τ_σ	schedule length
$\tau_{\sigma,min}$	minimized schedule length
$\tau_{\sigma_{det}}$	determination time of a schedule
t_i/n	robot tasks t_i using n time units to be processed
$A(P_S)$	accuracy of the heuristic scheduling algorithm

P_S	scheduling problem
$S(P_S)$	scheduling result
$O_{PT}(P_S)$	optimal value of the scheduling problem P_S

Performance

S_p	speedup
τ_1	execution time of robot tasks using a single transputer
τ_n	execution time of robot tasks using n transputer
E	efficiency
T_{post}	translation time used by the postprocessor
T_{mech}	time needed by the robot mechanics to perform the tasks
T_{robot}	execution time used by a robot system to perform a task
$T_{CS-Prolog}$	robot task translation time of the CS-Prolog system
$T_{PROLoop}$	translation time of the PROLoop of a robot task
T_{trans}	total translation time of object-oriented robot tasks
T_{com}	communication time
T_{ex}	total execution time of an object-oriented concurrent robot task
E_f	execution factor
T_l	data transfer startup time
T_c	average transfer time
APF	average parallelism factor
$C(P_S)$	communication cost of a schedule P_S
$\underline{V}$	volume matrix
$\underline{A}$	assignment matrix

$\underline{D}$	distance matrix
$v_{i,k}$	volume of data sent from object o_i to object o_k
$d_{i,j}$	communication cost between processor p_i and processor p_j
$a_{l,k}$	binary assignment values

Miscellaneous

$\mathcal{G}$	a directed graph
$E_{\mathcal{G}}$	the set of edges of a graph
$Z_{\mathcal{G}}$	the set of vertices of a graph
$a \wedge b$	a and b (logical AND)
$a \vee b$	a or b (logical OR)
$\mathbb{N}$	the set of all positive integers
$\mathbb{Z}_0^+$	the set of all non-negative integers
$F_{\mathcal{G}}$	a partial order over the set $Z_{\mathcal{G}}$
$O(f(n))$	order of $f(n)$
$\min_{k \in \mathbb{N}}\{a_1, a_2, \ldots, a_k\}$	minimum of the set $\{a_1, a_2, \ldots, a_k\}$
#	number of elements

Part I

General Concepts

Chapter 1
Introduction

1.1 Programming Aspects for Robot Controlling

Current control tasks of industrial robots require flexible and powerful programming methodologies. For the execution of these tasks, several robots and other involved manufacturing devices have to cooperate with each other within the manufacturing environment, i.e. they have to be coordinated in time and space. Apart from this overhead for the coordination, complex multi-robot control and application tasks often demand comprehensive computations which cause long execution times. To meet real-time conditions, the robot programming system should provide concurrent, decentralized (distributed) processing.

Commercially available robot programming languages such as SRL [20], PASRO [20], SIGLA [20], RAIL [20], VAL[20], or HELP [20] are used for several years to program industrial robots deploying explicit programming techniques, based on imperative high-level languages. Only a few of these languages support concurrency and none of them allow declarative programming, providing techniques to implicitly derive suitable robot commands from the specified task descriptions (e.g. for planning tasks). Moreover, existing robot programming languages hardly support the programming of different robot types or the programming of additional devices in the robot cell (e.g. complex sensors) in a uniform environment. Thus, each device has to be programmed by its own host usually applying different programming languages and/or programming techniques (e.g. interactive, teach-in). This local control requires greater hardware costs and also greater programming effort. To remove this lack, a global control of the manufacturing cell should be aimed also considering the above mentioned decentralization.

This book describes a robot programming approach, adopting the notation of object-orientation in logic programming to efficiently exploit the merits of concurrent, implicit and distributed programming in a global way, especially deploying the emerging transputer technology. For this purpose, the introduced approach adopts the object-orientation in logic programming and demonstrates that the concepts of object-orientation inherently materialize concurrency and distributedness. To support both features, relevant message passing modes are specified by means of Hoare's formalism of CSP (Communicating Sequential Processes) [57] and are implemented into the experimental PROLoop environment (PROLoop as the acronym of "Prolog-based language for object-oriented programming") [120, 34]. The message passing modes realize concurrency between objects, taking also concurrency of methods into account.

The concurrency mechanisms of the robot programming environment facilitate the global control of the robot in its working environment called the working cell or manufacturing cell. The feature of object-orientation to realize decentralization through distributed objects presents an appropriate basis for a uniform control of the manufacturing cell. Moreover, the integration of distinct postprocessors by defining additional classes and the concurrent activation of their instances support the global cell control to a great extent. The coordination of the involved machines (e.g. assembly lines, CNC machines, etc.) within the working cell is realized through the semaphore technique ensuring collision-free operations and through the evaluation of sensor data.

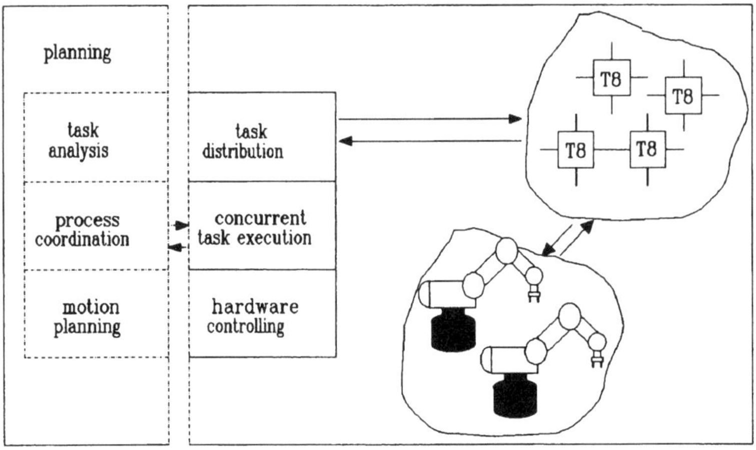

Figure 1.1: Topic of the introduced system

The introduced approach provides implicit robot programming using logic programming in Prolog. The benefits of logic programming stem from its declarativeness enabling precise mathematical characterizations of relationships between robot programs and their results. However, the topic of this book concentrates on concurrent processing for robot controlling. Planning problems for robot control that are often solved through implicit programming is the subject of other works involved on the robot programming project [122]. Figure 1.1 represents a scheme of all involved works marking the problems that are not solved by this approach by dotted lines.

In order to efficiently utilize the merits of concurrency, the introduced robot programming environment additionally supplies several scheduling techniques to map robot tasks to available transputers.

The robot task scheduler maps the robot tasks by means of scheduling constraints presented as heuristics in Prolog. The power of heuristics may significantly reduce the combinatorical complexity of the scheduling problem caused through the proliferation of alternatives. Further, the PROLoop strategy is guided by the fact that a heuristic scheduling algorithm alone cannot guarantee an optimal schedule for each scheduling problem. The robot programming system therefore also enables user-oriented scheduling allowing the programmer to define the granularity and the tasks and the system allocates the tasks to the processors.

An important criterion of the concurrent robot programs is connected with performance, i.e., a vital requirement PROLoop has to fulfill is that the costs of concurrent system management will not exceed a critical amount to prevent the real-time execution of time-critical robot applications. In order to evaluate the performance potential of the approach, typical multi-robot control tasks are implemented in an experimental environment, both in conventional programming languages and in PROLoop to compare the different programming paradigms. Empirical studies analyze the run time behaviour varying different criteria which are assumed to influence the performance level.

1.2 Parallelism and Concurrency

The notions concurrency and parallelism are often synonymously used to describe simultaneous processes. Below, a precise specification of both notions is given before these expressions are applied later in this work.

The ISO 2382/III 1976-05-01 standard specifies concurrency to be a processing mode in which two or more operations are performed simultaneously within a given interval of time.

The DIN 44300 standard specifies parallelism to be a processing mode in which operations are performed simultaneously. It is required that all operations are independent from each other.

Because of the characteristic of robot operations being frequently dependent from each other, this book uses the notion concurrency.

1.3 Structure of the Book

In combining theory and practice, the book is a user guide that seeks to follow tradition established by useful handbook and publications of robot experts. The book is organized in three parts followed by an appendix.

Part I of this book introduces general concepts. Chapter 1 surveys principles of concurrent robot programming depicting the difference between concurrency and parallelism. The introduction concludes with a view of the topics of each chapter.

Robot programming is the subject of Chapter 2. Typical robot controlling tasks are described and the features of different robot languages are discussed. A critical review of the languages illustrates their shortcomings according to user requirements on robot programming.

Chapter 3 compares features of object-orientation and logic programming fostering concurrency and explains the interferences between the inheritance mechanism of object-orientation and concurrent processing of logic programming.

Part II introduces the approach to concurrent object-oriented robot programming. First, Chapter 4 describes constructs and syntax for class and method definition in PROLoop, our experimental programming environment. It also deals with different message passing modes enabling concurrent processing between objects and methods. Subsequently, the message passing protocol for synchronous and asynchronous message passing is presented and the distinct message passing operators are specified by means of the CSP notation. The utilization of the operators is demonstrated by examples.

Chapter 5 introduces the class hierarchy of the programming environment presenting the fatherclasses and subclasses for robot and sensor control. Also the software structure and the hardware components of the experimental robot environment will be explained.

Part III discusses performance aspects. An algorithm for task scheduling for concurrent robot control will be introduced and analyzed. Following, some basic definitions and scheduling constraints are specified. The heuristics will be defined that enforces the scheduling algorithm.

Chapter 7 discusses the performance assessment of concurrent robot applications. According to basic principles of performance estimation of robot programming some criteria will be defined which may affect the performance of robot programs. Chapter 7 contains also a brief summary and results of the measurements. Chapter 8 concludes Part III with a summary of the book and outlooks on further problems.

Finally, Part IV consists of several appendices including the concept of the overall programming system, the formal representation of the experimental programming environment as well as a brief overview about CS-Prolog.

Chapter 2
Programming Languages for Robot Controlling

Current applications of industrial robots require flexible and powerful programming methodologies. Hence, the programming language has to provide features to fulfill these demands. The integration of concurrency into a robot programming system is one essential characteristic of a robot programming technique. In the following, these characteristics are introduced and completely discussed. For this purpose, typical robot controlling tasks are introduced and language features are given for their realization. Subsequently, this chapter surveys commercially available robot programming languages and robot languages being under development in industrial and academic environments. The chapter concludes with a review of the advantages and shortcomings of the robot programming languages and an introduction of an alternative approach to robot programming.

2.1 Robot Controlling Tasks

The subsections below survey essential robot capabilities current robot tasks are based on. Further, an overview on future robot applications is given.

2.1.1 Robot Capabilities

In general, robots possess three important capabilities which make them useful in manufacturing operations [101]:

- transport;
- manipulation;
- sensing.

Transport

One of the basic operations performed on a workpiece as it passes through the manufacturing process is material handling or physical displacement. The workpiece is transported from one position to another to be stored, machined, assembled, or packed. In these operations, the physical characteristics of the workpiece remain unchanged [101].

The ability of a robot to grasp, move and release a workpiece supports transport operations. Simple material handling tasks may only require one- or two-dimensional movements. Other parts handling operations may be more complicated and require varying degrees of manipulative capability in addition to transport capability. Examples of these more complex tasks include machine loading and unloading, palletizing, part sorting, and packaging. The requirements are specified for each task in detail below.

Manipulation

In addition to material handling, another basic operation performed on a workpiece is processing. Processing means the transformation of a workpiece from raw material to a finished product and generally requires some type of manipulation. Workpieces are inserted, oriented, or twisted to be in the proper position for machining, assembly, or some other operation [101].

The capability of a robot to manipulate workpieces and tools supports its use for processing applications. Examples include robot-assisted machining, spot and arc welding, and spray painting. More complex operations, such as assembly, also rely on the manipulation abilities of a robot.

Sensing

The capability of a robot to react by means of sensory feedback is also important, particularly in complex applications like assembly and inspection. The sensor data may be returned from different sensor types [77], including proximity switches, force sensors, machine vision systems, etc. Especially, the evaluation of sensor data of vision systems can support complex mobile and stationary robot tasks efficiently.

Available robots provide limited sensing capabilities. This lack is caused through the difficulty of robots to be interfaced with sensors and, to some extent, through the unavailability of suitable low-cost sensing devices. As the complexity of current robot applications increase, control capabilities by use of sensory feedback become more important.

2.1.2 Robot Applications

This section introduces robot applications in consideration of the mentioned robot capabilities containing:

Table 2.1: Required robot capabilities for particular applications [93]

Application	Examples	Transport	Manipulation	Sensing
material handling	parts handling palletizing transporting	•		
machine loading	die cast machines automatic presses NC milling machines lathes	•	•	
spraying	spray painting resin application		•	
welding	spot welding arc welding		•	
machining	drilling grinding routing cutting forming		•	•
assembly	mating parts fastening	•	•	•
inspection	position control tolerance			•

- material handling. Material handling applications [150] include the transport, palletizing and handling of parts;
- machine loading and unloading. Machine loading and unloading [58] is generally considered to be a more complex robot application than simple material handling. Robots can be used to grasp a workpiece from a conveyor belt, lift it to a machine, orient it correctly, and then insert or place it on the machine. After processing, the robot unloads the workpiece and transfers it to another machine or conveyor;
- spraying. In spraying applications [24], the robot manipulates a spray gun which is deployed to paint either a stationary or a moving part. These coatings are applied to a wide variety of parts, containing automotive body panels, appliances, and furniture;

- welding. The largest single robot application presents the spot welding of automotive bodies [124]. Spot welding is normally performed by a point-to-point servo robot, holding a welding gun. Arc welding can also be performed by robots [138];
- machining. In machining applications [93], the robot holds a powered spindle in order to perform drilling, grinding, routing, cutting, or forming on a workpiece;
- assembly. Assembly is the area with the greatest interest today [151, 33, 63]. However, assembly is one of the most complex application for robots including requirements such as planning and coordination of robot operations with other machines and the timed coordination of the assembly process;
- inspection. A small but rapidly growing number of robot applications is connected with inspection [93]. Considering these applications, robots are used in conjunction with sensors, such as vision systems, laser, or ultrasonic detector, to check part locations, identify defects, or recognize parts for sorting.

Survey of Current and Future Applications

Figure 2.1 shows in case of the U.S robot usage that the deployment of industrial robots has been increased dramatically during the last decade, and there

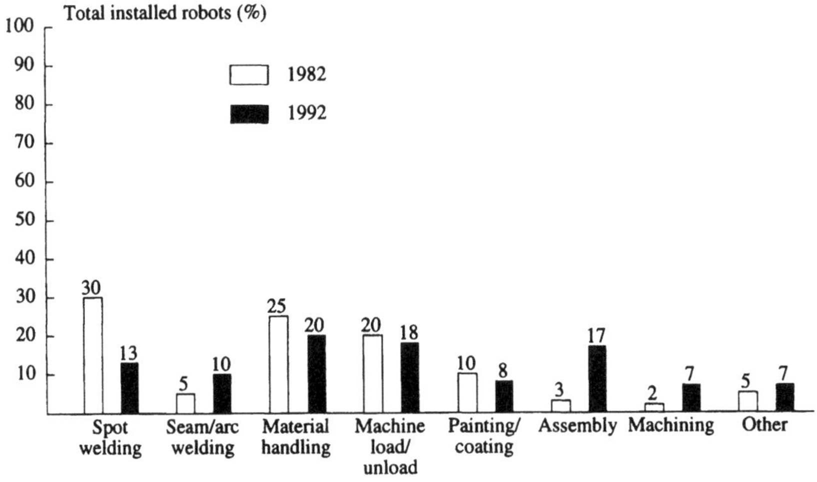

Figure 2.1: View of U.S. robot applications [93]

is almost universal agreement that this process will continue in the next years, due to further development of the robot programming languages. In order to implement complex robot tasks efficiently, a whole range of capabilities and operations are to be materialized. Therefore, current language characteristics are discussed in the following and their usability according to various robot applications is discussed.

Graphic 2.2 illustrates the robot applications in Germany. The amount of these machines increased during three years from 12400 (1986) up to 22395 manipulators in 1989.

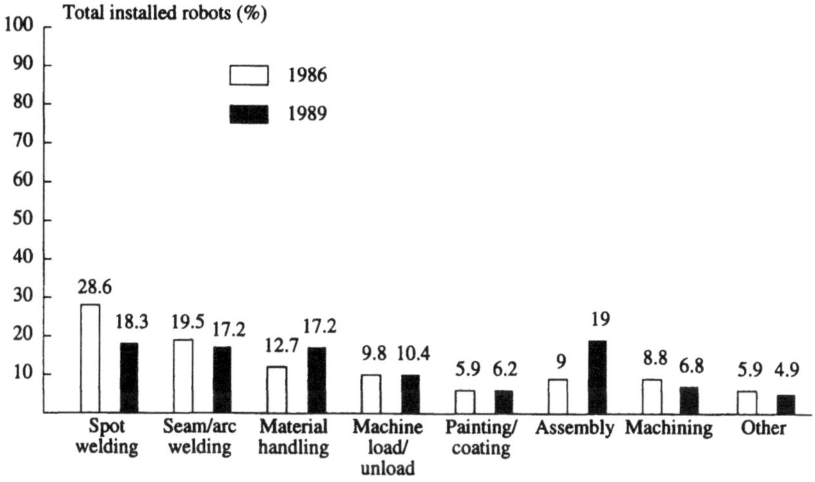

Figure 2.2: Survey of robot use in Germany [102]

2.2 Survey of Robot Programming Languages

This section describes commercial robot programming languages and surveys properties of robot programming systems that are under development.

- **T3**
  The language T3 [94, 22] is a system that uses guided teaching and function buttons to program robot tasks.

- **Anorad**
The Anomatic II Controller developed by the Anorad Corporation [6, 22] provides a numerical control language with programmable mathematical expressions and a self-configuring capability.
- **Emily**
Emily [46, 22] is an early attempt by IBM to develop a higher-level robot language with a reasonable simple processor as an extension to their robot control language ML. Emily was used for the development of later robot languages by IBM.
- **AML**
In the 1970s, IBM introduced a robot language to program their own robots, called AML (A Manufacturing Language) [60, 61]. AML is also a high-level programming language, influenced by PL/1. This language has a few peculiarities not usual in robot programming and not included in any of the languages discussed in this section. AML is formula-oriented, i.e., each instruction produces a value which may be reused. For this purpose, AML commands may be combined with each other in almost any way (orthogonality). Although this provides a flexible programming, it has inherent risks because it admits a vague programming style. AML may also be used interpretatively which is unusual for a language with Pascal-like block structure and strings. The syntax for movement instructions and other commands which are not used for program structuring are kept very simple. The simple version of AML, AML/E (Entry) [62], permits a teach-in by using terminals and a two-dimensional display of the IBM SCARA robot's working space.
- **AL**
AL (Assembly Language) [96, 20] was already derived from the high-level language ALGOL by Stanford University in the 1970s. This version of AL was not usable for industrial applications. Under a technology transfer in the early 1980s a new implementation was undertaken by the University of Karlsruhe. A number of improvements were made and used to program a PUMA 500 robot by Unimation. AL has served for design of numerous high-level robot programming languages in the United States, Europe, and Japan.
- **SRL**
SRL (Structured Robot Language) [20] was designed and implemented at the University of Karlsruhe. SRL is a high-level language based on AL (see above) with Pascal elements.
- **RCL**
Under development at Rensselaer Polytechnic Institute, RCL [133] is a command-oriented motion control language to program a sequence of steps used to accomplish a robot task.

- **RPL**
  RPL is a Fortran-like robot language developed by SRI International [104, 22] and designed to facilitate the writing and debugging of application programs for material-handling and assembly tasks.
- **Maple**
  Maple [36, 22] is a PL/1-like language for computation and several extensions for directing a robot to carry out complex tasks. Marple is developed by IBM.
- **MCL**
  MCL (Manufacturing Control Language) is an extension of the ATP numerical control language by McDonnell Douglas Corporation [90, 142] and is designed for the offline programming of industrial robots and their associated equipment under the same robotic control system.
- **PASRO**
  The teaching and demonstration system PASRO (PAScal for RObots) for robot programming was introduced in [21] and has been implemented on a number of computers and under various operating systems. PASRO includes Pascal completely and the geometrical data types of SRL.
- **VAL**
  A cooperation between Standfort University and the robot manufacturer Unimation has been enabled the development of VAL (Variable Assembly Language) [146, 20]. The language was determined initially by the robot's functions. As a consequence, the first version of VAL (VAL-I) has been provided with complex concepts such as frame variables. The handicap of VAL-I is the missing of e.g. inquiry request for coordinate values.
- **VAL-II**
  VAL-II is an enhanced version of VAL with some extensions. VAL-II is also designed by Unimation (USA) [147, 20].
- **HELP**
  HELP [39, 20] is designed by DEA, Italy, to program the PRAGMA robot. HELP includes high-level language elements and supports real-time processing for robot control. The PRAGMA robot moves in Cartesian coordinates, i.e., the programmer's positioning instructions can be directly processed by the controller. However, HELP contains no provision to indicate position and orientation of the robot.
- **SIGLA**
  SIGLA (SIGMA LAnguage) developed by Olivetti is designed for programming two-armed SIGMA portal robots [117, 20]. Since the syntax of SIGLA only consists of the statement of a two-lettered keyword and the enumeration of parameters, it is counted among the simple programming languages.

- **ROBEX**
  ROBEX (ROBot EXapt) is an extension of EXAPT (EXtended APT) and designed through the Technical Collage of Aachen [20]. ROBEX is similar to SRL.
- **PAL**
  In the PAL (Purdue Assembly Language) [142] programming system (developed at Purdue University), tasks are represented in terms of structured Cartesian coordinates. Every motion statement is a request to position and to orient the robot satisfying a position equation.
- **RAIL**
  RAIL is a high-level programming language for industrial robots with elements for graphic processing. The structuring properties are similar to those of Pascal. This language was developed by Automatix (USA) [7, 8].
- **AUTOPASS**
  AUTOPASS (AUTOmated Parts ASsembly System) [85] is a programming system for computer-controlled mechanical assembly under development at IBM. This system is oriented toward handling and assembly of objects and corresponding operations. It enables the programmer to concentrate on the overall assembly and handling sequence describing this sequence with English-like statements using familiar names and terminology.
- **RAPT**
  RAPT (Robot Automatically Programmed Tool) [4, 107] is a language for describing assembly tasks using geometric concepts and relations.
- **LAMA**
  LAMA (Language for Automatic Mechanical Assembly) [87, 86] transforms high-level assemble descriptions into programs for a computer-controlled manipulator. For this purpose, LAMA converts a human's assembly description into an assembly plan. Subsequently, this assembly plan is transformed into a manipulator program.

2.3 Robot Language Classification

The following section highlights general techniques of robot programming. The programming levels of each methodology is discussed and the introduced commercial and non-commercial robot programming languages are grouped to their corresponding classes.

Table 2.2: Robot language classification

Language	Robot-Level Prog.	Structured Prog.	Task-Level Prog.
T3	•		
Anorad	•		
Emily	•		
SIGLA	•		
RCL	•		
VAL (II)	•		
RPL	•		
Maple		•	
MCL		•	
PASRO		•	
AML		•	
AL		•	
SRL		•	
HELP		•	
PAL		•	
RAIL		•	
ROBEX			•
AUTOPASS			•
RAPT			•
LAMA			•

2.3.1 Robot-Level Programming

Robot-level programming provides point-to-point programming and primitive motion programming.

Point-to-Point Programming

Robot programming applying the point-to-point technique enables the user to save a series of points obtained by guiding the robot arm through the required motions. Usually, the guiding is executed by using a manual device to activate the joint motors in the robot and to save the desired locations. Sometimes, however, guiding is performed while moving the robot itself and saving points continuously (as with painting robots). Higher level guiding systems such as the T3 language provide specialized buttons which allow editing of programs and interaction with external signals. Further, T3 is operated manually through the use of a teach device. Robot motions are realized either in Cartesian, cylindrical, or joint coordinates. To revise a robot program, stepping forward and backward through the program will be carried out. Functions deploying external switches (e.g. a limit switch in the gripper) are provided. Furthermore, the T3 system can be interrupted by external signals and can signal itself to coordinate operations with external equipment in the robot working cell.

Primitive Motion Level

The primitive motion level for robot programming can be described as point-to-point programming in language form. Utilizing the constructs of the primitive motion language, simple branching and subroutines (generally with parameter passing), advanced sensing capabilities, primitive parallel execution, and frame definitions can be realized.

Anorad, Emily, RCL, and SIGLA are classified as primitive motion languages. They are based on interpreter, except RPL which has a compiler. These languages permit simple conditional and unconditional branching; Emily, RPL, and VAL also provide looping. Motions can be specified applying the joint angles directly or in Cartesian coordinates. Further, all languages support absolute movements. Anorad, RCL, and VAL also provide relative and straight-line motions.

Subroutines can be materialized in all robot controlling languages, except RCL. Further, Anorad and VAL only enable parameter passing. Anorad, Emily, SIGLA, and VAL allow files to be included as executable code; Anorad, SIGLA, and VAL achieve this by allowing all files to be run as subroutines. Emily uses statements that cause immediate execution of the desired file.

Sensing features of the primitive motion languages vary to a great extent. Anorad, RCL, SIGLA, and VAL are only provided with simple, binary touch sensing commands disabling vision functions (apart from the extended VAL-IIV system). Emily has several different kinds of tactile sensing, including touch sensors on one finger of the gripper, a sonar proximity sensor, and an infrared emitter and receiver to detect the presence of an object between the fingers. Emily monitors these sensors by using an on-off state to support the assembly process. RPL has only the simplest binary touch sensing command

and a very complex vision system capable of taking a picture, determining objects features, and recognizing an object which is defined in its database.

SIGLA and Emily allow simple, restricted parallel processing in terms of mutual exclusion of robot operations. SIGLA enables execution of several different subroutines to control the two-armed SIGLA portal robot. Emily synchronizes programs running simultaneously on different arms by synchronization statements.

VAL and RPL have limited coordinate transformation capabilities. Although they provide commands to define frames, invert transformations, and multiply matrices, the utilization of frames and transformations is not fully developed.

2.3.2 Structured Programming Level

The structured programming level represents a major improvement over the primitive motion level because these languages provide structured control primitives, coordinate transformations and the use of complex data structures (such as geometrical data structures). Further, sensor data processing is improved.

AL, HELP, Marple, AML, MCL, PAL, PASRO, and SRL belong to this language level. Each language provides user-defined subroutines with parameter passing (except PAL which has no subroutines, and HELP which allows no parameters). With the exception of HELP, each language is provided with distinct geometrical data structures such as points, lines, planes, frames, and rotations realized using structured data like arrays or records.

The physical properties of a robot are described by state variables. In PAL, the major state variables describe the top position of the arm (with respect to the environment) and the gripped tool (with respect to the end of the arm). The values of these variables change if the robot arm changes its orientation and position or when the tool is varied. Marple deploys state variables to monitor and perform tasks. For example, the state variables control the finger of the gripper or they monitor the current roll angle of the wrist and the size of the gap between the fingers. The programmer must define state variables for HELP, MCL, and AL. In PASRO and SRL, special effector instructions monitor the effector state. Further, constants can be defined, e.g. to involve the tool length or the size of gripped objects to ensure a collision-free motion of the arm.

The structured programming level provides sensor commands offering extended sensing capabilities. AL, HELP, and Marple include sensor operations for touch sensing in the fingers of the gripper. Additionally, Marple provides a proximity command. MCL is only equipped with simple binary touch sensing commands. However, MCL is the only language in this level with vision capabilities. The MCL system can locate, identify, and inspect objects. Although PASRO and SRL provide advanced sensing capabilities (e.g. instructions for program branching caused by sensory information, reading of sensor data, and the programming organization of sensory monitoring), both languages do not contain any commands for vision sensors.

The languages of the structured programming level support restricted concurrent processing. Excepting PAL, each language includes instructions for primitive concurrent processing. Marple, AL, HELP, and MCL allow specification of semaphores. AL and SRL deploy constructs defining a block structure to perform parallel blocks controlling, e.g. two robot arms. Nevertheless, collision avoidance is the user's responsibility. Concurrent processing in PASRO is implementation-dependent and possible, e.g. in CONCURRENT PASACL, MicroPower/Pascal or Modular/2 implementations.

The structured programming level defines motions in terms of transformations on the frame of the robot gripper. In PAL and AL, motions are specified directly in terms of the transformation. PAL uses mathematical symbols to cause movements whereas AL applies motion statements. Movements in AL can be programmed more specific with clauses to define intermediate points, approach vectors, velocities, and durations. In MCL and Marple, motions are separated into rotations and translations. The MCL motion statement will perform a translation and rotation but both must be specified as a point and two vectors. Marple uses separate commands for translations and for rotations of the robot arm. HELP only realizes motions through the specification of primitive joint coordinates. PASRO and SRL permit extensive motions such as relative motions, motions with specification of axis joints/distances, motion instructions with parameters like velocity, duration, or intermediate.

The RAIL language differs from the other language of this level since the robot programming by RAIL is supported through elements for graphic processing, i.e., RAIL contains special instructions for communication and control of a vision system.

2.3.3 Task-Level Programming

Task-oriented robot programming deploys abstract task specifications describing precisely the problem to be solved by robots. LAMA, RAPT, AUTOPASS, and ROBEX are languages of this level.

The concept of LAMA formulates relationships of task specifications, obstacle avoidance, and grasping, skeleton-based strategy synthesis, and error detection within one system. The lack of this system is the incomplete implementation. Although LAMA is often referenced [83, 101, 153], no information is available about the current state of development.

RAPT transforms symbolic specifications of geometrical goals (e.g. parallel, coplanar, aligned, against) together with a program into a sequence of end-effector positions. However, RAPT only concentrates on the evaluation of task specifications, i.e., it does not deal with obstacle avoidance, automatic grasping, or sensor operations.

AUTOPASS is designed to enable assembly by instructions humans might use. For this purpose, AUTOPASS applies commands considering state change, tool statements, or fastener statements. By means of these commands, AUTOPASS describes precisely what to do and are therefore easy to understand. To handle with objects and to operate with tools, this system absolutely requires a world modelling component and must also be capable of making assembly-oriented decisions, such as how to pick up an object. Commands are interpreted into a lower level code whose validity the user has to verify through altering any segment of code. Unfortunately, only a subset of the AUTOPASS system has been implemented [83]. Later information about AUTOPASS could not be found in literature.

The concept of ROBEX intends the automatical planning of collision-free motions and the generating of robot programs using sensor information available during execution. Because of the partial realization of ROBEX (e.g. missing functions for geometric reasoning and sensor planning), this system cannot be applied for complex robot tasks.

2.4 Essential Features of Robot Languages

Several robot soft- and hardware designers [19, 32, 16, 86, 83, 47] discussed important characteristics of robot controlling languages to control current and future industrial robot applications. In the following, a view of these features is given.

2.4.1 Concurrent Processing

Multi-robot systems exhibit a significant degree of concurrency. Concurrent programming primitives for robot controlling become more and more important. In reference to Volz's study [148], up to 30 % of the program involving two cooperating robots was concerned with interactions between these concurrently operating manipulators. Moreover, a robot programming language excluding concurrent programming mechanisms disables the programmer to design concurrent solutions for their problems. To sum up, following advantages arise deploying concurrency for robot programming [21, 86, 40, 32, 101, 148]:

- concurrency simplifies the coordination of the concurrent robot operations with other robots and other computer-controlled peripheral devices using a common programming system;
- concurrency supports notational convenience and conceptional elegance in describing robot systems;
- concurrent processing may shorten the run time of the manufacturing process by allocation of partial tasks to various processors;
- reducing program execution time by performing input/output operations concurrently with computations;
- mapping of concurrent activities to the programming language like:
  - concurrent processing to perform a single activity, e.g. in terms of a single instruction. Concurrent processing to perform a single activity is useful for complex operations such as a sensor-based robot motion. The essential calculation of the trajectory and the evaluation of the sensor data can be executed simultaneously;
  - concurrent execution of various activities, e.g. several instructions for controlling two or more robot arms. After the termination of the commands, the robot program continues either processing sequential or other concurrent statements;
  - execution of activities in form of parallel blocks. The parallel block structure is a more complex technique in concurrent processing and realizes concurrency through parallel blocks consisting of a number of instructions.

2.4.2 Knowledge Processing

A robot programming language should support knowledge processing [130, 109, 42] enabling intelligent decisions and task-level programming. The abstract task descriptions needed for task-level programs must be interpreted by a task planner generating suitable robot instructions. Knowledge processing additionally handles uncertainties within the robot cell, i.e., to decide what to do if an unexpected obstacle occurs or to plan a motion for passing an unknown area without collisions.

World Modelling

Without a world model, the robot is unable to recognize any element of its environment and, therefore, no task planning or trajectory planning is possible. A dynamic world modelling system does not only consider the initial state of the robot environment but also extends changes to the world model, i.e., a world model contains geometrical and physical descriptions of the manufacturing hardware and and information about current state of the manufacturing cell.

Motion Planning and Collision Detection

A motion planner guarantees a collision-free trajectory of the robot arm and the gripper. For this purpose, the motion planner distinguishes various planning tasks:

- gross motion planning. Gross motions are transfer movements with the only constraint that the robot and the gripped object should not collide with objects in the robot environment;
- fine motion planning. The presence of uncertainties in the world model affects the kind of motion that a robot may safely execute. In particular, positioning motions are not sufficient for all tasks; guarded motions are required when approaching a surface, and compliant motions are demanded when in contact with a surface;
- grasping planning. Grasping planning is associated with motion planning and determines where to grip an object neither to enable collisions during grasping or moving nor to loose the gripped object.

2.4.3 Object-Oriented Programming

Object-oriented robot applications deploy objects and methods presenting the robot's world and its activities. Significant benefits are connected with this paradigm for robot programming such as:

- the object-oriented system supports concurrency. The processes within a robot working cell are parallel in nature. An object-oriented environment may map these processes to objects and methods, i.e., these entities support concurrency where concurrency occurs (a detailed presentation of concurrent processing for robot controlling is given below);
- modelling virtually any real world object through object-orientation. The object characteristic splits the complete system into a number of self-contained modules including all necessary information. Thus, an object is an entire description of a part of the overall system;
- the object-oriented system is flexible and modular. The integration of a manipulator or manufacturing device to the robot programming system is simply realized by adding a new class or instance;
- human comprehensibility is high. The conversion-like control scheme of object-oriented systems facilitate object-oriented robot applications. The acceptance and utilization of any complex system depends in a high degree on the ability of the human user to understand how the system has to be handled for problem solving [101];
- object-orientation facilitates the design, maintenance, extensibility, and reusability of robot applications;

- similarity to general-purpose languages. Object-orientation also concentrates on data abstraction [32] for robot programming. Data abstraction is important because it facilitates program modularization and information hiding;
- the distributed characteristic of objects reflects the underlaying hardware model deploying a distributed multi-processor such as MIMD (multiple instruction, multiple data) architecture, e.g. a transputer system.

2.4.4 Global Control of the Working Cell

In this work, a system applying global control is considered to be a system consisting of several distributed components (e.g. processors) working locally and communicating with each other to fulfil a common task.

The increasing need for flexible integration and control of multiple robots of different types (e.g. gantry or elbow) and other manufacturing devices by means of a global controlling system is based on current requirements on robot tasks and, consequentially, on the advantages which are connected with this control mode [89, 139]:

- several robots must coordinate their actions with each other as they have
  - to execute different manipulation steps simultaneously;
  - to share their working space without collisions;
- the global control facilitates the design and programming of the robot applications since
  - only a single control system has to be programmed;
  - no coordination between several control systems is necessary;
- global control provides the flexibility to accommodate variations in the working environment and workpieces as they occur. Moreover, May [89] argues that global control becomes vitally necessary as the complexity of the manufacturing process increases;
- global control applying an underlaying multi-processor architecture increases the efficiency of the manufacturing cell through mapping of concurrent activities as processes to the available processors. The activities occurring within the cell arise through the control of several robots and additional computer-controlled peripheral devices at the same time. Alternatively, global control provides the facility to control the machines in a different manner dependent on special situations deploying
  - a single processor to control several robots;
  - several processors to control a single robot;
- global control facilitates programming and reduces the programming costs since all machines can be programmed by the same system only using one programming language. For this purpose, the post-processors of the

involved machines are embedded into the global programming environment. In contrast, local cell control demands the separate programming of each machine by its own host, frequently applying a particular hardware-oriented programming language;

- global control corresponds to object-orientation since this control mode provides typical characteristics of this programming paradigm [132]. The American National Bureau of Standards (NBS) has proposed that "the structure of a control system for a single robot system should be hierarchical, flexible, modular, and expandable. The hierarchy allows the control of the processes to be examined at different levels of detail, and flexibility can be incorporated to allow a variety of processes to be performed. Modularity permits the building of the control system in blocks by independent groups, as long as the interfaces to the blocks are well defined and respected." In later works, May, Kaye, Gentleman, Shin, and Epstein [131, 89, 53] have associated this recommendation with global multi-robot controlling arguing that the recommendation of the NBS is also valid for this purpose.

In another study of Shin and Epstein [131, 132] dealing with communication in a global multi-robot control system, both authors analyzed the communication behaviour between robot tasks considering the communication mechanisms of the NBS architecture. The study suggested that:

- the communication mechanisms should be based on message-passing enabling synchronous and asynchronous data transfer instead of the more complex communication system of the NBS architecture;
- the data transfer should be supported by ports as communication channels which also e.g. may improve the fault tolerance.

2.4.5 Programming Support and Language Type

A major problem in the development of robot languages arises regarding its design. Considering the programming support through general-purpose computer languages and the requirements of current robot tasks, Cox [32] and Blume [19] argue that a robot language should be a superset of an established computer programming language, not a subset. Consequentially, a high-level robot language should have the characteristics of a general-purpose programming language (e.g., Pascal, C, Prolog) and particular features for robot programming. Bonner and Shin [22] cite important characteristics of a robot language, based on a general-purpose language:

- debug and support facilities. Efficient debugging and support facilities are essential in development of robot programs. Facilities allowing quick,

efficient changes to create new application programs are as desirable as the most useful features of the language itself. Contrary to off-line robot programming, debugging time is especially crucial in on-line programming because the program design uses the robots themselves;
- ease of extension. The extensibility is important for robot languages. The language should have a modular expandable structure that meets the demands of robotics today and can be easily extended to handle the demands of the future as new applications for robots are discovered and sensing devices improve;
- transportability. The efficiency of a robot programming language also depends on the effort to adapt the language to a new environment. Robot languages should be adaptable to distinct computers and robots (different types and manufacturers);
- clarity of program structure. Structured and object-oriented programming techniques were developed to facilitate comprehension and debugging of programs;
- clarity, simplicity, and unity concept.

The disadvantages of an interpreter over a compiler are less essential considering robotics:

- interpreters are generally slower at execution time when parsing and interpretation take place;
- structured control constructs are more difficult to implement with an interpreter because of their more complex branching requirements.

2.4.6 Sensing

The sensing ability of a robot programming environment to perform tasks in the presence of uncertainties by means of sensors results in different language constructs enabling sensors to identify positions of parts, to inspect parts, to detect errors during manufacturing operations, and to accommodate unknown surfaces, i.e., the language constructs must ensure the solving of distinct sensor-based problems such as:

- initiating and terminating of motions. To do this, a robot programming system must include constructs for waiting and evaluation of interrupts, e.g. for synchronization of robots with other machines;
- identification of position and location of objects and identification of features of objects. Object identity, object features, and object location can be recognized by means of vision systems. The programming constructs therefore must enable the interfacing with the external recognition system and the evaluation of the more complex vision data often requiring comprehensive computations. Lozano-Pérez [86] therefore suggests separate

processors for the calculation of such data, and he encourages the support of several general input/output interfaces including communication channels to other computer hardware by the robot programming system. In contrast, existing systems frequently provide only binary or analog channels;

- selecting among alternative operations in programs and error checking. The selection of alternative operations in a robot program may be based on returned sensor data, e.g. the decision whether to place an object in a fixture or a disposal bin can depend on the result of an inspection test. Error checking requires the ability to obtain data from multiple sensors (like visual, force and position sensors) evaluating them and making decisions on the results;
- complying to external constraints. This mode of sensor interaction is necessary in situations requiring continuous motion in response to continuous sensor input. Data from force or visual sensors can modify the robot's motion in order to maintain or achieve a desired relationship with other objects.

2.4.7 Complex Motion Instructions

The robot system has to provide more complex motion instructions, such as motion instructions with sensor integration or motion statements with event monitoring. The complex motion instructions extend the more simple motion commands provided by e.g. the robot level languages.

2.5 Comparison of Robot Language Features

The following section compares the characteristics of robot programming languages. The shortcomings of the languages are summarized and an approach to robot programming is presented which will satisfy the essential demands discussed in Section 2.4.

2.5.1 A Uniform Representation

Concurrent Processing

Some languages permit concurrency through the simple signal/wait mechanism, such as VAL, AL, HELP, Marple and SIGLA. The more advanced parallel block technique is provided by SIGLA, HELP, SRL and AL. In PASRO, the ability to perform concurrent operations is implementation-dependent, i.e., using a general-purpose language, such as CONCURRENT PASCAL or Modular/2, processing of concurrent commands is possible. To do this, PASRO provides appropriate mechanisms which are similar to that of SRL. However, no information is available whether these languages support a parallel architecture such as a multi-processor or how parallel blocks may be scheduled to different processors. The other robot languages do not support concurrent processing.

Knowledge Processing

AL, RPL, and MCL support simple knowledge processing in terms of decision-making capabilities. However, these capabilities are connected with a robot vision system to recognize objects.

The concept of ROBEX, AUTOPASS, RAPT, and LAMA provide advanced knowledge processing capabilities according to task-level programming but all these languages have not been fully implemented.

Object-Oriented Programming

The robot languages analyzed in this work do not support object-orientation. Moreover, we only found one conception of an approach to object-oriented robot programming in literature [47] which is only partially implemented. The uncomplete description of this system disables an evaluation of the materialized features.

Global Control of the Working Cell

In order to support the global control of the working cell, AL and SRL are provided with advanced features for sensing and concurrent processing. The uncomplete information of the implementation state of AUTOPASS disable an evaluation of the mechanisms for this purpose. Global cell control with PASRO is implementation-dependent. The remaining languages do not offer suitable features for this task.

Programming Support and Language Type

In contrast to the robot-level programming languages, the robot languages based on established general-purpose languages provide advanced features for programming support adapted from these languages.

Most of the languages (T3, VAL, RCL, SIGLA, PAL, AUTOPASS, Marple, RAPT, and Anorad) are based on an interpreter. MCL and PASRO are based on a compiler. RPL, AL, HELP, and Emily provide an interpreter and a compiler. SRL is based on a compiler and provides additionally an interpreter (IRDATA [20]) for robot control.

Sensing

Excepting PAL and RAPT, all robot languages include some constructs to implement sensing mechanisms. T3, Anorad, Emily, RCL Maple, HELP, and SIGLA provide constructs to apply simple sensing abilities. The remaining languages support sensing either through advanced or through extensive sensing capabilities.

Motion Instructions

All languages include at least some constructs to implement simple, primitive motion capabilities (Emily, RCL, RPL, Maple, HELP, PAL). The other languages provide advanced motion features, and AL, SRL, and AUTOPASS support robot movements through extensive motion abilities.

2.5.2 A Critical Review

Table 2.3 surveys the results of the robot language investigation according to their language classification. The major shortcomings of the languages are separately summarized and in the following.

Robot-Level Programming

The philosophy of point-to-point languages is to program robot tasks applying simple motions. These languages disable off-line programming and suppress every ability based on a general-purpose language. Especially, restricted ability for concurrent processing and primitive sensing prevent global control of the robot cell, and the lack of complex robot motions disqualifies these languages to control current robot tasks.

Primitive-motion-level languages provide advanced sensor commands. Mechanisms for concurrency are introduced but not developed beyond an elemental level. Problems like off-line programming, knowledge processing, programming support (e.g. object-orientation), and global cell control cannot be solved. The lack of primitive-motion-level languages essentially limits the usability for current robot control tasks.

Structured Programming Level

Although structured-level-languages provide advanced capabilities (concerning programming support, robot movements, sensing) for robot control, important problems remain: unsufficient language constructs for concurrent processing and the lack of object-orientation complicate the global cell control in a great extent. Moreover, missing language features supporting knowledge processing restrict the usability of the languages of this level for current robot tasks.

Task-Level Programming

Task-oriented robot languages are still a subject of research with many unsolved problems, e.g. missing sensing. As illustrated in Table 2.3, some of the considered languages which fulfill the major part of the requirements have not been completely implemented, and a commercial task-oriented language for robot programming is not yet available. Moreover, some concepts of the analyzed languages are uncomplete and omit major criteria discussed above. Thus, a question arises whether these languages will ever be completely available in the future.

Table 2.3 outlines the robot language characteristics. In order to clearly arrange the representation, the language features have been abbreviated. The meaning of these abbreviations is listed below:

CP concurrent processing
KP knowledge processing
OO object orientation
GC global control
PS program support
S sensing
MI motion instruction

Table 2.3 not only surveys the characteristics of each robot language, but also evaluates its practical use for robot programming deploying one bullet for restricted capability, two bullets for advanced and three bullets for extended capability as mentioned in the discussion above.

Table 2.3: Survey of robot language characteristics

Language	CP	KP	OO	GC	PS	S	MI
T3	—	—	—	—	—	•	••
Anorad	—	—	—	—	—	•	••
Emily	•	—	—	—	—	•	•
SIGLA	••	—	—	—	—	•	••
RCL	—	—	—	—	—	•	•
VAL (II)	•	—	—	—	—	•••[a]	••
RPL	—	•	—	—	—	•••	•
Maple	•	—	—	—	••	•	•
MCL	••	•	—	—	••	••	••
PASRO	••[b]	—	—	••[b]	•••	••	••[b]
AML	•	—	—	—	••	••	••
AL	••	•[c]	—	••	•••	••	•••
SRL	••	—	—	••	•••	••	•••
HELP	•	—	—	—	•••	•	•
PAL	—	—	—	—	••	—	•
RAIL	—	—	—	—	•••	•••	••
ROBEX[d]	—	••	—	—	—	•••	••
AUTOPASS[d]	••	••	—	••	•••	•••	•••
RAPT[d]	—	••	—	—	•••	—	••
LAMA[d]	—	••	—	—	•••	••	••

• simple, restricted capability
•• advanced capability
••• extensive capability

[a] VAL extension for vision systems VAL-IIV
[b] implementation-dependent, e.g. in CONCURRENT PASCAL or Modula/2
[c] in research, but not integrated into AL
[d] only conceptional, not completely implemented

2.5.3 An Alternative Approach to Robot Programming

The essential characteristics of the approach presented in this book are:

- support of object-orientation through the object-oriented add-on;
- comprehensive capability of concurrent processing based on object-orientation and logic programming, achieved by particular operators realizing different granularity of concurrency;
- extensive sensing facility through the enlargement of the class hierarchy by sensor classes and integration of required methods to process the corresponding sensor data;

- global control of the working cell supporting object-orientation, concurrency, and sensing;
- facility of knowledge processing and programming support through the language primitives of logic programming;
- complex robot motions obtained through instructions integrated in the programming environment realizing e.g. continuous path motions or straight line motions;

A detailed description of this robot programming system is given in the following sections.

Chapter 3
Object-Orientation and Logic Programming

This chapter introduces basic elements of object-orientation and discusses characteristics of object-oriented and logic programming fostering concurrency. Significant side effects are discussed and alternative solutions for their avoidance are presented. Finally, the concept of the logic/object-oriented programming environment for robot programming is introduced.

3.1 Elements of Object-Orientation

Object-oriented programming is undergoing an evolution [5, 17, 35, 92, 141]. The various properties of this paradigm cannot be put in a simple and formalized definition. Hence, the basic principles and important features are described in a more detail in the following.

3.1.1 Principles of Object-Orientation

The following basic principles underline the essence of object-oriented computing. Each of the principles is discussed amply.

Data Abstraction

Data abstraction describes one major concept of object-oriented computing. This means, that programs should not make assumptions about implementations and internal representations. Any object can be requested for any required information or service by sending the suitable message. The requester is not bothered about how the object provides the information or service. It only gets what it asked for. The implementation and information generation is internal to the object and unvisible for the user. Thus, the emphasis is on what rather than on how when the interaction among objects is concerned. This provides the programmer an opportunity to think in terms of problem specification rather than be taken away by the implementation details. Data abstraction actually covers two separate but closely related concepts:

- modularization and
- information hiding.

Modularization is concerned with the splitting of complex systems into a number of self-contained entities (or modules). All information relating to a particular entity in the system is held within that module. Thus, a module is a self-contained and complete description of a part of the overall structure. In connection with computing, this means that a module will contain all the data structures and algorithms required for the implementation of the respective part of the system. The modularization benefits the programmer as there is an obvious place to go to if changes have to be made or problems occur. More fundamentally, modularization supports a particular design approach whereby the programmer splits the problem domain to be implemented into a number of recognizable conceptual modules and forms the essence of object-oriented computing.

Information hiding provides abstraction by hiding the implementation details of a module from the user. Using information hiding, the access of an object must be done through a protected interface. This interface normally consists of a number of operations which collectively define the behaviour of an entity. For the user, these internal details such as local procedures and data structures are unvisible. To handle complexity, information hiding enables the user to abstract over a level of detail in the system. Furthermore, the development of more reliable programs is supported by strictly controlling the entry points to a module. Thus, it is not possible to access data structures directly and hence not possible to perform unexpected actions on the data. The only way of accessing data structures is through the operational interface.

Behaviour Sharing

A further concept of object-orientation is connected with behaviour sharing. While data abstraction is realized through a defined external access interface, behaviour sharing extends this stage by allowing many entities to have the same interface set. As a consequence, the flexibility of a system can become greater.

One general approach for behaviour sharing can be provided by classification. The introduction of a classification into a system is formed on the basis of common behaviour of a group of entities. All these entities in a particular classification will therefore share common behaviour by definition.

Evolution

The next concept of object-oriented computing is concerned with evolution. Evolution is based on the observation that requirements change rapidly in computing environments. Over a period of time, systems change and additional functionality may be required. The object-oriented approach is to support this process of evolution as a fundamental aspect of the computational model. Two aspects of evolution have to be considered:

- requirement evolution;
- solution by evolution.

The requirement evolution is applied to already existing systems. Once such a system has been developed, it is likely that changes will occur which will require modifications or additions. This is particularly the case in dynamic environments, e.g. in design environments.

The solution by evolution is a more general view to develop solutions to problems step by step from an initial experimentation to a complete solution. This approach is particularly attractive where the final goals of a system are not well defined [17].

3.1.2 The Basic Concepts of Object-Orientation

The basic terms of object-orientation are highlighted below. As these terms are also the base of the object-oriented PROLoop environment, they are discussed here in a more detail. Therefore, the PROLoop explanations in Chapter 4 do not consider these basic terms.

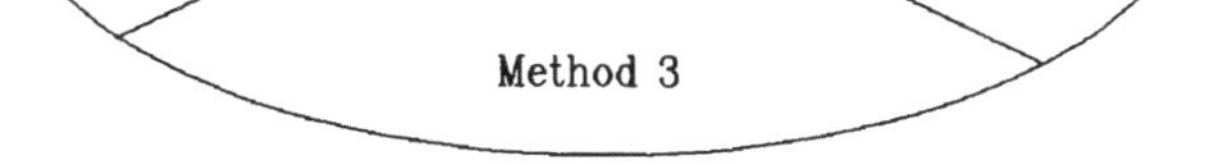

Figure 3.1: Encapsulated objects

Objects and Methods

Object-oriented software design is viewed as operational modeling of the real world which is made by objects. These objects simply reflect world objects at the level of abstraction appropriate for the application being constructed. The abstraction of an object supports the functionality required by the application developer.

In contrast, previous approaches (imperative languages, e.g. Pascal) have provided a set of abstractions which are more closely related to the underlying hardware architecture and therefore more work is required to produce an application. The methods of an object are a set of operations which are allowed to perform within the context of the object (Figure 3.1). They are the access procedures, i.e., the only procedures by which the object can be accessed. The physical realization of the objects meets the requirements of encapsulation.

Classes, Instances, and Class Hierarchy

The introduction of classes takes the system design one step further by introducing a rudimentary form of classification into the system. The mechanisms necessary to achieve this classification are class and object instantiation.

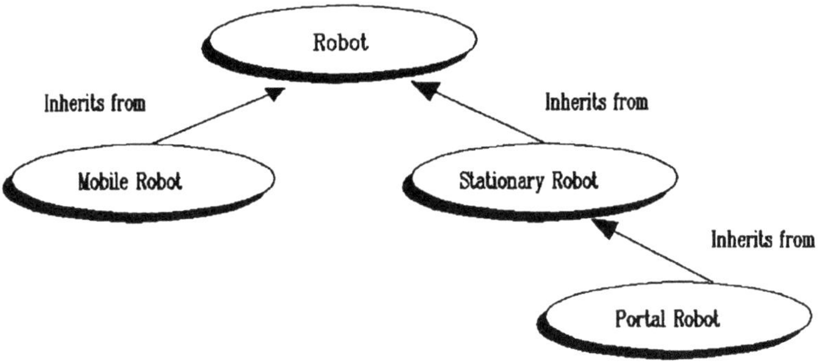

Figure 3.2: Example of a class hierarchy

Classes support classification by allowing groups of objects to be created sharing identical behaviour. More precisely, a class is a template from which objects may be created. It contains a definition of the state descriptors and methods for the object.

With the introduction of classes, it is necessary to provide a mechanism for materializing objects of a particular class. This object creation can be performed dynamically through an instantiation mechanism. An instantiation is done by calling a class to create a new object based on the template. This object is initialized and then exists in the environment to be accessed by other objects.

The design of an object-oriented system includes the construction of subclasses. These subclasses are created from existing classes until the appropriate functionality is developed. As a result, a class hierarchy is formed with nodes representing classes and arcs representing subclass relationships. The hierarchy is normally rooted by a special class, often referred to an object which contains a minimal set of behaviour common to all classes. Figure 3.2 illustrates a typical class hierarchy.

Inheritance

New classes must be generated to provide the overall appropriate functionality that is expressed in terms of data structures, algorithms and interfaces as universal components of the system. In some cases, the declaration of new classes can involve unnecessary effort because of the existence of similar classes. Therefore, inheritance provides a systematic way of specifying new classes by making use of existing classes, i.e., a new class can be described as an existing class but with modifications or extensions to meet the requirements of the new one. The new class therefore shares the behaviour of the old class but has modified or additional behaviour. This sharing of behaviour is the essential feature of inheritance: Inheritance is the incorporation of the behaviour of one class into another. This means, that a class inherits the methods and attributes (e.g. class variables) of that class. Furthermore, new methods and other attributes can be added. This new class is said to be a subclass of the old one. Similarly, the old class is the superclass of the new class.

Method Binding

One consequence of class hierarchy is connected with a decentralized representation of a complete knowledge of an object's behaviour. Classes inherit behaviour from superclasses which in turn inherit behaviour from their superclasses and so on. Thus, the complete behaviour of an object of a particular class is determined by the definitions in the class and in the subsequent line of superclasses. In practice, this means that a particular method may exist at any point in the search path. Therefore, it is necessary to carry out a binding from a method's name to implementation of a method whenever a method is invoked. Several techniques of method binding are considered:

- the static binding presents the simplest approach of method binding. This technique resolves all mappings at compile time. Hence, the compiler must build a table of classes and associated method implementations and then determine the subclass relationships between classes. Using this information, it is possible to determine the appropriate bindings from the method's name to its implementation. The actual calls to implementation would then be embedded in the code produced.

The advantage of static binding is connected with the missing of run time overhead in accessing methods. The binding of method names to implementations is carried out before the execution phase of an object-oriented program. Thus, invocation of a method may be no more expensive than a procedure call. A secondary advantage is that failed bindings are caught at compile time. The disadvantage of static bindings can be considered with several limitations such as the inability of changing these bindings without recompilation. A related problem is that an interpreted object-oriented environment cannot support compile time activity. Consequently, the dynamic binding is favoured against the static binding;

- with dynamic binding, the mapping of a method's name to implementation is carried out on every method invocation. Each time a method is invoked, the class hierarchy will be searched to find the suitable implementation. In practice, a message will be sent to the object requesting that a method will be applied to the object. This results in a search of the object's class, then it's superclass, and so on, until a method is found. If the search reaches the root of the class hierarchy, then an error message (e.g. method not found) must be sent back.

  The basic principle of dynamic binding is the changeability from invocation to invocation. Thus, if the class hierarchy changes between invocations, the change will be reflected in the final binding. Consequently, dynamic binding supports evolution of a program without requiring recompilation, and hence, it is suitable for an interpreted environment. The flexibility provided by dynamic binding is one of the key characteristics expected of an object-oriented environment. The ability to integrate changes is a central aspect of the object-oriented philosophy.

Polymorphism

A special kind of class construction is given by polymorphism. Polymorphism is informally defined as the ability to have more than one superclass. Thus, a method is defined over more than one class either through inheritance or by name overloading, i.e., the same name of a method is used in independent parts of a class hierarchy leading to an overloading of the term.

3.2 Object-Orientation and Logic Programming vs. Concurrency

This section briefly presents properties of object-orientation supporting concurrent processing [119, 2, 17, 143, 144], discusses the problems arising through the interference between inheritance and concurrency, and presents alternative solutions to avoid any influence between both features.

Logic programming fosters concurrent computations by various parallelism models. The models and their side effects are explained in detail. A brief survey of CS-Prolog (Communicating Sequential Prolog) to materialize concurrent logic programming concludes the section.

3.2.1 Features of Object-Orientation Supporting Concurrency

Object-orientation supports concurrency through following properties also enabling an efficient robot control such as:

Object/Method Allocation

Object-oriented systems are composed of a number of cooperating elements (objects and methods) residing on separate processors realizing concurrency. In order to assign objects and methods to processors, this work introduces a scheduling strategy in Chapter 6.

Distribution Transparency

Generally, in object-oriented concurrent systems the location of an object (or a method) may be transparent at the programming level. In either case, communication between objects is achieved by explicitly sending messages. Furthermore, an object does not distinguish between local message passing, i.e., between objects residing on the same processor or message passing between objects residing on different processors. Hence, object-oriented systems supporting concurrency can be programmed using the same abstractions as sequential ones.

Concurrency Level

A variety of different approaches to concurrency arises in object-oriented systems. One approach to concurrency occurs within objects. Systems having this kind of concurrency support multiple concurrent methods. Furthermore, the object-oriented programming system supports concurrent instructions for programming objects, in which case the unit of concurrency is the instruction, e.g. as a part of a method. Another model supports concurrency between objects, i.e., several objects are executed concurrently, but all methods of the same object are performed sequentially.

Communication

Communication via message passing is another characteristic of an object-oriented system [154]. Figure 3.3 illustrates these interactions (represented by an arrow) between objects (represented by an oval).

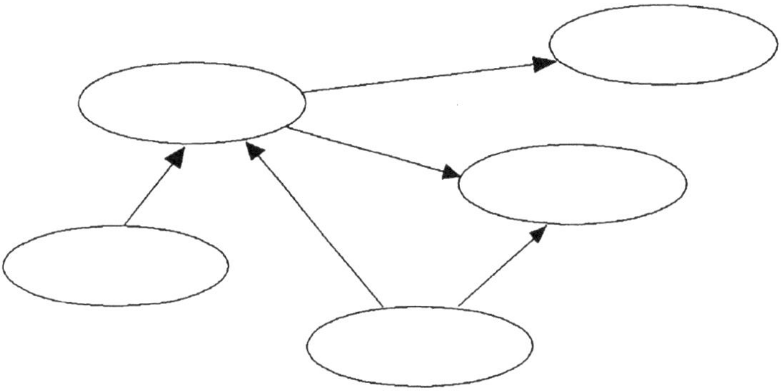

Figure 3.3: Object interactions

The message passing may be based on one of the following models:

- synchronous message passing in which the sending object is blocked until it receives a result after a period of time;
- asynchronous message passing in which the sender continues execution immediately after sending a message without waiting for a result.

3.2.2 Inheritance and Concurrency

Object-oriented systems applying conventional, class-based inheritance mechanisms and supporting concurrent processing have to provide primitives to prevent interferences between both features. Such interference has been discussed by different works distinguishing following reasons:

The Sharing Problem

Briot [23] and Wegener [149] investigated the locating and copying of methods at execution time in systems without shared memory. Deploying a distributed class hierarchy, distributed objects interact with each other. The interactions can be:

- interaction between instances;
- interaction between an instance and its corresponding class.

The latter form of interaction can also involve interaction between classes and their superclasses.

Several object-oriented models [23] view classes also as objects, such that the interaction between instances, classes, and superclasses can be treated uniformly. However, this approach has several disadvantages in distributed systems. The invocation of an operation on an object typically involves a number of interactions. First, the class of the instance must be contacted in order to access the code for the required operation. This code may be defined within the class of an instance, or it may have been inherited from a superclass. If it has been inherited, each superclass above the current position in the hierarchy must be contacted until the relevant partion of code has been located. If the instance, class and various superclasses are located on different processors, the costs of interaction will be extremely high.

The existing solutions to make the invocation of operations in distributed inheritance systems more efficient include following strategies:

- allow instances to reside only on processors which hold their associated classes;
- maintain a master copy of the hierarchy and cache slave copies on the different processors;
- associate pointers with instances which store the location of the appropriate class object.

The Concurrency Control Problem

The study of Kafura and Lee [74] results in another interference problem: interference between inheritance and concurrency control which is "fundamental and more deeply rooted". This interference results in concurrent object-oriented languages which either do not support inheritance or enable inheritance only by restricting some other properties such as object encapsulation or the reusability. In the following, this conflict is discussed and solutions are presented.

An object in an object-oriented concurrent system may interact with another object. Such an object has its own thread of control and is called an *active* object. In contrast, an object in a sequential object-oriented system cannot control itself because such an object has no own thread of control. This is a *passive* object. Concurrency implies the need for synchronization preventing data inconsistences of active objects. Since the internal state of an object can only be accessed through method invocation, some object-based concurrency control techniques are implemented inside the object. Two directions in providing concurrency control can be distinguished. One approach realizes concurrency control by a single procedure, called *centralized control.* The other approach materializes concurrency control without a centralized procedure, called *decentralized control.*

In *centralized control* the receiving of a message is explicitly programmed using mechanisms such as guarded commands [74]. The attempt to integrate inheritance into object-oriented concurrent systems causes the following problem: synchronization constraints specified in the centralized procedure cannot be inherited by a subclass [74].

Using the *decentralized control,* two different approaches to concurrency control can be found [74]. One attempt deploys *critical sections,* and the other one applies an *interface control.* In practice, the critical section approach is mainly adopted. Each method is responsible for ensuring a certain condition before entering a critical section. Another technique utilizes a locking mechanism whereby each method has to lock explicitly a variable before entering a critical section and must unlock the variable when exiting this section.

The disadvantages of the critical section technique are concerned with object encapsulation and violation of the critical section protocol. The use of a lock variable requires the visibility of this variable to any subclass in the class hierarchy which is a violation of encapsulation. Further, it is possible for a method to violate the critical section protocol. For instance, if explicit locking is used, a method may enter the critical section without performing the locking. This problem is especially given through inheritance. Since the subclass is separated from the superclass, there is a greater possibility that methods defined in a subclass may not observe the critical section protocol. Nevertheless, the weakening of the object encapsulation is not so grave since both inheritance and concurrency control are supported using the critical section technique.

The other approach in decentralized control is based on direct control of the object interface, *the interface control.* In this approach, receiving a message is implicit. A method execution is initiated only when the method is allowed to access the internal state of the object. The underlying control system delivers a message when the receiver is ready. However, a serious problem occurs in object-oriented concurrent systems applying this control methodology since the defining of a new method in a subclass may invalidate many superclass methods [74].

Chapter 5 describes the concurrency control technique of this work to ensure a conflict-free robot control.

3.2.3 Features of Logic Programming Fostering Concurrency

Logic programming supports concurrency by means of particular parallelism models that are briefly explained (see also Appendix A).

Sources of Concurrency

An interpreter of logic programs starts with a goal statement such as

$$? - p(X), q(X), r(Y).$$

and tries to derive the null clause through a series of resolutions. The interpreter must solve each subgoal in the goal statement by finding a clause in the program with a head matching the subgoal and then forming a new goal statement from the remaining subgoals and the body of the selected clause. In case of alternative program clauses having heads that match a subgoal, a tree of derived goal statements is defined. A sequential implementation (as implemented in standard Prolog interpreters) performs a depth-first search of this tree. Aiming to use concurrent processing, it is necessary to identify the steps in the interpretation that can be derived at the same time.

The simultaneous search of the tree and deriving goal statements is a possibility to realize concurrency: at each choice point, one has to interpret the goal statements of a node of an interpreter running on several processors. For example, if $p(X)$ in the above example matches the heads of two clauses (e.g. C_1 and C_2), one processor can solve the goal statement consisting of $q(X), r(Y)$ and the body of C_1. The other processor may solve the goal made from $q(X), r(Y)$ and the body from C_2. The expected speed up in execution will be obtained if one of these interpreters derives the null clause faster than an interpreter that performs a simple depth-first search [28]. The amount of time required in such a system (ignoring inter-processor communication times) will be directly proportional to the length of the shortest path in the search tree from the root to a null clause. In contrast, the amount of time required by a depth-first interpreter is proportional to the sum of path lengths in all branches to the left of the first branch that contains the null clause. However, this form of parallel search will not yield any speed up for programs that are implementations of deterministic functions (for more details see [28]).

The simultaneous search of the tree deriving the goal statements may be based on various parallelism models. The most promising models that have often been discussed are explained subsequently. These models include:

- Search parallelism;
- OR-parallelism;

- AND-parallelism;
- Stream parallelism

aiming to shorten the calculation time needed to derive goal statements. In addition, the Prolog program execution is frequently supported by intelligent backtracking aiming to reduce the amount of backtracking steps and, thus, to eliminate unnecessary goal derivations.

Search Parallelism Search-parallelism [123] enables a parallel search for clauses with heads matching a selected subgoal. The results of the parallel search are passed to a uniprocessor inference mechanism. This form of parallelism is useful for distributed database applications.

OR-Parallelism OR-parallelism [128] is exploited when a subgoal matches the heads of alternative clauses to be computed concurrently in order to derive a solution for the considered subgoal. OR-parallelism provides a large-scale, large-granularity parallelism across a wide range of applications and operates in the form of "generate and test" or "iterate and compute". Examples are processing of deductive databases, parsing a natural language sentence, searching for a string in a document, or compiling a set of objects.

AND-Parallelism In contrast to OR-parallelism, AND-parallelism [38] solves the goals sequentially. The aim of this strategy is to derive subgoals as much as possible at the same time, i.e., AND-parallelism arises when two or more subgoals from a single goal statement can be solved simultaneously. However, this model complicates concurrent processing causing possible binding conflicts, i.e., all common variables must be unified with the same value. Regarding the example above, $p(X)$ and $q(X)$ have a variable in common, and the system must ensure that the processes solving these subgoals will bind X to the same value.

Stream Parallelism Stream parallelism [25] considers subgoal solving processes as coroutines communicating via shared variables to be viewed as streams. According to the example clause above, subgoal $p(X)$ and $q(X)$ could be solved simultaneously by viewing the shared variable X as a stream. One of the subgoals will be the producer of values for the stream, the other will be the consumer. Execution of producers and consumers proceeds concurrently on different processors.

Intelligent Backtracking Intelligent backtracking [123] presents another methodology to shorten the execution time of Prolog programs and is often associated with the parallelism models.

The backtracking strategy of sequential Prolog (called *naive* backtracking) is primitive since this strategy always returns to the last deferred alternative. This simple method has no information about the failed situation. Hence, a multitude of unnecessary backtracking steps occur. In contrast, intelligent backtracking only tries to derive those subproblems alternatively which can exactly solve the failed problem. In order to determine these subproblems, intelligent backtracking strategies use a data dependence analysis.

Example 3.1 In order to demonstrate the process of intelligent backtracking, consider the rule

$$p(X,Y,Z) : -q(X,Y,Z), r(X), s(Y), t(Z).$$

and assume that during derivation of the subproblem $q(X,Y,Z)$ the variable Z can be bound to a constant value. If the other subproblems $r(X)$ and $s(Y)$ could be solved and the derivation of $t(Z)$ failed in consideration of the unification of Z, further alternative derivations of the subproblems $r(X)$ and $s(Y)$ are unnecessary since the cause of the fail of $t(Z)$ cannot be eliminated through another derivation attempt of $r(X)$ and $s(Y)$. As a consequence, the system backtracks to the subproblem $q(X,Y,Z)$ in order to find an alternative binding for the variable Z.

The AND/OR-Process Model

Prolog supports parallelism through inherent parallelism models distinguishing the AND- and OR-parallelism model. These models have influenced the
development of various practical logic programming languages such as Concurrent Prolog [127], PARLOG [25], Guarded Horn Clauses (GHC) [145], or Communicating Sequential Prolog (CS-Prolog) [97] concentrating on the AND/OR-process model in which goal statements are solved by sets of processes communicating only via messages. At any time, a process may decide to divide its input problem into subproblems and create descendant processes to solve those subproblems. Processes communicate only with their parents or descendants. The set of processes and their communication paths form a dynamic AND/OR-process (see Figure 3.4) changing as processes are created, executed, and terminated.

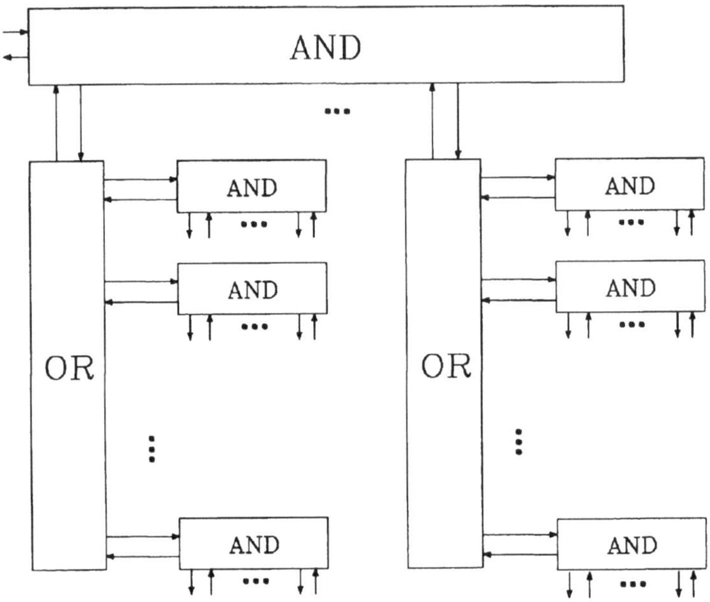

Figure 3.4: AND/OR-process model

3.3 Motivation for Object-Orientation in Prolog

This section summarizes the benefits of logic programming and concludes with the representation of the redesign of essential properties of the PROLoop (Prolog-based language for object-oriented programming) environment, especially regarding robot programming.

3.3.1 Benefits of PROLoop

The motivation to develop and to implement PROLoop has been carried by the benefits of both paradigms, logic programming and object-orientation. The benefits of logic programming using Prolog are:

- support of concurrency as discussed in Section 3.2.3;
- support of object-orientation by concurrent logic languages. Shapiro [126] argues that "concurrent languages also support object-orientation because several characteristics of logic programming meet Meyer's first four requirements [92] of an object-oriented languages: modularity, abstraction, memory management, and classes". Shapiro further emphasizes that, "according to Meyer, they can be called object based. Thus,

concurrent logic languages also meet Meyer's last three requirements: inheritance, polymorphism, and multiple and repeated inheritance which has been proved by the features of concurrent FCP system augmented with the inheritance mechanism";

- knowledge processing. The aim of knowledge processing is to enable problem solving by means of knowledge presented as elements of logic programming like:
  - facts, corresponding to a data base;
  - rules, giving relations between facts;
  - heuristics, determining the application of the given rules.

  Furthermore, the key idea of logic programming -to replace program and computation by a logical problem description and an automatical proof mechanism for testing the generated solution- corresponds exactly to the problem solving technique of knowledge based systems: to find and to apply the facts, rules, and heuristics in order to derive directly the solution of the problem from these rules and facts without intervening programming. Thus, logic programming is appropriate for knowledge processing since both paradigms derive the solutions by deduction and reasoning instead of program-controlled computing;
- basic characteristics of Prolog like:
  - the almost total absence of syntax and semantics;
  - only one name scoping rule for all program statements;
  - a single sequencing construct and a single statement format;
  - a minimal number of data types and data structuring operations.
- suitability of Prolog for technical applications. Gonzalez [54] demonstrated the effectiveness of Prolog for CAD applications. In comparison with Pascal, the CAD applications written in Prolog took shorter execution times than the Pascal version. In his experience, the Prolog-written CAD applications were developed more quickly and with minimum error, were more readable and more concise.

  The usability of Prolog for robot programming is also emphasized by Rathmill [112] in connection with a discussion about robot programming languages. He argues that "its applicability to robotics waits only to be fully demonstrated".

The importance of these benefits regarding robotics is discussed in Section 2.4.

3.3.2 Adding of PROLoop

In order to exploit the benefits of logic and object-oriented programming, the experimental environment has been implemented as described in [120].

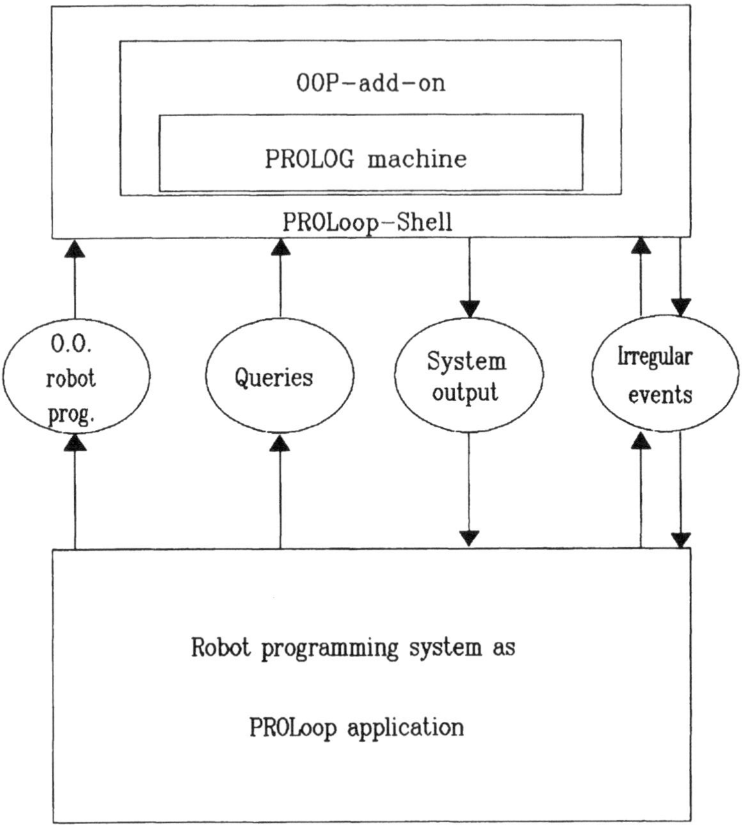

Figure 3.5: Scheme of PROLoop

However, this system had several serious shortcomings for robot programming. Adopting the key idea, the combination of logic programming and object-orientation, PROLoop has been redesigned [34] providing following improved and extended features [15, 14]. The first PROLoop version has only supported sequential processing. Extensions for concurrent robot control were necessary, such as:

- capability of concurrent processing. For this purpose, the system provides particular operators enabling
  - concurrency between objects;
  - concurrency between methods;
- concurrency control. The environment includes mechanisms materializing
  - access control of methods;

  - coordination of concurrent objects in time and space, e.g. for multi-robot control;
- support of scheduling and allocation of (robot) tasks to the transputers;
- extension of the message passing system. The message passing system of the first PROLoop system was insufficient since neither several messages could be transmitted at the same time nor various methods could be passed by the same message simultaneously;
- CS-Prolog supports concurrent processing of logic components being a part of the robot programming system, e.g. planning components. The first version was based on a sequential Prolog;
- ability to integrate user-defined built-in predicates into the CS-Prolog environment. These predicates can be developed in C using a Parallel-C compiler (the utilized Prolog system is written using this C-compiler) and invoked by means of an interface [97];
- name server to manage the name space within the object-oriented environment.

The following sections demonstrate the practical applicability of PROLoop for robot programming.

Part II

Robot Programming and Concurrency

Chapter 4
PROLoop for Robot Programming

In order to apply the logic/object-oriented programming environment for robot control, this chapter represents definitions and describes constructs of PROLoop. The message passing system is introduced by representing formal specifications of the message passing modes and the message passing operators. A discussion about concurrency control concludes this chapter presenting distinct concurrency control problems and corresponding solutions.

4.1 Specification of Basic PROLoop Properties

In the following, the characteristics of PROLoop such as class and method definition, generation and creation of instances and instance variables and the name server are presented. For this, corresponding PROLoop constructs are described and their use is demonstrated by means of examples.

4.1.1 Basic Notations

Concurrent logic/object-oriented programming for robot controlling can be considered as a tuple $(\mathcal{L}, \mathcal{O}, \mathcal{A}, \mathcal{P}, \mathcal{T})$ where $\mathcal{L}$ presents the object-oriented programming language based on first order predicate logic, $\mathcal{O}$ is an object representation of $\mathcal{L}$, $\mathcal{A}$ is a set of scheduling constraints, $\mathcal{P}$ is a set of transputers, and $\mathcal{T}$ the set of robot tasks consisting of a set $\mathcal{I}$ of logic and object-oriented robot instructions.

Let the class hierarchy of an object-oriented robot programming system be the finite set $\mathcal{H}$. For each class $c_j \in \mathcal{H}$, the subset $\mathcal{H}_{\mathcal{F}}$ is defined to be the superclasses and the subset $\mathcal{H}_{\mathcal{S}} \subseteq \mathcal{H}$ to be the subset of subclasses of c_j.

Each element of a class c_j is an object (instance) $o_i \in \mathcal{O}$ of that class denoted as $o_i \sqsubset c_j$. The set of instance variables is defined to be $\mathcal{V}$ and the set of methods to be $\mathcal{M}$ performing the activities within the manufacturing cell. The method m_j is an element of the set $\mathcal{M}$ and the instance variable v_k is an element of the set $\mathcal{V}$. The data transfer between the programming system and the hardware is supported through the set Π of ports. For this, every port $\pi_i \in \Pi$ can be assigned to an instance during instance generation.

4.1.2 Classes and Method Definition

Class Definition

A class definition in PROLoop describes the behaviour of a class and defines the methods $m_1, \ldots, m_n \in \mathcal{M}$, the set of instance variables $v_1, \ldots, v_m \in \mathcal{V}$, and the fatherclass $h_{\mathcal{F}i} \in \mathcal{H}_{\mathcal{F}}$. The corresponding syntax is given below:

def_class (<Class>, <Fatherclass>, <[Variables]>, <[Methods]>)

where:

<Class>	name of a class c_i to be defined
<Fatherclass>	name of the fatherclass $h_{\mathcal{F}i} \in \mathcal{H}_{\mathcal{F}}$
<[Variables]>	list of initialled instance variables $[v_1, \ldots, v_m]$
<[Methods]>	list of methods $[m_1, \ldots, m_n]$ of the specified class

Example 4.1 The definition of the class *robot* in PROLoop realizes the following expression:

$$def\_class(arm, robot, [pos\_nr], [method(move)]).$$

The clause *def_class* defines the class *arm* with the fatherclass *robot*. This class contains the instance variable *pos_nr* and the method *move*.

The enlargement of a class hierarchy can be achieved by means of the clause

subclass_fact (<Class>, <Fatherclass>, <[Variables]>)

where:

<Class>	name of a class c_i
<Fatherclass>	name of the fatherclass of the class c_i
<[Variables]>	list of instance variables $[v_1, \ldots, v_j]$

The list *Variables* contains the instance variables of *Class*, all its instance variables and their initial values inherited from the fatherclass.

Method Definition

A method definition describes a method m_i of a class c_j in PROLoop, i.e., the arguments and the subgoals are processed when the method is invoked. A method definition is based on following syntax:

method([<Name>(<[Arguments]>),<[Subgoals]>)

where:

<Name>	name of the method m_i to be defined
<[Arguments]>	list of arguments
<Subgoals>	subgoals to be processed

The materialization of a method definition through a Prolog clause is given in terms of:

head(class, [<Arguments>], Self) :- subgoal_1, subgoal_2, ..., subgoal_n

The argument *Name* is unified with the head of the clause *head*. The argument *Self* is used to enable the transmission of a message to itself, i.e., the sender of a message is also its receiver.

Example 4.2 By means of the method definition, the method *reset* of the class *robot* gets following structure:

$$reset(robot, [\,], Self) : -port < Mode > [write\_robot("RS")]$$

The method *reset* has only a single subgoal used for data transfer between the drive unit of the robot and the PROLoop environment. The expression *Mode* specifies the message passing mode described in Section 4.2. The string *RS* is a postprocessor instruction of the robot system enabling the desired function.

4.1.3 Instances and Instance Variables

A PROLoop instance $o_i \sqsubset c_j$ is able to generate new instances, to send messages, and to manipulate instance variables. In order to perform these procedures, the class hierarchy is provided with elementary methods that are defined in the root class *object* and inherited to all subclasses. In the following, these methods for static and dynamic instance creation and for manipulation of instance variables are presented.

Static and Dynamic Generation of Instances

The static instance generation, i.e., instance creation before program execution, is done using the method:

create(<Name>, <Port>)

where:

<Name>	instance o_j to be generated
<Port>	port π_i of the transputer system

Instances for manipulation of devices of the working cell (e.g. robots, sensors) need a port entry $\pi_i \in \Pi, 1 \leq i \leq 4$, to realize uni-directional data transfer with the equipment of the working cell. For this purpose, the transputer system provides four serial RS232 interfaces which can be accessed by an instance through unification of *Port*.

Example 4.3 The static instance generation of an additional robot arm materializes the expression:

create(robot_1, 2)

The dynamic generation of an instance, i.e., instance creation during program execution, realizes the construct:

<Class> <Mode> [create (<Name>, <Port>)]

where:

<Class>	class c_j of the instance o_k to be created: $o_k \sqsubset c_j$
<Mode>	message passing mode
<Name>	name of the instance o_k to be created
<Port>	port $\pi_i, 1 \leq i \leq 4$ of the transputer system

Example 4.4 The following expression demonstrates the dynamic instance generation in terms of a message:

$$arm < Mode > [create(robot\_1, 1)]$$

The message passing mode *Mode* is realized by one of the message passing operators introduced in Section 4.2.

The created instance then is added to the system by means of the clause

a_kind_of (<Name>, <Class>)

where:

<Name>	instance o_k to be added
<Class>	class c_j of the created instance: $o_k \sqsubset c_j$

Example 4.5 The following clause extends an object-oriented system by the entry:

$$a\_kind\_of(robot\_1, arm)$$

Every instance of a class is provided with the same instance variables. However, the values of these variables may differ since each instance variable has its own scope. In order to achieve data encapsulation, the access to each instance variable is handled by the clause

inst (<Name>, <Variable>, <Value>)

with:

<Name>	name of the instance
<Variable>	name of the instance variable
<Value>	value of the variable

which is additionally generated. During instance creation, the instance variables are initialized with default values.

Example 4.6 The generation of the instance *robot_1* of the class *arm* generates following clauses:

$a\_kind\_of(robot\_1, arm).$

$inst(robot\_1, pos\_nr1, 1).$
$inst(robot\_1, pos\_nr2, 2).$
$inst(robot\_1, grip\_stat, "O").$

The instance *robot_1* includes the instance variables *pos_nr1, pos_nr2* specifying positions and *grip_stat* specifying the gripper status. The position numbers are defined by the user. The are assigned to coordinates in the robot working area. During instance generation, the initial values (1 and 0) are assigned to the instance variables. The instance variable *grip_stat* specifies the status of the gripper of the robot.

Manipulation of Instance Variables

In order to manipulate instance variables, PROLoop provides the method

get_val (<Name>, <Value>)

with:

<Name>	instance variable to be manipulated
<Value>	value to be read

to read the values of instance variables. This procedure is based on unification of *Name* with *Value*.

Example 4.7 The method reads the value 20 from the instance variable *pos_nr*1:

$$get\_val(pos\_nr1, 20)$$

The method

set_val (<Name>, <Value>)

with:

<Name>	instance variable v_l to be manipulated
<Value>	value to be changed

replaces the value of the instance variable *Name*.

Example 4.8 In the following case, the method *set_val* assigns the value 20 to the instance variable *pos_nr*2:

$$set\_val(pos\_nr2, 20)$$

4.1.4 Name Server

In order to describe the task of the name server, it is useful to distinct between an object and its name. Object names are only references to objects and are just sufficient to distinguish the individual objects from each other. Hence, an object name has to be unique to activate that object it refers to.

In PROLoop, a valid object name can be an atom or a variable in Prolog. An object name is an element of the set $\mathcal{O}^{\mathcal{N}}$ which is defined to be the set of all object names. The set $\mathcal{O}^{\mathcal{N}}$ includes the set $\mathcal{O}^{\mathcal{A}}$ representing all object names based on Prolog atoms and the set $\mathcal{O}^{\mathcal{V}}$ representing the set of object names based on variables in Prolog, i.e., $\tilde{o}_i \in \mathcal{O}^{\mathcal{N}}$ where $\bigcup(\mathcal{O}^{\mathcal{A}}, \mathcal{O}^{\mathcal{V}}) = \mathcal{O}^{\mathcal{N}}$.

To ensure the uniqueness of object names, PROLoop supports the assignment of object names by means of the special constructs:

name_server (<Name>)

where:

<Name> object name

The *name_server* is called during object generation and controls the name assignment by the clause

name_space (<List>).

The list *List* contains all object names which are already used for object denotation. The check on uniqueness may return several error messages indicating:

- a name duplication, i.e., the selected name has already been used: $\exists \tilde{o}_i, \tilde{o}_j \in \mathcal{O}^{\mathcal{N}}(\tilde{o}_i = \tilde{o}_j)$;
- a convention, i.e., the selected identifier is neither a variable nor a Prolog atom: $\forall \tilde{o}_i \in \mathcal{O}^{\mathcal{N}}(\tilde{o}_i \notin \mathcal{O}^{\mathcal{A}}) \wedge (\tilde{o}_i \notin \mathcal{O}^{\mathcal{V}})$.

4.2 The Message Passing System

Concurrent processing in PROLoop is supported through a message passing system. Below, the message passing is introduced in detail and the corresponding protocol is described. The definition of the different message passing modes and their formal specification using Hoare's CSP notation concludes this section.

4.2.1 Notational Preliminaries

The robot activities are performed by methods of the classes represented as $c_i : m_j(x_1, \ldots, x_r, r_1, \ldots, r_p)$ where m_j is a method of class c_i with its input arguments $x_1, \ldots, x_r$ and its output $r_1, \ldots, r_p$. For representation of concurrency, the expression is extended by the $\|$-operator: $c_i : m_j \| c_x : m_y$ specifies concurrent processing of method m_j of class c_i and and method m_y of class c_x.

The set of messages passed between objects is defined to be $\mathcal{N}$. The messages are passed by means of the set of channels $\mathcal{K}$. The expression $message(n_i, k_j, o_s, o_e)$ specifies the message $n_i \in \mathcal{N}$ sent by object o_s and received by object o_e. The message n_i is transmitted by means of the channel k_j. Further, the function for determination of the receiver of a message n_i is defined to be $A_\psi(n_i)$.

The distribution of objects and methods to the set $\mathcal{P}$ of processors materializes a distribution process denoted as D_σ and presented through the expression: $D_\sigma(m_1, m_2, \ldots, m_n, o_1, o_2, \ldots, o_m) \rightsquigarrow \mathcal{P}$. The joint process J collects the results of the methods. The set of results is defined to be $\mathcal{R}$. The return of a result can be represented by the expression: $message(r_i, k_j, o_s, o_e)$ where $k_i \in \mathcal{K}, o_s, o_e \in \mathcal{O}, r_i \in \mathcal{R}$.

4.2.2 The Message Passing Protocol

PROLoop supports message passing by means of a protocol of the form [34]:

[Receiver, Mode, Message]

where:

<Receiver>	receiver o_e of a message
<Mode>	message passing mode
<Message>	message n_i given as a list of methods

The *Receiver* of a message is identified by its name. *Mode* specifies the message passing mode presented through a special operator. The unification of *Mode* with the different operators enables concurrent processing in a different manner. *Message* includes a number of methods which are passed to the receiving object. Concurrency between methods is based on this characteristic.

4.2.3 Formal Specification of the Message Passing Modes

The message passing modes can formally be presented by means of

- the definition of the operators;
- the derivation of their functional dependencies;
- the derivation of the corresponding CSP-description. The philosophy of CS-Prolog is similar to Hoare's CSP notation (Communicating Sequential Processes). This process concept is frequently applied to present concurrency and communication in a software application such as the introduced robot programming approach of this work;
- the presentation of the algorithms to implement the operators.

The *SEQ*-Operator

Definition 4.1 Let Θ be the set of message passing operators. Sequential processing of messages (no concurrency between methods and objects) realizes the operator $:<>: \in \Theta$ which is defined to be the SEQ-operator.

The receiving object o_e gets a message from an arbitrary object, the transmitting object o_s, within the class hierarchy using a channel k_i. The determination of the receiver distinguishes two cases:

- the sender is identical with the receiver of the message: $o_s = o_e$,
- the sender object is different from the receiver object: $o_s \neq o_e$,

i.e., after sending, the message n_j is checked by the function $A_\psi(n_i)$ whether the sending object is also the receiving object of a message. The transmitting object waits for the answer to continue its operation, i.e., the results will be returned to the transmitting object (if $o_s \neq o_e$). If $o_s = o_e$, the return of the results by sending a further message is not necessary.

In order to demonstrate the function of the SEQ-operator, the following formalism presents its functional dependencies:

$$\begin{aligned} o_s = o_e(message(n_i, k_j, o_s, o_e), A_\psi(n_i), message(n_j, k_j, o_s, o_e)),\ & s \neq e, \\ \vee\ o_s((message(n_i, k_j, o_s, o_s))),\ & s = e \end{aligned}$$

The process-based implementation of the SEQ-operator considers the process concept of CS-Prolog system which is similar to the formalism of Hoare's CSP. Thus, the corresponding CSP description is given below regarding objects and functions as processes:

$$\begin{aligned} O_s = (& message(k_j.n_i) \rightarrow A_\psi(n_i) \\ & \rightarrow (message(k_j.r_i) \rightarrow (O_e \rightarrow (message(k_{i_j}.n_i) \rightarrow O_s)),\ s \neq e \\ & \mid\ (message(k_j.n_i) \rightarrow O_s))),\ s = e \end{aligned}$$

The syntax of an object-oriented instruction using this operator is given below:

$object_1$:<>: $[m_1, \ldots, m_n]$.
$object_2$:<>: $[m_1, \ldots, m_p]$.

The methods $m_1, \ldots, m_n$ of *object_1* and the methods $m_1, \ldots, m_p$ of *object_2* are executed sequentially.

The PAR_I-Operator

Definition 4.2 Let Θ be the set of message passing operators. Concurrent processing between methods, i.e. within objects synchronous message passing materializes the operator, :<>$\in \Theta$ which is defined to be the PAR_I-operator.

A message n_i invokes the receiver to distribute the methods for concurrent execution to the nodes of the transputer system by means of the distribution process $D_\sigma(m_1, m_2, \ldots, m_n)$. The "succeeded" methods send the results to a special process J ("join process"). The join process collects the results and delivers them back to the transmitter of the message. Like deploying the SEQ-operator, the transmitter object has also to wait for the results. Further, the message sender can also be its receiver deploying this operator.

In order to demonstrate the function of the PAR_I-operator, the following formalism presents its functional dependencies:

$$
\begin{aligned}
o_s = {} & o_e(message(n_i, k_j, o_s, o_e), A_\psi(n_i), \\
& D_\sigma(o_i : m_1(x_1, x_2, \ldots, x_n, r_1, r_2, \ldots, r_p) \| \ o_i : m_2(x_1, x_2, \ldots, x_m, r_1, r_2, \ldots, r_o) \\
& \quad \| \ldots \| o_i : m_n(x_1, x_2, \ldots, x_v, r_1, r_2, \ldots, r_w)), message(r_i, k_j, o_s, o_e)), s \neq e \\
& \quad \vee\ o_s(message(n_i, k_j, o_s, o_e), D_\sigma(o_i : m_1(x_1, x_2, \ldots, x_n, r_1, r_2, \ldots, r_p) \\
& \quad \| \ o_i : m_2(x_1, x_2, \ldots, x_m, r_1, r_2, \ldots, r_o) \\
& \quad \| \ldots \| o_i : m_n(x_1, x_2, \ldots, x_v, r_1, r_2, \ldots, r_w)), message(r_i, k_j, o_s, o_e)), s = e
\end{aligned}
$$

The corresponding CSP process representation of the PAR_I-operator is:

$$
\begin{aligned}
O_s = {} & (message(k_j.n_i) \rightarrow A_\psi(n_i) \rightarrow (message(k_k.n_i) \\
& \rightarrow (O_e \rightarrow \tilde{d}_\sigma\ (m_1, \ldots, m_n) \rightarrow O_e)),\ s \neq e \\
& \mid\ (O_s \rightarrow \tilde{d}_\sigma\ (m_1, \ldots, m_n) \rightarrow O_s)),\ s = e
\end{aligned}
$$

where

$$
\begin{aligned}
\tilde{d}_\sigma\ (m_1, \ldots, m_n) \quad = \quad & D_\sigma(m_1) \rightarrow message(k_j.r_j) \rightarrow J \\
& \| \ D_\sigma(m_2) \rightarrow message(k_\ell.r_\ell) \rightarrow J \\
& \qquad \vdots \\
& \| \ D_\sigma(m_n) \rightarrow message(k_n.r_n) \rightarrow J \\
= \quad & \bigcup_{\substack{s>1 \\ s \in \mathbb{N}}} \| \ (D_\sigma(m_s) \rightarrow message(k_s.r_s) \rightarrow J)
\end{aligned}
$$

The following object-oriented commands illustrate the syntax of the PAR_I-operator:

$object_1 :<> [m_1, \ldots, m_n]$.
$object_2 :<> [m_1, \ldots, m_p]$.

The methods $m_1, \ldots, m_n$ and $m_1, \ldots, m_p$ of the objects $object_1$ and $object_2$ are performed concurrently. Consider that no concurrency arises between both objects.

The PAR_{II}-Operator

Definition 4.3 Let Θ be the set of message passing operators. Concurrency between objects realizes the operator $:<<:\in \Theta$ which is defined to be the PAR_{II}-operator.

This operator extends the function of the SEQ-operator by simultaneous sending of several messages to distinct objects effecting the sequential processing of the methods. In contrast to the previous operators, the PAR_{II}-operator presents asynchronous message passing, i.e., the sender object transmits several messages to receiver objects without waiting for the results.

To demonstrate the function of the PAR_{II}-operator, the following formalism presents its functional dependencies:

$$
\begin{aligned}
o_s = \; & o_{e_i}(message(n_i, k_{i_j}, o_s, o_{e_i}), A_\psi(n_i)), \; s \neq e_i, \\
& \qquad \vee \; o_s(message(n_i, k_{i_k}, o_s, o_s)), \; s = e_i, \\
& \| \; o_{e_j}(message(n_j, k_{j_i}, o_s, o_{e_j}), A_\psi(n_j)), \; s \neq e_j, \\
& \qquad \vee \; o_s(message(n_j, k_{j_k}, o_s, o_s)), \; s = e_j \\
& \qquad \vdots \\
& \| \; o_{e_n}(message(n_n, k_{n_i}, o_s, o_{e_n}), A_\psi(n_n)), \; s \neq e_n, \\
& \qquad \vee \; o_s(message(n_n, k_{n_k}, o_s, o_s)), \; s = e_n \\
= \; & \bigcup_{\substack{i>1 \\ i,j,k,\ell \in N}} \| \; o_{e_i}(message(n_i, k_{i_j}, o_s, o_{e_i}), \; s \neq e_j, \\
& \qquad \vee \; o_s(message(n_i, k_{i_k}, o_s, o_{e_i}), \; s \neq e_i
\end{aligned}
$$

The corresponding CSP-description of the function of this operator is given below:

$$
\begin{aligned}
O_s = \; & (message(k_{i_j}.n_i) \rightarrow A_\psi(n_i) && \rightarrow \; (message(k_{i_\ell}.n_i) \rightarrow O_{e_i}), s \neq e_i, \\
& && | \; (message(k_{i_k}.n_i) \rightarrow O_s)), s = e_i, \\
& \|(message(k_{j_i}, n_j) \rightarrow A_\psi(n_j) && \rightarrow \; (message(k_{j_\ell}.n_j) \rightarrow O_{e_j}), s \neq e_j,
\end{aligned}
$$

$$
\begin{aligned}
&& \mid\ & (message(k_{j_k}.n_j) \rightarrow O_s)), s = e_j,\\
&& & \vdots\\
&\|(message(k_{s_i}.n_s) \rightarrow A_\psi(n_s) & \rightarrow\ & (message(k_{s_\ell}.n_s) \rightarrow O_{e_s}), s \neq e_s,\\
&& \mid\ & (message(k_{s_k}.n_s) \rightarrow O_s)), s = e_s,\\
= \bigcup_{\substack{i>1\\ i,j,k,\ell\in\mathbb{N}}} &\|(message(k_{i_j}.n_i) \rightarrow A_\psi(n_i) & \rightarrow\ & (message(k_{i_\ell}.n_i) \rightarrow O_{e_i}), s \neq e_i,\\
&& \mid\ & (message(k_{i_k}.n_i) \rightarrow O_s)), s = e_i
\end{aligned}
$$

The ensuing object-oriented statement show the syntax applying the PAR_{II}-operator:

$object_1$:<<: $[m_1, \ldots, m_n]$.
$object_2$:<<: $[m_1, \ldots, m_p]$.

Two messages are simultaneously sent to $object_1$ and $object_2$. Consider that the methods $m_1, \ldots, m_n$ and $m_1, \ldots, m_n$ of these objects are executed sequentially.

The PAR_{III}-Operator

Definition 4.4 Let Θ be the set of message passing operators. Concurrency between objects and between methods enables the operator $:<<\in \Theta$ which is defined to be the PAR_{III}-operator.

This operator provides the highest degree of concurrency and extends the function of the preceding operator through distribution and execution of methods in parallel. In contrast to the PAR_I-operator, no result management is necessary, i.e., the sender does not wait for the results.

In order to demonstrate the function of the PAR_{II}-operator, the following formalism presents its functional dependencies:

$$
\begin{aligned}
o_s \;=\;& o_{e_i}(message(n_i, k_{i_i}, o_s, o_{e_i}), A_\psi(n_i), \tilde{d}_\sigma\ (m_1, \ldots, m_n)),\ s \neq e_i,\\
& \quad \vee\ o_s(message(n_i, k_{i_j}, o_s, o_s), \tilde{d}_\sigma\ (m_1, \ldots, m_n)),\ s = e_i\\
& \|\ o_{e_j}(message(n_j, k_{j_i}, o_s, o_{e_j}), A_\psi(n_j), \tilde{d}_\sigma\ (m_1, \ldots, m_o)),\ s \neq e_j,\\
& \quad \vee\ o_s(message(n_j, k_{j_j}, o_s, o_s)), \tilde{d}_\sigma\ (m_1, \ldots, m_o))\ s = e_j\\
& \qquad \vdots\\
& \|\ o_{e_n}(message(n_n, k_{n_i}, o_s, o_{e_n}), A_\psi(n_n)\ \tilde{d}_\sigma\ (m_1, \ldots, m_p)),\ s \neq e_n,
\end{aligned}
$$

$$\vee\ o_s(message(n_n, k_{n_j}, o_s, o_s), \tilde{d_\sigma}\ (m_1, \ldots, m_p)),\ s = e_n$$

$$= \bigcup_{\substack{i>1 \\ e,i,j,n,s \in N}} \|\ o_{e_i}(message(n_i, k_{i_i}, o_s, o_{e_j} A_\psi(n_n), \tilde{d_\sigma}\ (m_1, \ldots, m_n)),\ s \neq e_i$$

$$\vee\ o_s(message(n_i, k_{i_j}, o_s, o_{e_j}), \tilde{d_\sigma}\ (m_1, \ldots, m_n)),\ s = e_i$$

where

$$\begin{aligned}
\tilde{d_\sigma}\ (m_1, \ldots, m_n) &= D_\sigma(o_{s,e_\ell} : m_1(x_1, x_2, \ldots, x_n, r_1, r_2, \ldots, r_o) \\
&\qquad \|\ o_{s,e_\ell} : m_2(x_1, x_2, \ldots, x_m, r_1, r_2, \ldots, r_p) \\
&\qquad\qquad \vdots \\
&\qquad \|\ o_{s,e_\ell} : m_n(x_1, x_2, \ldots, x_v, r_1, r_2, \ldots, r_w)) \\
&= D_\sigma(\bigcup_{\substack{i>1, i \leq \ell \leq n \\ i,n,o,p,s \in N}} \|\ o_{s,e_\ell} : m_i(x_1, x_2, \ldots, x_o, r_1, r_2, \ldots, r_p)
\end{aligned}$$

The corresponding CSP-description of the functional dependencies of the PAR_{III}-operator can be specified as:

$$\begin{aligned}
O_s = (&message(k_{i_j}, n_i) \rightarrow A_\psi(n_i) \\
&\qquad \rightarrow (message(k_{i_\ell}.n_i) \rightarrow \tilde{d_\sigma}\ (m_1, \ldots, m_n) \rightarrow O_{e_i}),\ s \neq e_i \\
&\qquad \mid\ (message(k_{i_k}.n_i) \rightarrow \tilde{d_\sigma}\ (m_1, \ldots, m_n) \rightarrow O_s)),\ s = e_i \\
\|\ (&message(k_{j_i}.n_j) \rightarrow A_\psi(n_j) \\
&\qquad \rightarrow (message(k_{j_\ell}.n_j) \rightarrow \tilde{d_\sigma}\ (m_1, \ldots, m_o) \rightarrow O_{e_j}),\ s \neq e_j \\
&\qquad \mid\ (message(k_{j_k}.n_j) \rightarrow \tilde{d_\sigma}\ (m_1, \ldots, m_o) \rightarrow O_s)),\ s = e_j \\
&\qquad\qquad \vdots \\
\|\ (&message(k_{n_i}.n_n) \rightarrow A_\psi(n_n) \\
&\qquad \rightarrow (message(k_{n_\ell}.n_s) \rightarrow \tilde{d_\sigma}\ (m_1, \ldots, m_p) \rightarrow O_{e_n}),\ s \neq e_n \\
&\qquad \mid\ (message(k_{n_k}.n_n) \rightarrow \tilde{d_\sigma}\ (m_1, \ldots, m_p) \rightarrow O_s)),\ s = e_n
\end{aligned}$$

$$= \bigcup_{\substack{i>1 \\ i,\ell,k,n \in N}} \|\ (message(k_{i_j}.n_i) \rightarrow A_\psi(n_i)$$

$$\rightarrow (message(k_{i_\ell}.n_i) \rightarrow \tilde{d}_\sigma\ (m_1,\ldots,m_n) \rightarrow O_{e_i}),\ s \neq e_i$$
$$\mid (message(k_{i_k}.n_i) \rightarrow \tilde{d}_\sigma\ (m_1,\ldots,m_n) \rightarrow O_s)),\ s = e_i$$

where

$$\begin{aligned}\tilde{d}_\sigma\ (m_1,\ldots,m_n) &= D_\sigma(m_1) \rightarrow message(k_{j_1}.r_{j_1}) \rightarrow J \\ &\quad \| \ D_\sigma(m_2) \rightarrow message(k_{j_2}.r_{j_2}) \rightarrow J \\ &\quad \vdots \\ &\quad \| \ D_\sigma(m_n) \rightarrow message(k_{j_n}.r_{j_n}) \rightarrow J \\ &= \bigcup_{\substack{i,s>1 \\ i,s\in N}} \| \ (D_\sigma(m_s) \rightarrow message(k_{s_i}.r_{s_i}) \rightarrow J)\end{aligned}$$

The syntax of object-oriented instructions is shown in the following:

$object_1$:<< $[m_1,\ldots,m_n]$.
$object_2$:<< $[m_1,\ldots,m_p]$.

Like in the previous example, concurrency between objects, $object_1$ and $object_2$, occurs through sending simultaneously several messages. Additionally, concurrency arises through the execution of the methods of these objects, $m_1,\ldots,m_n$ and $m_1,\ldots,m_p$, in parallel.

4.2.4 Synchronous Message Passing for Robot Controlling

After introduction of the PROLoop operators, the algorithms of the SEQ and the PAR_I- operator are represented and their practical use is illustrated by means of robot examples.

Synchronous Message Passing by the SEQ-Operator

Example 4.9 demonstrates the utilization of the SEQ-operator introduced by Definition 4.1 disabling any concurrent processing. The message passing between the involved objects is illustrated in Figure 4.1. Algorithm 4.1 grossly describes the function of this operator formally.

Algorithm 4.1 (*SEQ*-operator)

begin
Input: the message $n_j \in \mathcal{N}$ given as a list L_{n_j} of methods $[m_1, \ldots, m_n]$ to be executed sequentially:
check the existence of the receiving object $\exists o_e \in \mathcal{O}((o_e \sqsubset c_i) \wedge (c_i \in \mathcal{H}))$:
if $(o_e \not\sqsubset c_i)$ **then**
  Output: corresponding error message
  terminating of the message processing
else
  method execution supported by the functions *check_meth* and *exe_meth*

  begin
  the methods can be unified and the message list is not empty:

  if $(L_{n_j} \neq [\,])$
    while $(L_{n_j} \neq [\,])$ (* 1 *)
      if $(m_i \notin \mathcal{M})$ **then**
        break message processing
        Output: corresponding error message
      else
        execution of the method m_i
        if $(o_e \neq o_s)$ **then**
          return of the result $r_i \in \mathcal{R}$ to the sender o_s
        end if
        remove the element m_i from the list:
        $L_{n_j} = L_{n_j} \backslash m_i$
      end if
    end while (method execution)
  else
    Output: error message
  end if (list processing)
  end (method handling)
end if (message processing)
end. (algorithm *SEQ*-operator)

Theorem 4.1

1. Algorithm 4.1 terminates for any finite message length, i.e., for any finite set of methods $\mathcal{M}_{n_i}$ of a message n_i.
2. The complexity of Algorithm 4.1 is $O(n)$.

Proof

1. Let $\mathcal{M}_{n_i} \subseteq \mathcal{M}$. The cardinality $|\mathcal{M}_{n_i}| = n, 1 \leq n < \infty$. Then the *while*-construct (* 1 *) will be performed n times. Hence, the algorithm terminates assuming that the algorithms of the methods terminate.
2. The complexity of Algorithm 4.1 depends on the algorithms of the methods to be processed. In order to access the complexity of Algorithm 4.1, the complexity of the method algorithms is considered to be an elementary unit. In the following, this unit is assumed to be 1.

   The complexity for processing of a message consisting of n methods is obvious: for each method following operations must be done: the existence check, the execution, the return of the result, and the list manipulation (remove of a method). Hence, the complexity (upper bound) is $O(n)$.

□

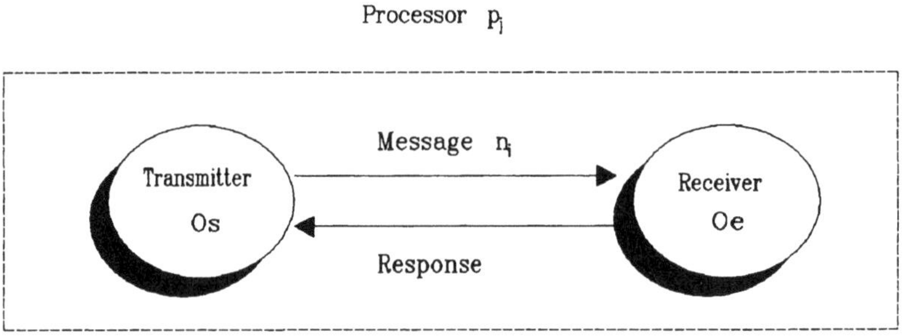

Figure 4.1: Principle of message passing using the *SEQ*-operator ($o_e \neq o_s$)

Example 4.9 Consider the following simple robot application:

arm :<>: [*create*(*robot_1*, 0)].

robot_1 :<>: [*close*].
robot_1 :<>: [*set_val*(*pos_nr*1, 20), *move*].

The simple robot application consists of two parts. At the beginning, the instance *robot_1* is generated by means of the method *create*. The message is passed to the object *robot_1* and invokes the manipulator to close the effector. The method *set_val* of the following command assigns a position to the instance variable *pos_nr1*. The method *move* then causes the motion to the specified position. An execution of both methods (*set_val* and *move*) in parallel is impossible since the method *set_val* specifies the position to which the robot should be moved to.

Synchronous Message Passing by the PAR_I-Operator

Figure 4.2 presents the message passing scheme of the PAR_I-operator introduced by Definition 4.2. In order to keep an easy survey of the figure, this example considers only two methods to be distributed to various transputers.

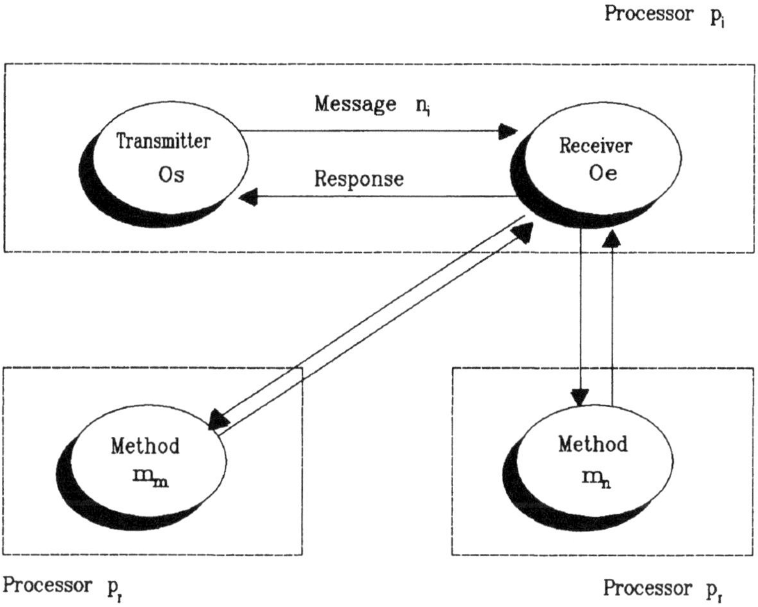

Figure 4.2: Concurrency within objects by means of the PAR_I-operator ($o_s \neq o_e$)

The formal representation of Algorithm 4.2 includes a *par*-construct (see also [64]) indicating that all statements within the scope of this construct are executed simultaneously.

Algorithm 4.2 (PAR_I-operator)
begin
Input: message $n_j \in \mathcal{N}$ given as the list L_{n_j} ($[m_1, \ldots, m_n]$) consisting of the set of methods $\mathcal{M}_{n_j}$ to be executed concurrently:
check the existence of the receiving object $\exists o_e \in \mathcal{O}((o_e \sqsubset c_i) \wedge (c_i \in \mathcal{H}))$:

if $(o_e \not\sqsubset c_i)$ **then**
Output: corresponding error message
terminating of the message processing
else
create the joint process J
method execution supported by *check_meth* and *exe_meth*:

if $((L_{n_j} \neq [\,]) \wedge (|\mathcal{M}_{n_j}| \geq 2))$ **then**
for (all methods $m_i \in L_{n_j}$) (∗ 1 ∗)
if $(m_i \notin \mathcal{M})$ **then**
break message processing
Output: corresponding error message
end if
end for (existence check)
for (all methods $m_i \in L_{n_j}$) (∗ 2 ∗)
method assignment to the transputers by means of the function *new* (...)
end for (method assignment)
par (for all methods $m_i \in L_{n_j}$) (∗ 3 ∗)
concurrent execution of the methods $m_1, \ldots, m_n$
if $(o_e \neq o_s)$ **then**
collection of the results $r_i \in \mathcal{R}$ by J
end if (method processing)
end par (concurrent method execution)
else
Output: corresponding error message
end if (message list processing)
for (all results $r_i \in \mathcal{R}$) (∗ 4 ∗)
return of the results to the sender o_s
end for (return of the results)
end if (message processing)
end. (algorithm PAR_I-operator)

Theorem 4.2

1. Algorithm 4.2 terminates for an arbitrary message n_j consisting of a finite set of methods $\mathcal{M}_{n_j}$.
2. The complexity of Algorithm 4.2 is $O(n)$.

Proof

1. Let $\mathcal{M}_{n_j} \subseteq \mathcal{M}$. The cardinality $|\mathcal{M}_{n_j}| = n, 1 \leq n < \infty$. Then the algorithm parts enabling the existence check $(* \ 1 \ *)$, the method assignment $(* \ 2 \ *)$, the concurrent execution, the collection of the results $(* \ 3 \ *)$, and the return of the results $(* \ 4 \ *)$ terminate on the assumption that the algorithms of the methods terminate. In case of occurrences of methods $m_i \notin \mathcal{M}$ the message processing breaks immediately.
2. The complexity of Algorithm 4.2 is mainly influenced by the *for*-loops $(* \ 1 \ *)$, $(* \ 2 \ *)$, $(* \ 4 \ *)$, and the *par*-construct. Considering the loops, it is obvious that the complexity of Algorithm 4.2 is $O(n)$ processing n methods (worst case) assuming that the complexity of the algorithms of the methods is 1.

$\square$

Example 4.10 demonstrates the utilization of this operator by means of a simple robot application.

Example 4.10 Consider the simple part of a robot application:

$object\_data$:<>: $[create(camera, 1)]$.
arm :<>: $[create(robot\_1, 0)]$.
$task$:<>: $[create(robot\_task, \_)]$.

$camera$:<>: $[read\_code(1, Value)]$.
$robot\_task$:<> $[take\_defined(camera, robot\_1, 1, 2, 3), set\_val(pos\_nr1, 10)]$.

At the beginning, the instances *robot_1*, *camera*, and *robot_task* are generated. The activated methods of *robot_task*, *take_defined()* and *set_val()*, are independent and may be executed in parallel. The method *create* also assigns a port π_n $(1 \leq n \leq 4)$ to the instances in order to enable the data transfer between the programming system and the involved hardware. If no port has been unified, the instance has no access to the robots or other devices.

The method *read_code* of the instance *camera* initiates the reading of sensor data (*Value*) provided by the specified port. The method *take_defined()* then compares the sensor data with a programmer-specified code by means of an instance variable of *camera*. If the object can be identified this method causes *robot_1* to move to the given position 1 gripping an identified workpiece to move it via position 2 to the given position 3. Otherwise, this progress will be broken. In order to realize concurrency, a second independent action is executed simultaneously. The method *set_val()* assigns a position number to the instance variable *pos_nr1* the robot arm has to move to during another activity that is not further considered in this short example.

4.2.5 Asynchronous Message Passing for Robot Controlling

As mentioned above, asynchronous message passing is allowed by the PAR_{II} and the PAR_{III}-operator omitting waiting for the return of the results.

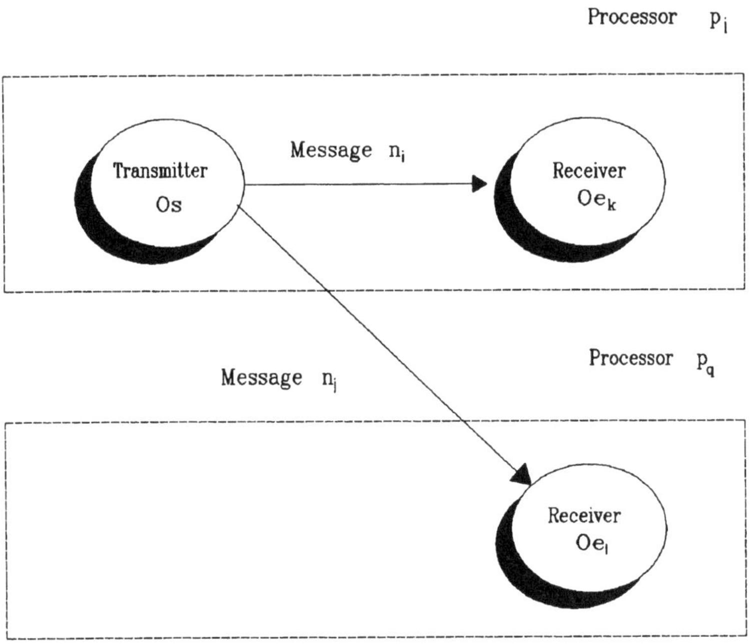

Figure 4.3: Concurrency principle of the PAR_{II}-operator ($o_e \neq o_s$)

Asynchronous Message Passing by the PAR_{II}-Operator

Figure 4.3 shows the message passing principle of the PAR_{II}-operator in case of two messages sent simultaneously. Definition 4.3 introduced this operator, and Example 4.11 demonstrates its application. The algorithm of this operator is grossly given below.

Algorithm 4.3 (PAR_{II}-operator)
begin
Input: several messages $n_1, \ldots, n_k \in \mathcal{N}$ to be sent simultaneously and given as lists $L_{n_1}, \ldots, L_{n_k}$.
for (all methods of the messages $n_i \in \mathcal{N}$) (* 1 *)
assign the methods $m_1, \ldots, m_n$ of the message $n_i \in \mathcal{N}$ to a transputer $p_j \in \mathcal{P}$
end for (method assignment)
par (for all messages $n_i \in \mathcal{N}$) (* 2 *)
execute the methods $m_1, \ldots, m_n$ of the message n_j sequentially. For this, check the existence of the receiving object
$\exists o_e \in \mathcal{O}((o_e \sqsubset c_i) \wedge (c_i \in \mathcal{H}))$:

if ($o_e \not\sqsubset c_i$) **then**
Output: corresponding error message
terminating of the message processing
else
method execution supported by the functions *check_meth* and *exe_meth*
the methods can be unified and the message list is not empty:
if ($L_{n_j} \neq [\,]$)
while ($L_{n_j} \neq [\,]$) (* 3 *)
if ($m_i \notin \mathcal{M}$) **then**
break message processing
Output: corresponding error message
else
execution of the method m_i
remove the element m_i from the list:
$L_{n_j} = L_{n_j} \backslash m_i$
end if
end while (method execution)
else
Output: corresponding error message
end if (list processing)
end if (message processing)
end par (processing of all messages)
end. (algorithm PAR_{II}-operator)

Theorem 4.3

1. Algorithm 4.3 terminates for an arbitrary number of messages $n_1, \ldots, n_k$ sent simultaneously consisting of finite sets of methods $\{\mathcal{M}_{n_1}, \ldots, \mathcal{M}_{n_n}\}$.
2. The complexity of Algorithm 4.3 is $O(kn)$. The complexity assessment assumes the simple case of messages consisting of n methods.

Proof

1. Consider the termination proof of Theorem 4.1 evidencing the termination of Algorithm 4.1. Assuming a finite set of messages $n_i \in \{n_1, \ldots, n_k\}, k < \infty$ and $\forall \mathcal{M}_{n_i} \in \{\mathcal{M}_{n_1}, \ldots, \mathcal{M}_{n_n}\}\ |\mathcal{M}_{n_i}| < \infty$ the algorithm parts (* 1 *), (* 2 *), and (* 3 *) terminate. Since the algorithm has no further loops and recursions, it terminates.
2. Consider the complexity proof of Theorem 4.1 demonstrating the complexity of Algorithm 4.1. Also assuming that the complexity of a method algorithm is 1, it is obvious that the complexity of Algorithm 4.3 results in $O(kn)$ regarding k messages.

   In the more general case considering methods with a different number of methods the complexity varies insignificantly.

□

Example 4.11 Consider the robot application involving two manipulators:

arm :<<: $[create(robot\_1, 1)]$.
arm :<<: $[create(robot\_2, 2)]$.

$robot\_1$:<<: $[move\_straight(10, 30, "O")]$.
$robot\_2$:<<: $[move\_continuous(20, 60), close]$.

The method *create* generates the instances *robot_1* and *robot_2*. Concurrency between objects arises through simultaneous sending of two messages to these instances. Both messages cause a motion of the robots.

After specification of the final position, *robot_1* moves through 30 intermediate points on a straight line to the destination position 10. The intermediate positions are calculated by the system. The other robot (*robot_2*) moves continuously through 20 predefined intermediate positions to the final position 60 closing the gripper subsequently. The concurrent processing of the methods *move_continuous* and *close* prevents their dependence as mentioned in Example 4.1.

Asynchronous Message Passing by the PAR_{III}-Operator

In reference to Definition 4.4, asynchronous message passing applying the PAR_{III}-operator is demonstrated in Example 4.12. Figure 4.4 shows the principle of this procedure in case of two messages sent concurrently and consisting of several methods distributed to various processors. The algorithm of this operator is grossly given below.

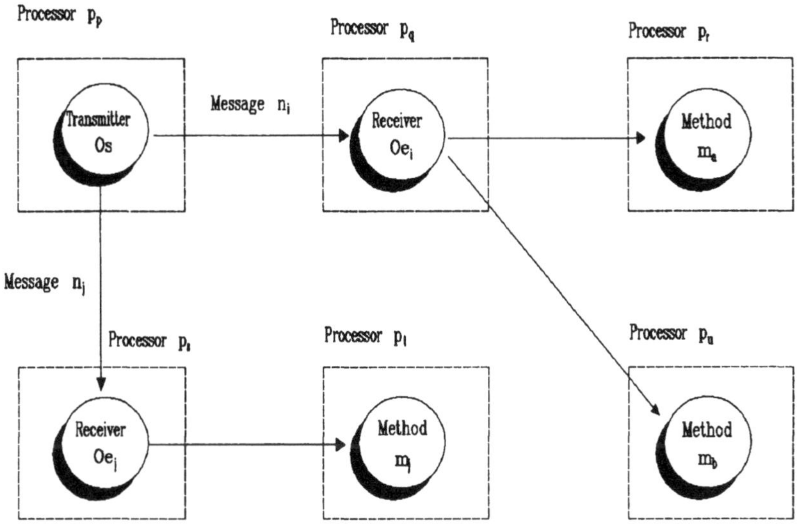

Figure 4.4: Concurrency principle of the PAR_{III}-operator ($o_e \neq o_s$)

Theorem 4.4

1. The Algorithm 4.4 terminates for an arbitrary finite set of concurrent messages $n_1, \ldots, n_k$ consisting of finite sets of methods $\{\mathcal{M}_{n_1}, \ldots, \mathcal{M}_{n_k}\}$.
2. The complexity of Algorithm 4.4 is $O(kn)$ assuming the simple case of messages containing n methods.

Proof

1. Consider the termination proof of Algorithm 4.2 and Algorithm 4.3. Also assuming $|\{n_1, \ldots, n_k\}| = k < \infty$ and $\forall \mathcal{M}_{n_j} \in \{\mathcal{M}_{n_1}, \ldots, \mathcal{M}_{n_k}\} |\mathcal{M}_{n_j}| = n < \infty$ it is obvious that the *for*-loops (* 1 *), (* 3 *), and (* 4 *) terminate. The *par*-constructs (* 2 *) and (* 5 *) also enable the concurrent execution of a finite set of objects/methods. Thus, this algorithm terminates.

2. Considering Algorithm 4.2 and Algorithm 4.3 since the complexity assessment of this algorithm can be derived similarly. The complexity of the inner *par*-construct (concurrent method execution) results in $O(n)$ since n methods have to be carried out each requiring four processing steps, and the complexity of outer *par*-construct (concurrency between objects) is $O(k)$ since k messages have to be processed. Hence, the complexity is $O(kn)$.

□

Note that a message generally includes not more than two or three methods.

Example 4.12 Consider the robot statements of a program part given below:

```
object_data :<>: [create(camera, 1)].
arm         :<>: [create(robot_1, 0)].
arm         :<>: [create(robot_2, 2)].
task        :<>: [create(robot_task, _)].
```

```
camera     :<>: [read_code].
robot_task :<< [take_defined(camera, robot_1, 1, 2, 3), set_val(pos_nr1, 10)].
robot_2    :<< [move_continuous(10, 20), open].
```

At the beginning, the instances *robot_1*, *camera*, *robot_2*, and *robot_task* are generated. The activated methods of *robot_task*, *take_defined()* and *set_val()*, are independent and may be executed in parallel.

The method *take_defined()* causes *robot_1* to move to the given position 1 gripping an identified workpiece. If the workpiece could be identified, *robot_1* moves it via position 2 to the given position 3. In order to realize concurrency, a second independent action is executed simultaneously. The method *set_val()* assigns a position number to the instance variable *pos_nr1* the robot arm has to move to in another activity that is not further considered in this short example.

The simultaneous sending of the second message to the instance *robot_2* materializes concurrency between the instances *robot_2* and *robot_task*. The activating of the instance *robot_2* also enforces concurrency between the methods *move_continuous()* and *set_val()* moving the robot arm continuously from position 10 to position 20 opening the gripper in parallel.

Algorithm 4.4 (PAR_{III}-operator)

begin

Input: several messages $n_1, \ldots, n_k \in \mathcal{N}$ specified as lists $L_{n_1}, \ldots, L_{n_k}$ consisting of the finite set of methods $\{\mathcal{M}_{n_1}, \ldots, \mathcal{M}_{n_k}\}$ to be processed concurrently:

for (all methods of the messages $n_i \in \mathcal{N}$) (* 1 *)

  assign the methods $m_1, \ldots, m_n$ of the message $n_i \in \mathcal{N}$

end for (method assignment)

par (for all messages $n_j \in \mathcal{N}$) (* 2 *)

  check the existence of the receiving object $\exists o_e \in \mathcal{O}((o_e \sqsubset c_i) \wedge (c_i \in \mathcal{H}))$:

  if ($o_e \not\sqsubset c_i$) **then**

    Output: corresponding error message

    terminating of the message processing

  else

    method execution supported by *check_meth* and *exe_meth*:

    if $((L_{n_j} \neq [\,]) \wedge (|\mathcal{M}_{n_j}| \geq 2))$ **then**

      for (all methods $m_i \in L_{n_j}$) (* 3 *)

        if ($m_i \notin \mathcal{M}$) **then**

          break message processing

          Output: corresponding error message

        end if

      end for (existence check)

      for (all methods $m_i \in L_{n_j}$) (* 4 *)

        assign the methods of list L_{n_j} to the transputers by means of the function *new* (...)

      end for (method assignment)

      par (for all methods $m_i \in L_{n_j}$) (* 5 *)

        concurrent execution of the methods $m_1, \ldots, m_n$

      end par (concurrent method execution)

    else

      Output: corresponding error message

    end if (message list processing)

  end if (message processing)

end par (processing of all messages)

end. (algorithm PAR_{III}-operator)

4.3 An Approach to Solve Concurrency Control Problems

PROLoop permits concurrency control either by synchronization mechanisms or by data sharing in order to prevent the discussed interferences (see Section 3.2.2) considering following problems:

- the sharing problem;
- access control of instances and of instance variables;
- collision-free multi-robot control.

4.3.1 The Sharing Problem

To avoid problems during locating or copying methods at run time in systems without shared memory, PROLoop provides information about the hierarchical class structure to any transputer in the transputer net. This information is available in terms of the clause:

subclass_fact (**<Class>**, **<Fatherclass>**, **<[Variables]>**)

where:

<Class>	name of the class c_i
<Fatherclass>	fatherclass $h_{\mathcal{F},i}$ of class c_i
<Variables>	instance variables $[v_1, \ldots, v_n]$

To execute a desired method, the class hierarchy information is searched until the method can be found. Subsequently, the code is copied to the node in the transputer net that has required the method.

4.3.2 Concurrency Control during Instance Accessment

The access control of an object by synchronization is two-fold:

- controlling of the instance itself to prevent multiple invocation;
- controlling of the instance variables to avoid data inconsistences.

Instance Access Control

Instance access control prevents multiple access to an instance, i.e., a multiple invocation of methods of an instance at the same time. PROLoop supports the decentralized control technique [74] to synchronize any method invocation of instances. The decentralized control is based on the semaphore concept which is implemented in the logic/object-oriented environment in terms of the clause

semaphore (<Name>, <Status>)

where:

<Name>	name $\tilde{o}_i$ of the instance o_i to be controlled
<Status>	state of the semaphore

The semaphores can adopt the status *close* and *open*. The corresponding operations *unlock* and *lock* manipulate the states: *lock* unifies the variable *Status* with the atom *close*. Analogously, *unlock* unifies *Status* with the atom *open*. The clause *execute()* returns the assigned value of *Status*. Figure 4.5 illustrates the object scheme including the access control.

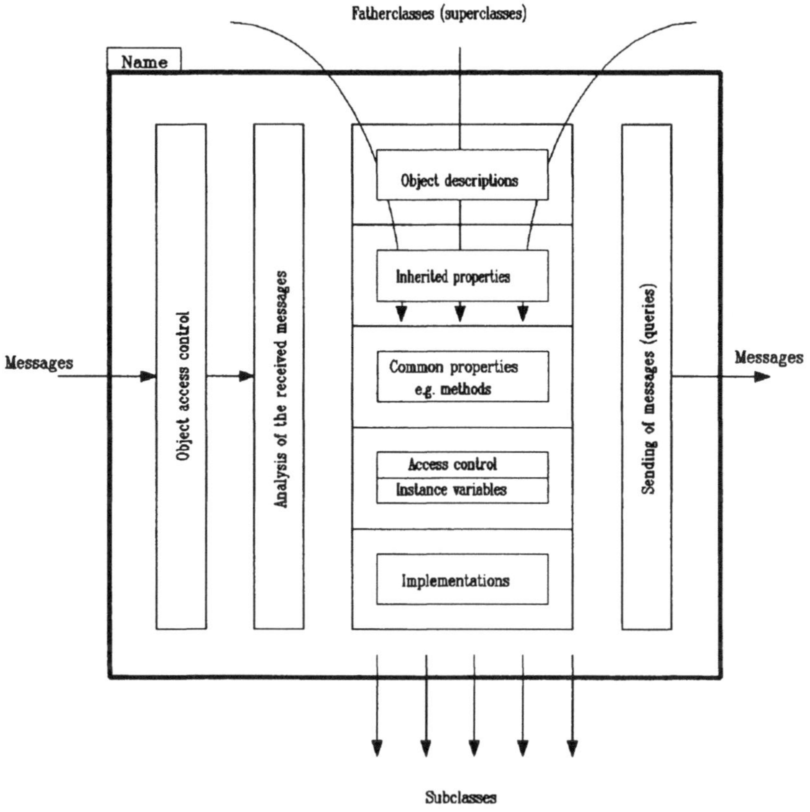

Figure 4.5: Object scheme in PROLoop

Access Control of Instance Variables

Concurrency control to synchronize the simultaneous access of instance variables is handled through the programming environment also by adopting the semaphore technique. Considering the defined operators, the multiple access of instance variables is possible deploying the PAR_I and PAR_{III}-operator. In order to avoid data inconsistency, a semaphore is declared for each instance variable presenting its status. Further, the separation of the semaphores from the data scope of an instance prevents any influence between inheritance and access control of the instance variables.

PROLoop supports the access control of instance variables by means of the clause:

main_queue (<Queue>)

where:

<Queue> list including accessible methods to the instance variables

The manipulation of the semaphores is also realized by the functions mentioned above. The variables are locked during method processing and unlocked after the termination of this procedure.

4.3.3 Multi-Robot Control

For multi-robot control, the synchronization of the involved manipulators is necessary to coordinate the robots in time and space, i.e., the timing of the robot activities and the control of common overlapping operational areas preventing collisions. PROLoop handles the timing of manipulator operations using wait primitives and sensors. To avoid collisions, the more complex *critical sections* technique is applied. The mechanism of this methodology is introduced in more detail below.

Notational Preliminaries

Definition 4.5 Let Ω^W be the overall robot operational space of a working cell W. Further, let ϱ be a set of robots operating in W. Ω_{ϱ_i} is defined to be a local robot operational space with $\Omega^W = \{\Omega_{\varrho_1}, \Omega_{\varrho_2}, \ldots, \Omega_{\varrho_n}\}$. Every local robot operational space consists of n robot positions ω with $\Omega_{\varrho_i} = \{\omega_{\rho_i,1}, \omega_{\rho_i,2}, \ldots, \omega_{\rho_i,n}\}$.

Definition 4.6 Consider the working cell W. A critical section Ω^{κ} is defined as:

$$\Omega^{\kappa} = \begin{cases} \phi, & \text{if } \Omega_{\varrho_i} = \phi \\ \phi, & \text{if } \bigcap\limits_{k \in \Omega^W} \Omega_{\varrho_k} = \phi \\ \bigcap\limits_{k \in \Omega^W} \Omega_{\varrho_k}, & \text{if } (\Omega_{\varrho_i} \neq \phi \wedge \Omega_{\varrho_j} \neq \phi) \wedge (\Omega_{\varrho_i} \cap \Omega_{\varrho_j} = \phi) \end{cases}$$

Theorem 4.5 Let Ω^{κ} be a critical section. For every $\varrho_i \in \varrho$, a collision may be occur if:

$$\forall \varrho_i \in \varrho \, \exists \, \Omega_{\varrho_i} \in \Omega^W (\Omega_{\varrho_i} \cap \Omega^W \neq \phi)$$

Proof Follows from Definition 4.5. □

Control of Critical Sections

The introduced robot programming system supports the control of the critical sections using semaphores. The semaphores are manipulated by the system in order

- to indicate a desired operation of a robot ϱ_i within the critical section;
- to indicate the finish of a robot operation within this section.

For this purpose, the clause

critical_section (<Name>, <Status>)

where:

<Name>	name of the critical section
<Status>	status of the critical section

documents the current status of a specified critical section. The status of this section (*open* or *close*) can be specified by the variable *Status*. The semaphore operations

lock_sec (<Name>) and **unlock_sec (<Name>)**

are similar to the semaphore operations for controlling the instance variables. The *lock_sec()*-operation locks a critical section. Analogously, *unlock_sec()* releases the locked section. The desired access of robots to the critical section manages the system clause:

queue_sec (<Queue>)

by means of the list *Queue* denoted as L_{Ω^κ}. The control of a critical section is presented by Algorithm 4.5.

Algorithm 4.5 (Control of a critical section)
Control of a critical section Ω^κ by the *lock_sec*() and *unlock_sec*()-operations.

begin
initialize Ω^κ by *unlock_sec*(),
query of robot ϱ_i to enter the critical section,
append of the query as i^{th} element into the list L_{Ω^κ}
if ($L_{\Omega^\kappa} \neq [\,]$) **then**
in order to enter Ω^κ, eliminate the next element of L_{Ω^κ}
if ($L_{\Omega^\kappa} = [\,]$) **then**
lock the critical section Ω^κ by *lock_sec*()
execution of the activities of robot ϱ_i
unlock Ω^κ by the operation *unlock_sec*()
else
lock the critical section Ω^κ by *lock_sec*()
execution of the activities of robot ϱ_j
eliminate query of robot ϱ_j from L_{Ω^κ}
unlock Ω^κ by the operation *unlock_sec*()
end if (processing of a single query to enter Ω^κ)
end if (processing of all queries to enter Ω^κ)
end. (algorithm 4.5)

Theorem 4.6
Algorithm 4.5 terminates for an arbitrary critical section Ω^κ.

Proof
The missing of any loops and recursions leads to the termination of Algorithm 4.5. □

Example 4.13 The following simple robot program demonstrates the use of the mechanisms to synchronize the access to a critical section:

```
arm :<>: [create(robot_1, 1)].
arm :<>: [create(robot_2, 2)].


robot_1 :<<: [set_val(pos_nr1, 10),
              lock(critical_section(1)),
              move,
              unlock(critical_section(1))].
```

$robot\_2$:<<: $[set\_val(pos\_nr1, 10),$
$lock(critical\_section(1)),$
$move,$
$unlock(critical\_section(1))].$

The instances *robot_1* and *robot_2* are activated deploying the PAR_{II}-operator. For the execution of the robot tasks, motion to the position 10 is necessary. Thus, a collision is possible without synchronization. The operations *lock()* and *unlock()* enable the collision-free movement (caused by the method *move*) of both robots into the critical section.

Chapter 5
The Object-Oriented Robot Programming Environment

This chapter introduces the class hierarchy of the programming environment and presents the experimental environment for execution of robot tasks. This environment is used to implement and perform the robot programs of the performance analysis.

The first section describes the super- and subclasses of the object-oriented programming environment. The following sections present the software structure and the hardware components of the experimental robot environment. The chapter concludes with the representation of typical multi-robot control examples.

5.1 Class Hierarchy of the Programming System

The class hierarchy of the introduced robot programming approach includes the classes:

- environment model;
- planning;
- sensor configuration;
- robot configuration.

The class structure is based on the work of [99, 34, 77, 59] and is shown in Figure 5.1. The classes and the subclasses are presented in the following and their task for robot controlling is explained. Note that the classes connected by a dotted line are not fully or not yet implemented since the corresponding works are still under development or the sensor equipment and robot hardware have not been integrated into the robot programming system. An overview of the overall concept of the experimental robot programming system can be found in Appendix B.

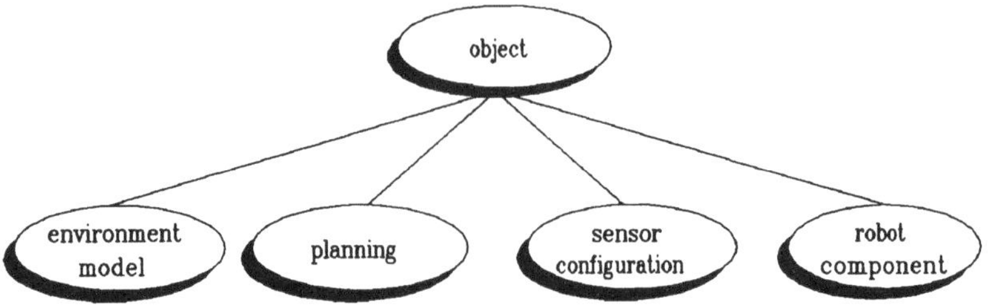

Figure 5.1: Class hierarchy of the programming system

5.1.1 Class "environment_model"

The class *environment_model* contains subclasses providing geometrical and technical data of the working cell, the used robots and other manufacturing devices, i.e., the subclasses of *environment_model* (Figure 5.2) represent data bases with corresponding methods for their manipulation. The methods enforce:

- search of the data base for a specified object description and return of the description to the calling instance;
- comparison of object features given by lists;
- manipulation of lists in terms of
  - appending list elements to an existing list;
  - deleting of a specified list element;
  - search for a given list element;
- generation and saving of new data base entries.

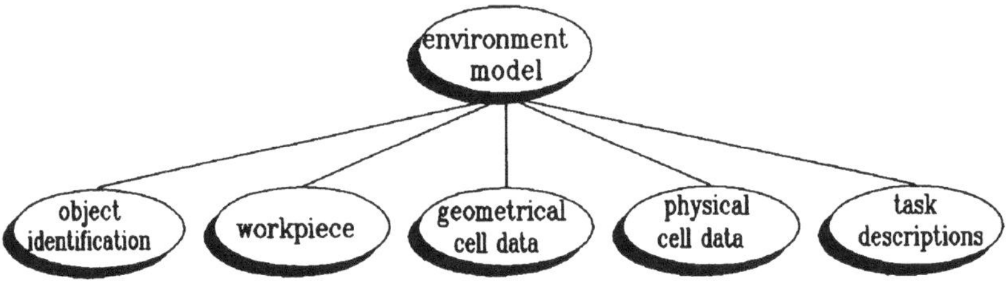

Figure 5.2: Subclasses of *environment_model*

Class "object_identification"

The class *object_identification* provides universal methods for list processing. The lists presenting the data base of this class include object characteristics in order to identify a workpiece of an assembly part. At present, the data base contains entries especially applied to identify objects by means of a bar-code system through comparison of the list entries with the processed sensor data, e.g. c10034567,[pin, black, short]. The additional integration of other appropriate sensors for object identification requires the implementation of corresponding data bases.

Class "workpiece"

The class *workpiece* provides lists consisting of workpiece orientations and workpiece positions. This information is necessary for gripper operations of a robot.

Class "geometrical_cell_data"

The class *geometrical_cell_data* provides geometrical descriptions of all manufacturing devices in the robot environment, e.g. the dimension of the working cell and the equipment, their positions and orientations. The information is also given through lists and is available through list manipulations.

Class "physical_cell_data"

The class *physical_cell_data* offers physical descriptions of the cell equipment such as robot system characteristics (e.g. speed and acceleration bounds). The design of this data base and its manipulation is similar to that of the previous classes.

Class "task_descriptions"

The class *task_descriptions* enables robot actions only by specifying their effects on workpieces [59]. At the current state of implementation, several sensor-controlled and nonsensor-controlled robot tasks (e.g. material handling tasks) are available.

Example 5.1 Material handling problems are concerned with transport and repacking of parts or workpieces considering an initial state and a final state. The user has only to specify the material handling process instead of specifying the sequence of robot motions needed to perform the same task. This palletizing task can be translated and executed if

- all positions and orientations of the workpieces are known;
- the initial state of the task environment is known;
- all robot motions are collision-free.

The introduced robot programming environment realizes material handling without sensing by the following task:

transfer (<Position_1>, <Position_2>, <Position_3>)

where:

<Position_1>	initial position
<Position_2>	intermediate position
<Position_3>	final position

For execution of this task, the robot arm moves to the position *Position_1*, opens the gripper, grasps the object, closes the gripper, and moves to the reference position *Position_2* to ensure a collision-free motion. Finally, the robot moves to the final position *Position_3* in order to replace the grasped object.

The sensor-controlled material handling tasks utilize sensors, e.g. to support decision making. To do this, the sensor data are evaluated and applied during program execution to influence the robot work. For this purpose, the robot programming environment provides the task:

take_defined (<Sensor>, <Robot>, <Position_1>, <Position_2>, <Position_3>)

where:

<Sensor> instance of the subclass *object_data*
<Robot> instance of the class *arm*
<Position_1> initial position
<Position_2> intermediate position
<Position_3> final position

This task initiates the grasping of an object (e.g. a workpiece) and its transport to a defined position. The returned sensor data are evaluated to obtain the corresponding object identity through comparison with the user's object specification. If the expected object can be identified, the robot *Robot* grasps the identified object lying on position *Position_1* and moves it via the intermediate position *Position_2* to the final position *Position_3* in order to replace the grasped object. If an unexpected object is identified, the object identification procedure is repeated.

The execution of sensor-controlled material handling tasks meets several conditions to ensure a correct handling process:

- the initial state of the robot cell is known;
- the applied sensors are initialized and are in stand-by mode;
- collision-free robot motions;
- the used instances are generated.

Other sensor-controlled tasks provided by this class cause similar material handling operations, e.g., the task *take_object()* causes the grasping and moving of any identifiable object.

5.1.2 Class "sensor"

The robot sensor classification of [84] subdivides the sensors according to their characteristics. This classification distinguishes between contact and noncontact sensors. Figure 5.3 illustrates the corresponding class hierarchy.

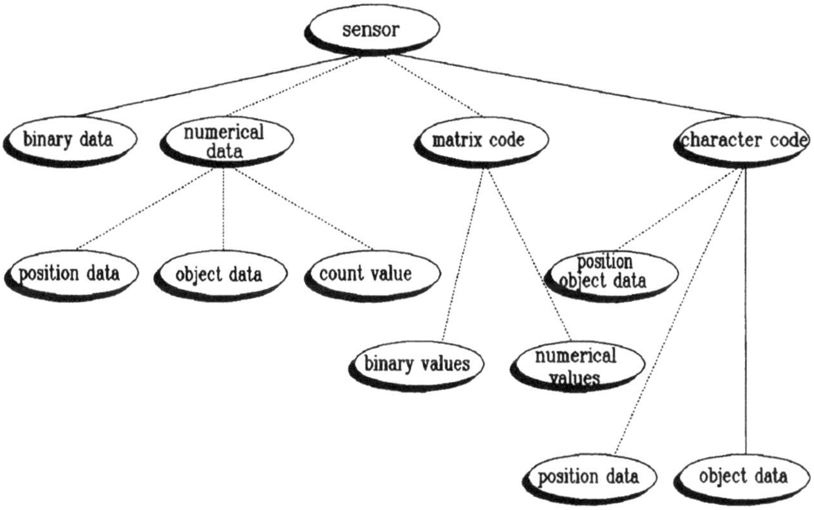

Figure 5.3: Subclasses of *sensor*

Contact sensors are further grouped into tactile, touch, and force/torque sensors whereas noncontact sensors are divided into proximity and vision sensors. Unfortunately, this classification does not supply any detail about the preprocessed sensor data. For example, the preprocessed data of a vision sensor can include the object identification and the determination of the orientation and position of an object. However, other vision sensors only return matrices which have still to be processed to determine e.g. the orientation and position of an object. This example illustrates that the classification of [84] is insufficient for an object-oriented system regarding the inheritance of methods. In order to deploy this mechanism efficiently, it is useful to classify the sensors considering the returned character of the sensor data. Hence, the classification approach of this work is based on this property and consists of the subclasses *binary_data*, *numerical_data*, *matrix_code*, and *character_code*. The subclasses of the class hierarchy (Figure 5.3) marked by dotted lines are not implemented since the corresponding sensors have not been available for robot programming. Nevertheless, the utilization of these sensors only requires the implementation of respective methods, Therefore, these subclasses are briefly introduced. The object-oriented design of the programming environment supports a facile extension of the class hierarchy to integrate them into the existing class structure.

General Methods for Sensor Data Processing

The superclass *sensor* provides universal methods enabling data transfer between the sensors and the programming system such as:

- writing data to a sensor;
- synchronous and asynchronous reading of sensor data.
  - The synchronous reading is realized by methods providing hand shake signals, e.g. the execution of the robot application is interrupted for reading of sensory information which are necessary for the further program execution.
  - The asynchronous reading of sensor does not interrupt the robot execution, e.g. the robot application can continue its work without waiting for the returned sensor data. The received sensor data are buffered and can read back for demand.

The special methods for sensor data processing are provided by the subclasses presented in the following.

Class "binary_data"

Binary data are returned from sensors such as light barriers or inductive sensors and utilized by methods enabling simple decision making.

Class "numerical_data"

The subclass *numerical_data* provides methods for processing numerical sensor data. According to the character of the numerical data, this subclass may be subdivided into the classes *count_value*, *distance_data*, and *object_data*.

Subclass "count_value" The methods of *count_value* may be deployed for event counting and comparison of counting values with user-specified ones.

Subclass "distance_data" The methods of *distance_value* evaluate the sensor data to determine positions of objects within the robot cell. The computed positions then may be used for robot activations.

Subclass "object_data" The subclass *object_data* provides methods converting object information in terms of binary vectors into object descriptions.

Class "matrix_code"

The class *matrix_code* supports matrix processing including binary and integer elements. A further classification subdivides this class into the subclasses *binary_values* and *numerical_values.* Typical sensors returning matrices are vision sensors or sensor arrays such as pressure-sensitive arrays [101].

Subclass "binary_values" Object features such as orientation and position may be specified by matrices including binary values. The determination of these object characteristics frequently require comprehensive computations. Thus, the support of parallel processing through the corresponding methods is useful.

Subclass "numerical_values" The processing of matrices including numerical elements is similar to that of binary matrices. In contrast to the binary elements, the numerical values require more comprehensive computations for determination of object features.

Class "character_code"

The subclass *character_code* provides methods for string processing. A string may consist of integers, characters, and special characters also supplying information about the object features. This class can be subdivided distinguishing object and position code and a combination of both.

Subclass "position_code" The methods of this class analyze the string to estimate the position of an object, i.e., it is aimed to determine the coordinate values (e.g. in Cartesian coordinates) of the recognized object. The estimated position then may be utilized in a robot application.

Subclass "object_code" An object code may be used to identify an object. Analogously to the procedure of the subclass *object_data*, it is helpful to transform this code into an object description aiming to facilitate its handling in a program. In case of an object-identifying barcode system, the sensor data processing and the error handling is discussed below.

Preliminary Notations Let $\mathcal{B}$ be the set of barcodes where a barcode b_i is an element of $\mathcal{B}$. Further, let $\mathcal{F}_\mathcal{S}$ be the set of system error codes where the system error code $f_{\mathcal{S}i}$ is an element of $\mathcal{F}_\mathcal{S}$. $\mathcal{F}_\mathcal{R}$ is defined to be the set of read error codes where the read error code $f_{\mathcal{R}i}$ is an element of $\mathcal{F}_\mathcal{R}$. Let $\mathcal{F}$ be the union set of all error codes: $\mathcal{F} \overset{def}{=} \{\mathcal{F}_\mathcal{S}, \mathcal{F}_\mathcal{R} \mid \mathcal{F} = \bigcup (\mathcal{F}_\mathcal{S}, \mathcal{F}_\mathcal{R})\}$. In addition, let $\mathcal{E}_\mathcal{S}$ be the set of corresponding system error messages printed on screen where $e_{\mathcal{S}i} \in \mathcal{E}_\mathcal{S}$ is defined to be the corresponding error message to the system error mode $f_{\mathcal{S}i}$. Analogously, $\mathcal{E}_\mathcal{R}$ is defined to be the corresponding read error messages to the set $\mathcal{F}_\mathcal{R}$ where $e_{\mathcal{R}i}$ is the corresponding error message to the event $f_{\mathcal{R}i}$.

Sensor Data Processing of a Barcode System The processing of the returned barcode needs distinct methods for

- error detection;
- conditional handling;
- code conversion.

Error Detection An error detection routine tests the ASCII-string for correctness. For this purpose, the barcode b_i is compared with the system error codes $\mathcal{F}_\mathcal{S}$ and read error codes $\mathcal{F}_\mathcal{R}$ determining an existing system error $f_{\mathcal{S}i}$ or and read error $f_{\mathcal{S}i}$. An incorrect barcode causes the output of an error message to inform the user what happened and what to do. The error messages are organized as lists. The entries of the lists are also lists including an error code such as:

$$system\_error\_message :=$$
$$[[[18], Code\ cannot\ be\ read], [[19], Camera\ out\ of\ order], \ldots]$$

In the example above the number 18 specifies the error code and the following entry the corresponding error message.

In case of read errors, an acknowledge from the user repeats the barcode reading. In contrast, a system errors (e.g. missing barcode camera) immediately aborts the error detection procedure, i.e., there is no further attempt reading a barcode as depicted in Algorithm 5.1.

Algorithm 5.1 (Error detection)

begin

Detection of system errors $\mathcal{F}_S \subset \mathcal{F}$ and read errors $\mathcal{F}_\mathcal{R} \subset \mathcal{F}$ by methods:

for (all error codes $\mathcal{F}$)

barcode comparison to detect system errors:

if ($b_i \equiv f_j \in \mathcal{F}_S$) **then**

output of error message $e_{S_i} \in \mathcal{E}_S$

immediate break of the error detection procedure

end if ($b_i \notin \mathcal{F}_S$)

comparison with read error codes:

else

if ($b_i \equiv f_{\mathcal{R}i} \in \mathcal{F}_\mathcal{R}$) **then**

output of the error message $e_{\mathcal{R}i}, e_{\mathcal{R}i} \subset \mathcal{E}_\mathcal{R}$

wait for user acknowledge

end if (detection of read errors $\mathcal{F}_\mathcal{R}$)

end if (error detection $\mathcal{F}$)

end for (error detection)

correct barcode $b_i \notin \mathcal{F}$ for another utilization in a program

end (Error Detection)

Theorem 5.1

1. Algorithm 5.1 terminates for an arbitrary barcode b_i.
2. The complexity of Algorithm 5.1 is $O(n)$.

Proof

1. Consider the sets $\mathcal{F}_S$ and $\mathcal{F}_\mathcal{R}$ where $|\mathcal{F}_S| \leq k < \infty$ and $|\mathcal{F}_\mathcal{R}| \leq n < \infty$. The comparison of a barcode with both sets to determine existing errors terminates since the sets $\mathcal{F}_S$ and $\mathcal{F}_\mathcal{R}$ are finite, i.e., Algorithm 5.1 terminates.
2. Consider the termination proof of Theorem 5.1. The upper bound of Algorithm 5.1 is $O(n)$ since the *for*-loop has to be carried out n times where $n > k$.

□

Conditional Handling Methods for conditional handling compare programmer specifications with barcodes features estimated by the system to enable conditional program execution (e.g. branching in order to perform alternatives for problem solving).

Example 5.2 The following simple program part demonstrates the conditional method execution (*grip_object* and *replace_object*) which is dependent on the identified object:

$$\mathit{alternative} :<>: \mathit{if\_code\_then\_else}(\mathit{grip\_object}, \mathit{replace\_object}).$$

The method *if_code_then_else()* causes the execution of the method *grip_object* if the user-defined object is identical with the system-determined one. In the other case, the alternative method *replace_object* will be performed.

Code Conversion The methods for code conversion transform the returned ASCII-string of the barcode system into object descriptions.

Example 5.3 The statement

$$\mathit{object\_description} :<>: \mathit{convert\_code}.$$

utilizes the method *convert_code* to convert the sensor data by searching a data base including the defined object descriptions. If the data base search fails, the method invokes the error detection routine for testing the string on existing errors.

Subclass "position_object_code" Combined object and position code (e.g. returned by a vision sensor) require methods separating the string in order to estimate object position and object data.

5.1.3 Class "robot"

The class hierarchy of the programming system provides classes and subclasses to integrate distinct robot hardware of different robot types. The robot classification is similar to that of [47, 101, 55] and subdivides *robot* into the subclasses *mobile_robot*, *stationary_robot*. The class *stationary_robot* additionally includes the subclasses *gantry*, *vertical_articulated*, and *fixed_arm*. Figure 5.4 illustrates this classification approach.

Class "mobile_robot"

A mobile robot is defined as a freely programmable robot for industrial applications. The special feature of this robot type is connected with its degree of mobility since this robot type can be automatically moved in space, i.e., in addition to its usual five or six axes, the robot is provided with a vehicle. The motion of the vehicle can either be programmed or the vehicle can be e.g. inductively guided by a particular equipment. Since there is no mobile robot available to be controlled by the robot programming system at present, the methods manipulating the robot of this class have not been implemented.

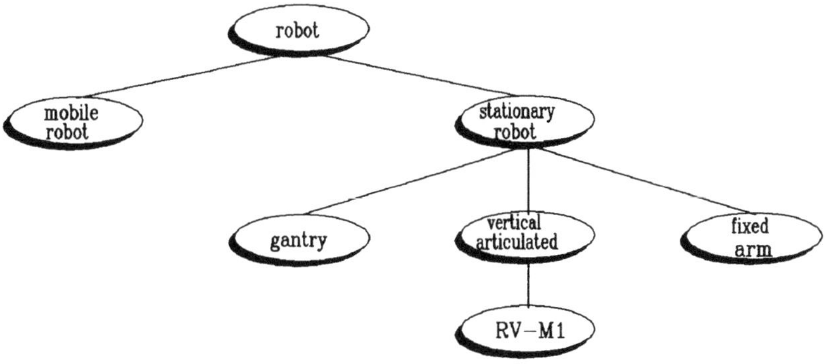

Figure 5.4: Subclass *robot*

Class "stationary_robot"

In contrast to the mobile robots, the stationary manipulators are fixed on the ground, or they are hanging from the ceiling or from a supporting construction. Hence, the class may be further subdivided into the subclasses *gantry*, *fixed_arm* and *vertical_articulated.*

Class "gantry" A gantry is an overhead-mounted rectilinear robot with three (minimal) to six (maximal) degrees of freedom. Large work envelops, heavy payloads, overhead mounting, and the capability and flexibility to perform the tasks of several pedestal-mounted robots are some of the benefits of this robot type.

Class "fixed_arm" The class *fixed_arm* distinguishes several configurations:

- polar configuration. This configuration uses a telescoping arm that can be raised or lowered about a horizontal pivot. The pivot is mounted on a rotating base. These various joints provide the robot with the capability to move its arm within a spherical space;
- cylindrical configuration. A robot with a cylindrical configuration utilizes a vertical column and a slide which can be moved up or down along the column. The robot arm is attached to the slide so it can be moved radially according to the column. By rotating the column, the robot is capable to achieve a work space that approximates a cylinder;

- Cartesian configuration. The Cartesian robot deploys perpendicular slides to construct the x-, y-, and z-axes. By moving the three slides relative to one another, the robot is capable of operating within a rectangular work space.

Class "vertical_articulated" At present, the programming environment controls two articulated-arm robots (Mitsubishi RV-M1 robots). For this, various methods are implemented according to the robot actions and the functions of the drive unit [99, 34, 59]:

- position/motion control. The methods for robot positioning and motion control realize defining, replacing, assigning, and calculating of position data effecting the articulated and linear interpolations as well as continuous-path motions. Additionally, these methods enable speed-setting, origin setting, and basic palletizing operations;
- program control. Program control operations include methods concerning counter operations (the counter are positioned in the drive unit of the robot) and declarations of interrupt operations by means of external signals which is done by the I/O port of the drive unit;
- gripper control. Gripper control permits the setting of the gripping force, manipulating of the gripper, the setting of open/close time of the grip, and for definition of gripper flags;
- I/O control. The I/O control methods cause input and output of data through the general-purpose I/O port. For both the inputs and outputs, the data can be exchanged synchronously and asynchronously. The data can be processed in bits or parallel;
- drive unit control. To control the drive unit, methods for error resetting, for exchanging data with the host, and for reading data from the memory of the drive unit. The readable data are position data, program data, and counter data.

An overview of the available methods can be found in Appendix C. In order to integrate other articulated arm robots, the programmer defines new subclasses and implements the methods for controlling the corresponding robot mechanics. Considering object-orientation, Freund [47] has demonstrated the advantage of the effortless extensibility because the object-oriented modelling of articulated-arm robot (VW-G8-robot) has only taken about two hours.

5.1.4 Class "planning"

The class *planning* provides methods for task-level programming considering collision-free path planning, task analysis, and task coordination. As mentioned in the introduction, task-level programming is aimed to extend the robot programming system. Planning aspects are not subject of this work, however, other works concentrate on path planning [122], task analysis and task coordination [12]. The results of these works will be integrated into the programming system.

5.2 Software Structure

The combination of object-orientation and logic programming results in the software structure shown in Figure 5.5. This composition allows the implementation and execution of logic as well as object-oriented applications. The motivation to combine both paradigms is discussed in the previous chapters.

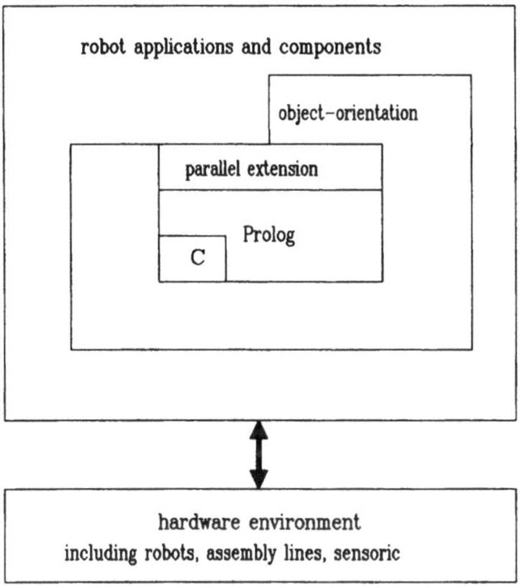

Figure 5.5: Software structure of the programming environment

In the following, the languages C (a parallel C compiler) and CS-Prolog as components of the robot programming system are briefly presented.

5.2.1 The C-Interface

The C-interface supports the developing of user-defined built-in predicates in C [1] and their integration into the Prolog environment. For this purpose, the C-interface provides a C function set supplying parameter handling, memory allocation, and choice point handling of nondeterministic built-in predicates.

For robotics, the Prolog environment has been extended by appropriate predicates materializing:

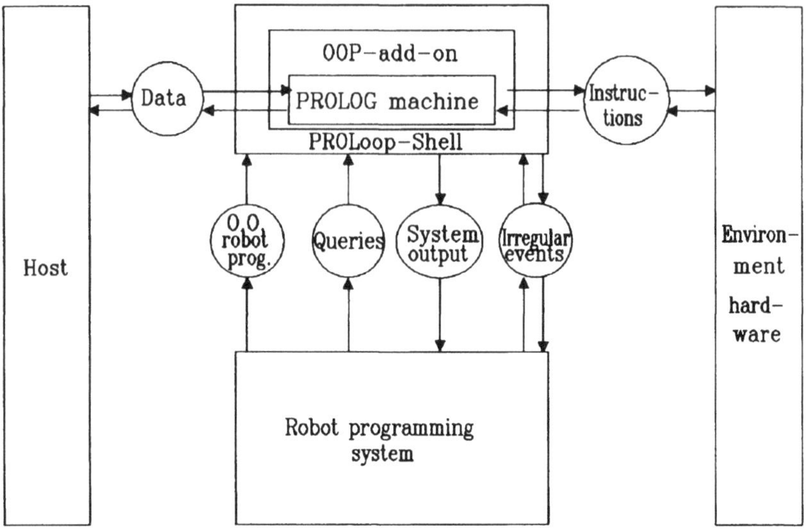

Figure 5.6: Interactions of the system

- the connection of additional hardware devices such as different robot types, stored-program controller, or different sensors [77] to the programming environment through special predicates. These predicates enforce e.g. the initialization of hardware to be controlled or the data transfer between the programming environment and the hardware [79];
- solving of complex mathematical problems occurring e.g. for evaluation of sensor data. Mathematical problems can be solved more efficient in C than in Prolog. Moreover, the use of transputers also allows the processing of these problems concurrently.

5.2.2 CS-Prolog — A Communicating Sequential Prolog

CS-Prolog [97] is a process-oriented Prolog language based on the language concept of Clocksin and Mellish [26] with an extended set of built-in predicates. These predicates support parallel execution and communication in a distributed multi-processor environment. A special feature of CS-Prolog is its full support of exhaustive search through the logical state space achieved by a restricted AND-parallelism and by distributed backtracking.

Considering the declarative aspect, CS-Prolog explicitly permits concurrency by declaring certain goals to be "hypotheses" in the proof procedure, i.e., the goals considered to be "hypotheses" may be accepted true without proof and be proved by an independent proof process. Hence, CS-Prolog ensures declarative logic programming while permitting simultaneous proof processes. The speed of the proof processes is only partially determined by the language. The only restriction is that a proof process must succeed before the initial goal statement is accepted true. However, if a "hypothesis" cannot be proved true, all the considerations connected with that particular "hypothesis" must be rejected. In procedural terms, the computation of the whole system must be rejected to the point where the false "hypothesis" was set in order to keep the whole system consistent.

The Difference from Other Prolog Systems

In contrast to Prolog systems executing application programs through implicit parallelism (see Aurora [88]), CS-Prolog has explicit language constructs to describe separate proof procedures and to arrange their interactions such as concurrency and communication. Communication in CS-Prolog is based on generalized data base manipulating built-in predicates. Thus, no communication by means of logical variables exists between concurrent processes as realized in Prolog systems deploying stream parallelism (see Concurrent Prolog [128], Guarded Horn Clauses [145], or Parlog [25]). Additionally, CS-Prolog applies the concept of *Guarded Commands* to handle nondeterminism occurring from interactions among the resolution processes of different "hypotheses".

The Concept of CS-Prolog

CS-Prolog consists of a set of Prolog inference machines (PIM) working simultaneously and communicating by messages. The activity of a PIM results in a single process. The number of PIMs changes dynamically during execution. PIMs can initiate backtracking as it is usual in Prolog. However, backtracking may be influenced by messages the PIMs have accepted and emitted. Communication is also backtrackable in CS-Prolog. Appendix A describes the communication mechanisms in detail.

The basic element of CS-Prolog is a process. A process is defined by the clauses of the CS-Prolog program, a goal and the resolution rules. A process terminates after the resolution of its initial goal. Explicit termination is possible by built-in predicates.

The restricted AND-parallelism is also supported by the process concept of CS-Prolog: the processes are considered as AND-processes solving AND-parallel goals. These AND-parallel processes cannot contain unbound variables [72, 73]. Thus, binding conflicts do not occur and, therefore, conflict resolution is unnecessary. However, to explicitly establish the consistency of the values of two different variables in two different AND-parallel processes, the values have to be established by explicit message exchange. The sending of a value and an accepting of the same value yields a single binding action which is just the same as in OCCAM: the parallel output of a value and the input of the same value results in a parallel or distributed assignment.

The following simple example demonstrates the single binding and the problem solving using "hypotheses".

Example 5.4 Consider the "hypothesis" indicated in the clause body by using a special predicate: *assume(H, T)*. The first argument is the subgoal to be accepted true, i.e., the working "hypothesis", and the second argument, if present, associates a dynamic partition of the data base from which the "hypothesis" can apply facts. The search tree given by Figure 5.7 represents the search space underlaying to the goal. Such a search tree can be constructed considering the goal, the clauses of the data base, and the resolution rules.

The declarative reading of the first clause of the program below is the same as that of the corresponding Prolog clause without the assume annotation: for all X, $a(X)$ is true if g and $b(X)$ and $c(X)$ and d are true. During the proof of a goal $a(X)$, subgoals g and $c(X)$ are accepted to be true immediately without any proof and, therefore, goal $a(X)$ is reduced to $b(X), d$. Before the program terminates, goals g and $c(X)$ must be proved, too. The proof procedures of goals g and $c(X)$ denote separate Prolog programs, hence processes.

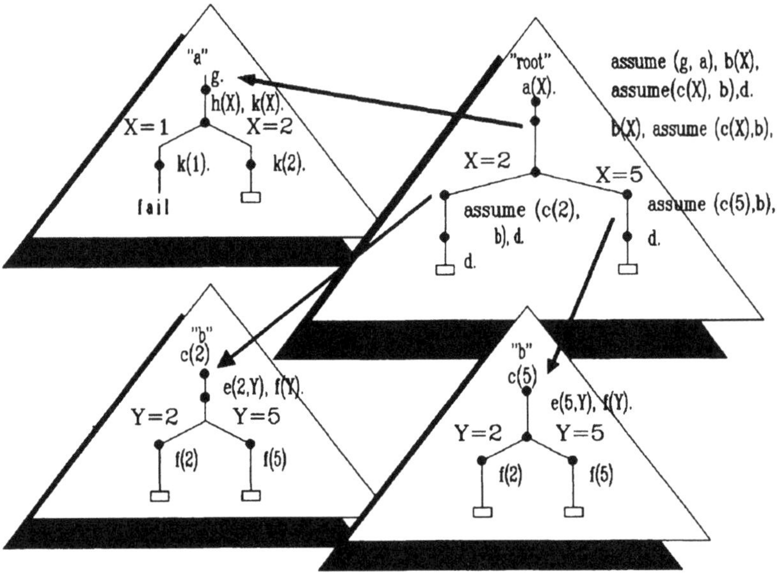

Figure 5.7: Search tree of Example 5.4

$$
\begin{aligned}
a(X) &:- \ assume(g,a), b(X), assume(c(X),b), d.\\
c(X) &:- \ e(X,Y), f(Y).\\
g \quad &:- \ h(X), k(X).
\end{aligned}
$$

$b(2).$
$b(5).$
$h(1).$
$h(2).$
$e(2,5).$
$e(X,X).$
$k(2).$
$k(3).$
$f(2).$
$f(5).$
$d.$

Support of Concurrent Processing

In CS-Prolog process objects and methods will be materialized as concurrent processes executable on various transputers. After creation the processes will be assinged to the nodes in the network. A simple example demonstrates this strategy:

PROLoop notation:

position_1 :<> [set_val(pos_nt1, 10), set_val(grip_stat, C)]

The methods *set_val* with their distinct arguments are processed simultaneously. The statement *set_val(pos_nr*1, 10) initializes the instance variable *pos_nr*1 with the value 10, and the statement *set_val(grip_stat, C)* invokes the robot to close the gripper. This PROLoop expression will be translated into CS-Prolog as follows:

set_val(position, [10,C]) :- write_robot(10), write_robot(C)

The predicate "write_robot()" is a robot-oriented predicate which is especially implemented for robot controlling in the CS-Prolog environment. In the simple example, both "write_robot()" predicates are not dependent and can be executed in parallel. The transformation into concurrent processes supports the construct "new(< Arguments >)":

Process$_1$:

new(write_robot(10), process identifier, transputer_number)

$Process_2$:

new(write_robot(C), process identifier, transputer_number)

"Process identifier" is the name of the process which is executed on the transputer with the specified number. More details about the features of CS-Prolog can be found in Appendix A.

5.3 The Hardware Components

The following explanations represent the experimental environment beginning with a brief introduction of the transputer technology. Finally, details about each hardware component are given.

5.3.1 Brief Introduction to Transputer Technology

A transputer is a single VLSI device with processor, memory and communication links for direct connection to other transputers [68, 69]. The advantage of the transputer stems from its property to construct multi-processor systems. For this purpose, a collection of transputers is coupled by serial bi-directional interfaces, called links, which are also used for interprocessor communication.

In order to realize transputer systems, the transputer family includes various transputer types like the

- 16 bit T222;
- 32 bit T414 and T425;
- 32 bit T800, T801 and T805;
- 32 bit T9000 (planned future type of the next family)

transputers which can be combined arbitrarily in a system.

Although the transputer software is compatible to each transputer type the performance potential of such applications differs in a high degree. It is dependent on the applied transputer type. Considering the T222 with 20 MIPS (million instructions per second) instruction rate the performance increases up to 200 MIPS regarding the T9000 [69]. Further, the transputer types T800, T801 and T805 with an integral high speed floating point processor achieve 4.3 MFLOPS (million floating point instructions per second) instruction rate; the T9000 increases up to 25 MFLOPS instruction rate. The performance level is also influenced through the data transfer rate between the transputers. The link speed varies from 20MBit/s (T222, T414, T425, T800, T801, T805) up to 80MBytes/s using the T9000. The application of transputer/transputer systems contains areas such as [68, 66, 65, 69]:

- scientific and mathematical applications;
- high performance graphics processing;
- digital signal processing;
- distributed data bases;
- robotics;
- fault tolerant systems;
- artificial intelligence;
- pattern recognition;
- image processing.

5.3.2 The Experimental Environment

Figure 5.8 illustrates the scheme of the experimental environment. The experimental environment consists of different equipment such as

- a transputer system [106] controlling the hardware of the environment. The transputer system provides five T800 transputers and an I/O module to transfer data between the transputers and the environment hardware. The I/O module also provides a T800 transputer which can be connected optionally by means of links to the other transputer modules. The task of this tranputer is two-fold:
  - as node in the transputer net in order to process the assigned robot tasks;
  - as converter transforming the serial data stream received by the links into the serial RS232 format in order to communicate with the hardware (robots, sensors, etc.) that are connected to four RS232 interfaces also provided by this I/O module. In Figure 5.8, these interfaces are denoted as *Serial 1, Serial 2, Serial 3* and *Serial 4*;
- a host system enabling input and output operations. The host, a PC or a SUN workstation, is provided with a PC-bus adapter or a SUN S-bus interface;
- the robot arms [95] with their drive units;
- a barcode camera [37] as visual sensor for object identification (see Section 5.1.2). For the applications, a barcode system is an appropriate visual sensor since the position and the orientation of all objects are known and given by
  - assembly line model;
  - defined object depots within the robot working cell;
- a programmable modular I/O control unit for 32 digital inputs and outputs. The amount of controllable inputs/outputs can be varied through adding of additional I/O modules;

- an assembly line model to transport objects during execution of robot applications. These applications concentrate on material handling.

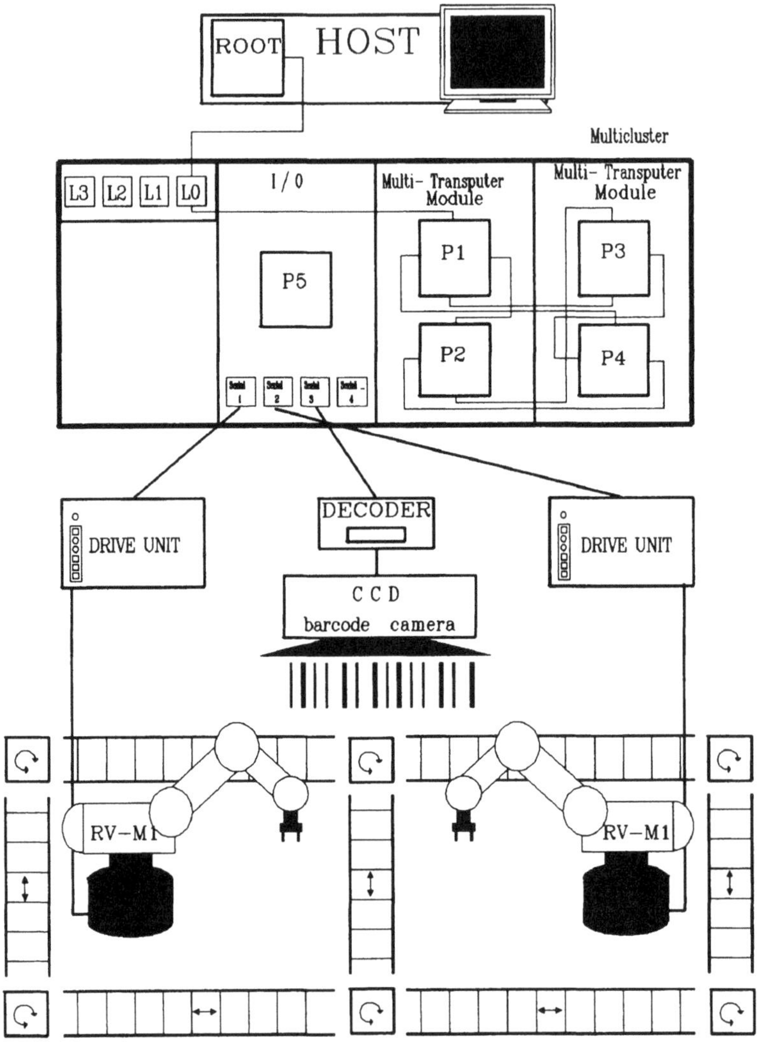

Figure 5.8: Scheme of the experimental environment

5.4 Multi-Robot Control Examples

The application programs below demonstrate the use of the robot programming environment.

Example 5.5 Consider the simple scenario given in Figure 5.9. The robots *robot_1* and *robot_2* have to repack the workpieces lying on the pallets *pallet_1* and *pallet_2*. The task should be partitioned to both manipulators, i.e., *robot_1* has to repack the workpieces lying on the positions 11 and 13 of *pallet_1* to the positions 12 and 14 of *pallet_2*. Analogously, *robot_2* has to repack the remaining workpieces to the positions 16 and 18 of *pallet_2*. Every robot motion of *robot_1* and *robot_2* is guided through a reference position representing a safety distance. Further, the task is executed on the condition that:

- all positions of the workpieces and their orientations are known, e.g. by position teaching;
- the robot tasks are independent;
- the simultaneous execution of the tasks causes no collision between the both robots;
- at the beginning of this procedure, both robots are positioned in a specified initial position.

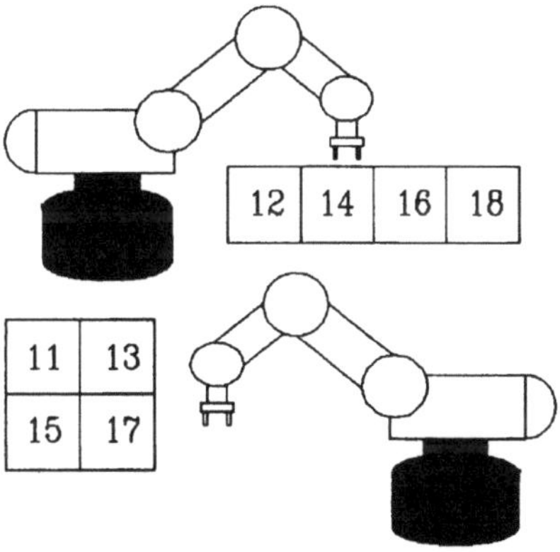

Figure 5.9: The simple scenario of Example 5.5

Program 5.1 The following program provides the required instructions to solve the given problem. Note that the percent sign % marks comment:

```
arm :<>: [create(robot_1, 1)].   %Instance generation
arm :<>: [create(robot_2, 2)].   %Instance generation

robot_1 :<<: [transfer(11, 50, 12), transfer(13, 50, 14)].
robot_2 :<<: [transfer(15, 60, 16), transfer(17, 60, 18)].
```

% The tasks "robot_1" and "robot_2 enable the transport of the workpieces also considering the reference positions 50 and 60 used in the listing of Program 5.2

Program 5.2 exemplarily specifys the program of *robot_1* using the low-level language of the manufacturer.

Program 5.2 Program listing of *robot_1:*

```
GO         % opening the gripper
SP 9       % highest speed for gross motion
MO 50      % gross motion to reference position
MA 11,5    % gross motion to the start position of the fine motion
SP 3       % slower speed for fine motion
MC 11,15   % fine motion through 15 specified intermediate points
GC         % closing the gripper
MA 11,6    % lifting the workpiece
SP 9       % highest speed
MO 50      % gross motion to reference position
MA 12,5    % gross motion to the start position of the fine motion
SP 3       % slower speed for fine motion
MC 12,15   % fine motion through 15 specified intermediate points
GO         % closing the gripper
MA 12,6    % lifting the workpiece
SP 9       % highest speed
MO 50      % gross motion to reference position
GO         % opening the gripper
MA 13,5    % gross motion to the start position of the fine motion
SP 3       % slower speed for fine motion
MC 13,15   % fine motion through 15 specified intermediate points
GC         % closing the gripper
MA 13,6    % lifting the workpiece
SP 9       % highest speed
MO 50      % gross motion to reference position
MA 14,5    % gross motion to the start position of the fine motion
SP 3       % slower speed for fine motion
MC 14,15   % fine motion through 15 specified intermediate points
```

GO	*% closing the gripper*
MA 14, 6	*% deposing the workpiece*
SP 9	*% highest speed*
MO 50	*% gross motion to the reference position*

This language offers assembler-like instructions for robot control. According to the robot language analysis of Chapter 2, important features of a robot language are missing to fulfill the requirements of current robot tasks. A comparison of both programs demonstrates the power of the introduced programming approach underlying the lack of the manufacturer's programming language. Program 5.2 is not only more compact, but also provides a higher flexibility regarding robot task variations.

The program of *robot_2* is similar; the only difference of both programs is connected with the distinct working positions of the robots.

The following example deals with a sensor-supported robot application. Analogously to the previous example, Example 5.6 also concentrates on material handling.

Example 5.6 Consider the working cell (Figure 5.10) consisting of *robot_1* and *robot_2*, the conveyors, *conveyor_1* and *conveyor_2*, a barcode camera, a manufacturing device, and two different types of workpieces, *workpiece_1* and *workpiece_2*, arriving on *conveyor_1*.

The arriving workpieces are identified by means of the barcode camera. For this purpose, an inductive sensor stops *conveyor_1* and triggers the visual sensor. The methods *wait_for_data, get_data* describe the data reading process. Then, the barcode is evaluated (*test_code, convert_code*), returned by means of the instance variable *term*, and, according to the identified workpiece, *task_1* or *task_2* will be invoked. The instruction by the method *activate_output()* restarts *conveyor_1* or *conveyor_2*.

The method *if_code_then_else* identifies the workpiece through comparison, i.e., the expression given by the instance variable *term* is compared with the expression stored in the instance variable *condition_term*. This assignment is not considered in this simple program, because it is not important for the understanding of the scenario.

In case of the identification of *workpiece_1*, *task_1* is invoked to cause the further manipulation by the manufacturing device. For this, *robot_1* grasps the workpiece at *position_1* and transports it to *position_3*. If *workpiece_2* will be identified, *robot_2* replaces the workpiece on *conveyor_2* in order to transport it to another manufacturing process. These processes are recursive and repeated until the user breaks.

The problem solving assumes that the following requirements are met:

- all robot motions are collision-free. To avoid collisions, the robot moves through predefined reference positions to achieve a safety distance to the equipment in the working cell;
- the programming environment controls the manufacturing devices in the cell;
- all robot working positions are known including the reference positions for the robot motions;
- the robot program consists of endless tasks, i.e., the robot tasks are performed as often as they are terminated by user.

The described scenario with its involved manufacturing equipment:

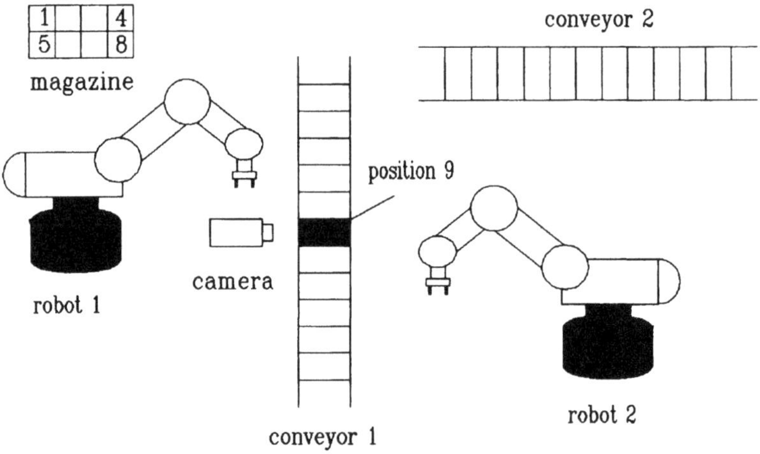

Figure 5.10: Scheme of the working cell of Example 5.6

The expressions *task*, *task_1*, and *task_2* are logical objects that must not be declared or instanced. The object-oriented robot program deploying the experimental robot programming system is given below.

Program 5.3 Listing of both robot tasks:

```
object_code :<>: [create(camera, 2)].  % instance generation
arm         :<>: [create(robot_1, 0)]. % instance generation
arm         :<>: [create(robot_2, 1)]. % instance generation

% sensor data evaluation:
task :-
        camera :<>: [wait_for_data, get_data, test_code, convert_code],
        camera :<>: [if_code_then_else(task_1, task_2)].
```

```
% task of robot_1:
task_1 :-
        robot_1 :<>: [transfer(1,10,3)],
        robot_1 :<>: [activate_output(1), desactivate_output(1)],
        task.

% task of robot_2:
task_2 :-
        robot_2 :<>: [transfer(1,20,2)],
                     [activate_output(1), desactivate_output(1)],
        robot_2 :<>: [activate_output(2), desactivate_output(2)],
        task.
```

The following example demonstrates the collision avoidance by means of the critical section technique. Semaphores control the common working area of two robots.

Example 5.7 Consider the working cell in Figure 5.11 consisting of *robot_1* and *robot_2*, the local working areas *working_area_1* and *working_area_2* and a common working space representing the critical section *critical_section_1*.

The workpieces arriving at *working_area_1* should be transported from *position_1* via *position_3* to *position_5*. The second robot then grasps the workpieces and transports them via *position_4* to *position_2* where they are processed by other manufacturing devices. These manufacturing processes are not further considered in this example.

The problem to be solved by *robot_1* and *robot_2* is based on the inclusion of *position_5* located within the *critical_section_1*. For problem solving, each robot has to enter the critical section. Thus, this section will be locked by a robot and unlocked after finishing its work. The other robot has to wait for release of the section. The method *set_timer()* initiates a time delay of 5 s (50 x 0.1 s) ensuring the release of the critical section by *robot_1*, since both robot activities are executed concurrently. All robot motions are performed either with closed or open gripper. The endeffector status is indicated by the constant (O or C) of the method *move_to()* and set before starting the robot operation. The control of the critical section is a part of the program solving the described problem under following assumptions:

- the scenario ensures that the arrival of the workpieces at *position_1* and their further transportation from *position_2* will always be done correctly;
- all robot working positions are known including the reference positions;
- both robots execute their tasks concurrently;

- both robot tasks are synchronized, i.e., the timing of the activities excludes further operations such as buffering of workpieces within the critical section;
- the robot motions are collision-free.

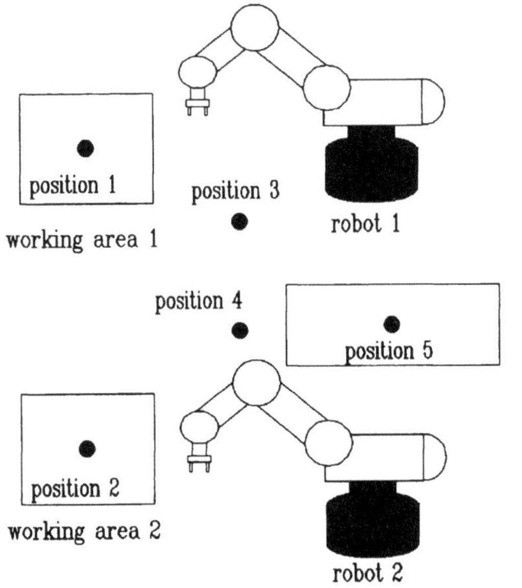

Figure 5.11: Scheme of the working cell of Example 5.7

The scenario of Figure 5.11 illustrates the working areas, the working positions, and the critical section.

Program 5.4 Listing of the object-oriented robot statements:

```
arm :<>: [create(robot_1, 0)].   % instance generation
arm :<>: [create(robot_2, 1)].   % instance generation

% task of robot_1:
robot_1 :<<: [move_to(1, "O"),
              move_to(3, "C"),
              lock_sec(critical_section_1),
              move_to(5, "C"),
              move_to(3, "O"),
              unlock_sec(critical_section_1),
              move_to(1, "O")].
```

```
% task of robot_2:
robot_2 :<<: [move_to(2,"C"),
              move_to(4,"O"),
              set_timer(50),
              lock_sec(critical_section_1),
              move_to(5,"O"),
              unlock_sec(critical_section_1),
              move_to(4,"C"),
              move_to(2,"C")].
```

Part III

Performance Aspects

Chapter 6
Task Scheduling for Concurrent Robot Control

The efficient utilization of the multi-transputer technology may decrease the execution times of robot applications. However, the efficiency of robot applications depends on the scheduling of the robot tasks in a high degree. This section presents a user-based scheduling methodology and a system-supported one using heuristics in Prolog. For this purpose, basic notations of scheduling are introduced and the scheduling criteria of the presented scheduling strategies are explained. The section concludes with the description of the scheduling heuristics and a representation of various scheduling examples using the scheduling environment of PROLoop.

6.1 Scheduling — Definitions, Criteria, Methodologies

The scheduling problem has become a wide area of research and many scheduling problems have been introduced (e.g. [118, 18, 155]). This work concentrates on the static scheduling of robot tasks and discusses suitable scheduling criteria and strategies aiming to optimize the schedule length [50]. However, scheduling optimization leads to a NP-complete problem [18, 43], i.e., the combinatorical complexity of scheduling problems increases in such a high degree augmenting the problem size that the processing time of a schedule rises significantly yielding unsufficient results. To handle this combinatorical complexity, the introduced scheduling attempt applies heuristic information, without guaranteeing an optimal schedule. Moreover, it is possible that the heuristic schedule cannot find a solution at all. However, the research efforts of the scheduling area have focused on heuristics methods. Shirazi [135, 134] analyzed and evaluated heuristic static tasks scheduling; the work of Sih [137] has concentrated on dynamical scheduling strategies and Ramamritham [111] has characterized heuristic scheduling by tasks with worst case computation times, deadlines, and resource requirements. Price [110] and El-Rewini [45] analyzed the communication behaviour of communication-intensive applications also scheduled by heuristics.

The heuristics for robot task scheduling of this work are similar to that of Shirazi's weighted length algorithm. The scheduling objective is to minimize the schedule length (makespan). To underline the use of heuristics of this optimality criterion, the complexity of exact enumerative algorithms varying the number of processors, tasks, and precedence constraints is discussed.

6.1.1 Basic Notations

Let the multi-transputer system be a system with a set $\mathcal{P}$ of identical transputer elements. It is assumed that the computations submitted to this system are a finite set of robot tasks $\mathcal{T}$ consisting of a finite set of instructions $\mathcal{I}$. The tasks are given in a partial order $\prec$ on $\mathcal{T}$. If $t', t'' \in \mathcal{T}$ $(t' \prec t'')$, t' is defined to be the predecessor of t'' and t'' to be the successor of t'. In addition, if there exists no $t''' \in \mathcal{T}$ such that $t' \prec t''' \prec t''$ then t' is defined to be an immediate predecessor of t'' and t'' is defined to be an immediate successor of t'.

In order to present and discuss scheduling problems, a notation is introduced consisting of three entries $\langle\alpha|\beta|\gamma\rangle$ specifying the scheduling of robot tasks and the underlying hardware.

The first entry $\alpha = \alpha_1, \alpha_2$ describes the transputer environment. Parameter α_1 characterizes the processor type. Since this work only considers transputer elements with identical (arithmetic) features, α_1 is replaced by $\mathcal{P}$. Parameter α_2 denotes the number of transputers in the problem. The number is equal to $m, m \in \mathbb{N}$.

The second entry $\beta = \beta_1, \beta_2$ describes robot task characteristics. The parameter β_1 reflects the precedence constraints (see below). The parameter β_2 specifies the task processing times. Finally, the last entry γ presents a scheduling aim, e.g. the minimization of the schedule length τ_σ.

Example 6.1 Consider the given problem consisting of several robot tasks:

$$\langle\mathcal{P}, 2||\tau_{\sigma,min}\rangle$$

This notation reads as follows: Scheduling of robot tasks aiming to minimize the schedule length. The tasks are performed by means of two identical processor elements, p_1 and p_2.

Precedence Graphs

Precedence graphs belong to the set of directed graphs. A directed graph is a pair $\mathcal{G} = (Z_\mathcal{G}, E_\mathcal{G})$ where $Z_\mathcal{G}$ is the set of vertices or nodes, and $E_\mathcal{G}$ is the set of edges. If a directed graph $\mathcal{G}$ contains no directed cycles, it can always be enlarged to a partially ordered set by adding transitive edges, i.e., those pairs (u, w) of vertices for which there exists a directed path from u to w, and all reflexive pairs $(z, z), (z \in Z_{\mathcal{G}})$ to $E_{\mathcal{G}}$. For a given partially ordered set $(Z_{\mathcal{G}}, F_{\mathcal{G}})$, where $F_{\mathcal{G}}$ is a partial order over the set $Z_{\mathcal{G}}$ always a smallest directed graph can be constructed in the following way: $E_{\mathcal{G}}$ is obtained by taking those pairs of elements $(u, w), u \neq w$, for which no sequence $z_1, \ldots, z_k$ of elements with $(u, z_1) \in F_{\mathcal{G}}, (z_i, z_{i+1}) \in F_{\mathcal{G}}$ for $i = 1, \ldots, k-1$, and $(z_k, w) \in F_{\mathcal{G}}$ can be found. Such a smallest directed graph without transitive edges is called precedence graph.

Example 6.2 Figure 6.1 shows a precedence graph $(\{t_a, t_b, t_c, t_d\}, \prec)$ describing the precedence between the given tasks as $t_a \prec t_c, t_b \prec t_c, t_b \prec t_d, t_a \not\prec t_d, t_d \not\prec t_a, t_a \not\prec t_b, t_b \not\prec t_a, t_c \not\prec t_d, t_d \not\prec t_c$:

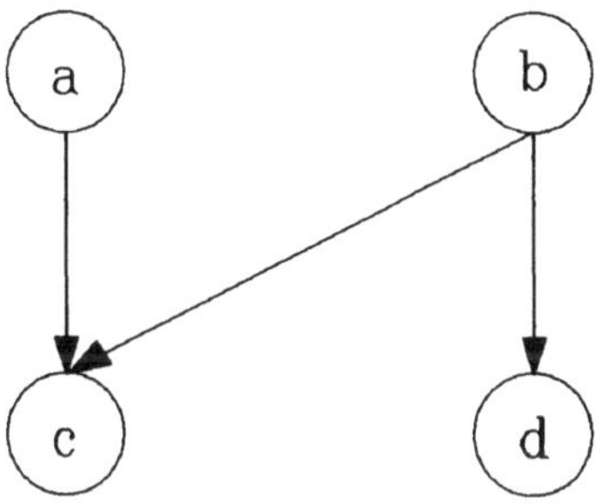

Figure 6.1: Precedence graph of Example 6.2

Scheduling Criteria

In the following, appropriate scheduling criteria are defined for robot task scheduling. In the following, the summed processing times of the tasks assigned to a transputer p_i are called processor load and denoted as $[\![p_i]\!]$.

Definition 6.1 Consider a robot application consisting of a set of robot tasks T. A subset $T_A \subset T$ is defined to be partially ordered by a precedence relation $\prec_A$. $t' \prec_A t''$ means that t'' is *task-dependent* from the task t', i.e., the processing of t' must be completed before t'' can be started. The precedence relation $\prec_A$ on t', t'' is given by:

$$t' \prec_A t'' \Longrightarrow \tau' \leq \tau''_o, \tau', \tau'' > 0$$

where:

τ'_o start time of the task t'
τ''_o start time of the task t''
τ' termination time of task t'
τ'' termination time of the task t''

Task dependency frequently arises controlling several robot simultaneously, i.e., solving a common problem by means of various robots.

Definition 6.2 Consider a robot application to be a finite set of $\mathcal{T}$. A subset $\mathcal{T}_\mathcal{D} \subset \mathcal{T}$ is defined to be partially ordered by the precedence relation $\prec_\mathcal{D}$. $t' \prec_\mathcal{D} t''$ means that t'' is *data-dependent* from t' and, therefore, the task processing of the task t'' needs data computed during the processing of the task t'. The data dependency of tasks can be specified as:

$$t' \prec_\mathcal{D} t'' \Longrightarrow (\tau'_o \leq \tau''_o \wedge \tau' \leq \tau'') \vee (\tau''_o < \tau'_o \wedge \tau' \leq \tau''), \tau', \tau'' > 0$$

where:

τ'_o start time of the task t'
τ''_o start time of the task t''
τ' termination time of task t'
τ'' termination time of the task t''

Data dependency can occur through computing sensor data by means of several methods.

Definition 6.3 Consider a robot application consisting of a finite set of robot tasks $\mathcal{T}$. The tasks $\tilde{\mathcal{T}} \subset \mathcal{T}$ are called *independent* if the tasks are neither task-dependent nor data-dependent denoted by the symbol $\not\prec_{\mathcal{A},\mathcal{D}}$. Thus, the independence of the tasks $t', t'' \subset \mathcal{T}$, can be specified as follows:

$$\begin{aligned} t' \not\prec_{\mathcal{A},\mathcal{D}} t'' \Longrightarrow & (\tau''_o < \tau') \vee (\tau''_o < \tau'_o \wedge \tau'' \leq \tau') \vee (\tau''_o < \tau'_o \wedge \tau' < \tau'') \\ \vee & (\tau'_o \leq \tau''_o \wedge \tau' \leq \tau'' \leq \tau_\sigma) \vee (\tau'_o < \tau''_o \wedge \tau' < \tau'' \leq \tau_\sigma), \tau', \tau'' > 0 \end{aligned}$$

where:

τ'_o start time of the task t'
τ''_o start time of the task t''
τ' termination time of task t'
τ'' termination time of the task t''
τ_σ schedule length

6.1.2 Scheduling as State-Space Search

The scheduling starts with the empty schedule and gradually inserts robot tasks into the schedule until all the robot tasks have been inserted. Usually, alternatives exist at any insertion step because there are several robot tasks waiting to be scheduled. Thus, the scheduling problem is a search problem. Accordingly, scheduling can be formulated as a state-space search problem:

- states are partial schedules;
- a successor state of some partial schedule is obtained by adding a not yet scheduled robot task to this schedule. Another possibility is to leave a processor idle that has completed its current task;
- the initial state is the empty schedule;
- any schedule including all the robot tasks in the problem is a goal state (a solution of the scheduling problem);
- the cost of a solution is the schedule length τ_σ of a goal schedule. The schedule length is roughly estimated by means of the execution time classification.

6.1.3 Complexity of Schedule Length Optimization

The combinatorical complexity of optimization problems is caused through the proliferation of alternatives for finding an optimal solution. However, not for all optimization problems a polynomial time optimization algorithm can be constructed because some of these problems are NP-hard. A decision problem being outside of NP to which a NP-complete problem can be transformed will have the property that it cannot be solved in polynomial time. Such a problem is NP-hard, since it is, in a sense, at least as hard as the NP-complete problem [50]. In this case, it is meaningful to use heuristic (also called suboptimal) algorithms which tend towards but do not guarantee the finding of optimal solutions.

This section is devoted to the complexity discussion for minimizing the schedule length τ_σ emphasizing following scheduling aspects:

- a variable number of identical processors m;
- precedence constraints between tasks;
- number of tasks $t_1, \ldots, t_n$ and their processing times $\tau_1, \ldots, \tau_n$

demonstrating that this problem cannot be solved with an enumerative algorithm for an increase of the input size.

Variable Number of Processors

The problem $\langle \mathcal{P}, m|\tau_\ell|\tau_{\sigma,min}\rangle$ is based on a finite set $\tilde{\mathcal{T}}$ of independent tasks with the length $\tau_\ell \in \mathbb{Z}^+$ for each $t \in \tilde{\mathcal{T}}$, a variable number of processors

$m \in \mathbb{N}$, and the schedule length $\tau_{\sigma,min}, \tau_\sigma \in (0, \infty)$ in order to minimize the schedule length. The complexity analysis investigates the problem whether an m-processor schedule exists minimizing the schedule length $\tau_{\sigma,min}$, i.e., does a function $\sigma : \tilde{\mathcal{T}} \rightarrow \mathbb{Z}_0^+$ exist such that, for $u \geq 0$, the number of tasks $t \in \mathcal{T}_\sigma$ for which $\sigma(t) \leq u < \sigma(t) + \tau_\ell(t)$ is no more than m and such that $\forall t \in \tilde{\mathcal{T}}\ [\sigma(t) + \tau_\ell \leq \tau_{\sigma,min}]$.

The analysis leads to the result that for even simple cases such as scheduling on two processors this problem can be proved to be NP-hard [Karp 1972] [18, 76]. Since there is no hope of finding an optimization polynomial time algorithm for $\langle \mathcal{P}, m || \tau_{\sigma,min} \rangle$, only an algorithm using heuristic information may solve this problem efficiently. However, for tasks with identical processing times, this problem is trivial to solve in polynomial time.

Precedence Constrained Scheduling

The case $\langle \mathcal{P}, m | \prec, \tau_\ell | \tau_{\sigma,min} \rangle$ considers the finite set $\mathcal{T}'$ of dependent tasks (these tasks are task- and/or data-dependent), each having the length $\tau_\ell = 1$, number $m \in \mathbb{N}$ of processors, and the general precedence relation $\prec$ on t to be minimized to $\tau_{\sigma,min} \in (0, \infty)$.

To determine the complexity of this problem minimizing the schedule length $\tau_{\sigma,min}$, it is necessary to analyze whether there exists an m-processor schedule σ for t_σ that meets the minimal schedule length $\tau_{\sigma,min}$ and obeys the precedence constraints, i.e., such that $t_\sigma \prec t'_\sigma$ implies $\sigma(t') \geq \sigma(t) + \tau_\ell = \sigma(t) + 1$.

The complexity of the problem for unit task processing times has been determined [Coffman and Graham, 1972] [27]. The problem can be solved in polynomial time $O(n^2)$ for $m = 2$. If the number of processors $m > 2$ is variable, the problem becomes NP-hard [18].

If the task processing times may take two values, the complexity results in $O(nlogn)$ for $\tau_\ell = 1$ or 2 [Nakajima, Leung, Hakimi, 1981] [98] or it results in $O(n^2logn)$ [Du and Leung, 1989] [44, 82] for $\tau_\ell = 1$ or 3 with $m = 2$ and a tree-structured precedence graph.

Arbitrary Task Processing Times

The complexity investigation of the problem $\langle \mathcal{P}, m | \prec, \tau_\ell | \tau_{\sigma,min} \rangle$ is based on the finite set of dependent tasks $\mathcal{T}'$ with an arbitrary processing time $\tau_\ell \leq \tau_{\sigma,min}$, a number of $m \in \mathbb{N}$ processors, precedence constraints $\prec$ between tasks, and a schedule length $\tau_{\sigma,min} \in (0, \infty)$. In order to evaluate the complexity of this problem, it is essential to investigate whether there an m-processor schedule σ exists for $\mathcal{T}'$ that meets the scheduling length $\tau_{\sigma,min}$ in consideration of the precedence constraints, i.e., such that $t \prec t'$ implies $\forall t, t' \in \mathcal{T}'[\sigma(t) + \tau_\ell(t') \leq \sigma(t') \leq \tau_{\sigma,min}]$.

It is obvious that a polynomial time optimization algorithm for scheduling tasks of arbitrary task processing times cannot be found since $\langle \mathcal{P}, 2 || \tau_{\sigma,min} \rangle$ is already NP-hard. The problem $\langle \mathcal{P}, m | \prec | \tau_{\sigma,min} \rangle$ results in a NP-hardness even for two processors [Du, Leung, and Young, 1991] [43].

6.2 The Algorithm for Parallel Processor Scheduling

In consideration of the discussion above, the heuristics of the scheduling algorithm are introduced aiming to estimate a schedule for a variable number of transputers. The schedule consists of a finite set of dependent robot tasks with various processing times aiming to minimize the schedule length τ_σ.

6.2.1 Scheduling Assumptions

The heuristic scheduling approach is based on conditions influencing the mapping of the robot tasks to the transputers:

- a processor p_i is assigned to at least a load $[\![p_i]\!] \neq 0$. This condition excludes the idleness of an available transputer;
- the robot tasks $\mathcal{T}$ are processed in time interval $[0, \infty)$;
- task preemptions are neglected, i.e., the robot task schedules are non-preemptive. A preemptive task may be interrupted at any time and restarted later at no costs, perhaps on another processor;
- regard of constraints such as data and task dependency between the robot tasks;
- the robot tasks $\mathcal{T}$ are assigned to transputers providing identical arithmetical and physical properties;
- the heuristic scheduling algorithm cannot guarantee an optimal schedule with the schedule length $\tau_{\sigma,min}$;
- resource constraints, if any, are satisfied;
- using of a variable number of transputers. The robot tasks are distributed to a number of transputers specified in the input file *schedule.dat*;
- consideration of experimentally determined task processing times for distinct robot and sensor operations.

6.2.2 The Heuristics of the Scheduling Algorithm

The scheduling algorithm needs a list of robot tasks and their execution time. The current processor load is evaluated during the scheduling process. The heuristics are:

- repeat the scheduling procedure if there is at least one assignable robot task waiting to be scheduled;
- determine and assign all tasks without predecessor;
- fill the schedule according to increasing times so that robot tasks are inserted to the schedule one by one;
- in order to add a robot task to the schedule, check the corresponding precedence relations;
- determine the current processor load of each transputer;
- try to shorten the schedule length τ_σ in consideration of the current load of the transputers, i.e., if possible, assign a robot task to that processor with a less work load. For this purpose, the best-first search strategy determines the most promising node guaranteeing the shortest schedule length from a current node considering the remaining, undistributed tasks.

Task Scheduling

The first presentation surveys the main part of the scheduling algorithm.

Theorem 6.1
Algorithm 6.1 terminates for an arbitrary number of robot tasks.

Proof
Let $\{t_1, \ldots, t_n\} \subseteq \mathcal{T}$ be the set of robot tasks to solve a given problem and $\{p_1, \ldots, p_m\} \subseteq \mathcal{P}$ be the set of transputers. For $(|\{t_1, \ldots, t_n\}| \leq n < \infty \wedge |\{p_1, \ldots, p_m\}| \leq m < \infty)$ it is obvious that the *for*-loop (∗ 1 ∗) terminates.

The second part of the algorithm terminates if the nested *for*-loop (∗ 2 ∗) terminates, i.e., the inner *for*-loops (∗ 3 ∗), (∗ 4 ∗), and (∗ 5 ∗) must terminate. The loops (∗ 4 ∗) and (∗ 5 ∗) determine the processor loads. Since $|\{p_1, \ldots, p_m\}| \leq m < \infty$ and $|\{t_1, \ldots, t_n\}| \leq n < \infty$ the summation of the task processing times terminates. Then loop (∗ 3 ∗) terminates. In consideration that Algorithm 6.2 and Algorithm 6.3 terminate, Algorithm 6.1 terminates.

□

The complexity of this algorithm cannot be determined generally, since the amount of computation steps depends on the problem, i.e., no prediction about the way how the heuristics will solve the problem is possible and thus about the number of computation steps. The examples of Section 6.4 demonstrate this behaviour.

Algorithm 6.1 (task scheduling)
Scheduling a $\langle \mathcal{P}, m| \prec_{\mathcal{A}}, \prec_{\mathcal{D}}, \tau_i | \tau_{\sigma,min}\rangle$ problem:
begin
Input: robot tasks $\mathcal{T}$, precedence constraints $\prec_{\mathcal{A}}, \prec_{\mathcal{D}}$, number m of available transputers through the input file *schedule.dat*
for (all robot tasks $t_i \in \mathcal{T}$) (∗ 1 ∗)
search all nodes except t_i $(\mathcal{T} \setminus t_i)$ in the task precedence graph in order to determine the existence of a predecessor:
if $(t_i \not\prec_{\mathcal{A}} (\mathcal{T} \setminus t_i))$ **then**
if($[\![p_j]\!] = 0$) **then**
assignment of t_i to a processor with no load:
$t_i \rightsquigarrow p_j, p_j \in \mathcal{P}$
else
assignment of t_i to the processor p_k with a minimum of load:
$t_i \rightsquigarrow p_k, [\![p_k]\!] = \min_{k \neq j}\{[\![p_1]\!], \ldots, [\![p_m]\!]\}$
eliminate t_i from the robot tasks list: $\mathcal{T} = \mathcal{T} \setminus t_i$
end if (assignment of tasks without predecessor: $\mathcal{T} \setminus \tilde{\mathcal{T}}$)
end if (determination of a task without predecessor)
end for (task list only includes dependent tasks now)
scheduling of $\mathcal{T}_{\mathcal{D}} \subseteq \mathcal{T}$ and $\mathcal{T}_{\mathcal{A}} \subseteq \mathcal{T}$:
for (all robot tasks $\mathcal{T}_{\mathcal{A}}, \mathcal{T}_{\mathcal{D}} \subseteq \mathcal{T}$) (∗ 2 ∗)
for (each task $t_i \in \mathcal{T}_{\mathcal{A}} \vee t_i \in \mathcal{T}_{\mathcal{D}}$) (∗ 3 ∗)
if $(t_i \prec_{\mathcal{A}} t_k, t_k \in \mathcal{T}_{\mathcal{A}})$ **then**
for (all processors $p_\ell \in \mathcal{P}$) (∗ 4 ∗)
consider the current workload of the processor p_ℓ : $[\![p_\ell]\!]$
determine the most promising task from the current one minimizing τ_σ
$\tau_\sigma = \tau_i + \min_{i<k\leq n} (\sum_i^n \tau_k)$
end for (estimation of processor loads)
insert t_i into task list of processor p_ℓ:
$t_i \rightsquigarrow p_\ell, [\![p_\ell]\!] = \min_{1\leq i\leq m}\{[\![p_1]\!], \ldots, [\![p_m]\!]\}$
end if (consideration of one precedence relation of task t_i)
data dependence handling: substitute all tasks of a sublist $\mathrm{L}_{\mathcal{S}i}$ through $\tilde{t}_i$:
if $((t_i \prec_{\mathcal{D}} \tilde{t}_i, \tilde{t}_i \in \mathcal{T}_{\mathcal{D}}) \wedge (\mathrm{L}_{\mathcal{D}} \neq \phi))$ **then**
for (all processors $p_\ell \in \mathcal{P}$) (∗ 5 ∗)
consider the current workload of the processor p_ℓ : $[\![p_\ell]\!]$

determine the most promising task from the current one:

$\tau_\sigma = \tilde{\tau}_i + \min\limits_{i<k\leq n} (\sum\limits_i^n \tau_k)$

end for (estimation of processor loads)

insert $\tilde{t}_i$ into task list of processor p_ℓ:

$\tilde{t}_i \rightsquigarrow p_\ell, [\![p_\ell]\!] = \min\limits_{1\leq i\leq m} \{[\![p_1]\!], \ldots, [\![p_m]\!]\}$

end if (consideration of one precedence relation)

end for (consideration of all precedence relations)

end for (schedule of all robot tasks)

resubstitution of data-dependent tasks

Output: expressions in terms of tuples:

at (*<Scheduling_Entity>*, *<Transputer>*) by means of the file *allocate.pro*

screen print of the Gantt diagram

end. (algorithm task scheduling)

Data Dependency Handling

The scheduling mechanism of the robot programming environment enables the user to specify data-dependent tasks in order to suppress waiting periods during these tasks. Data-dependent robot tasks are given by the list $L_\mathcal{D}$ consisting of sublists L_{Si} containing data-dependent tasks in the order of execution. The specification of data-dependent tasks is optional and can be omitted if no such tasks exist or if the specification is not desired by the programmer. In this case, the entry of the input file consists of empty brackets.

Algorithm 6.2 (data dependency handling)

begin

check the existence of data-dependent tasks $\mathcal{T}_\mathcal{D} \neq \phi$:

if ($L_\mathcal{D} \neq \phi$) **then**

for (q sublists $\{L_{S1}, \ldots, L_{Sq}\} \in L_\mathcal{D}$) (* 1 *)

for (k robot tasks $\{t_1, \ldots, t_k\} \subseteq \mathcal{T}_\mathcal{D}$) (* 2 *)

sum up the processing times of each sublist:

$\left(\sum\limits_i \tau_i = \tilde{\tau}_i\right), 1 \leq i \leq k$

substitute $\tilde{t}_i$ for all robot tasks in the sublist and replace the tasks of through $\tilde{t}_i$

end for (substitution of the tasks of a sublist)

end for (substitution of all tasks of all sublists of $L_\mathcal{D}$)

end if (existence of data dependent tasks)

end. (algorithm data dependency handling)

Theorem 6.2

1. Algorithm 6.2 terminates for an arbitrary set of data-dependent tasks $\mathcal{T}_{\mathcal{D}}$.
2. The complexity of Algorithm 6.2 is $O(kq)$.

Proof

1. Consider the set of robot tasks $\mathcal{T}$ of a given problem where $|\mathcal{T}| \leq n < \infty$. The sublists processed by the inner *for*-loop $(* \ 2 \ *)$ contain a finite number of list elements: $|\mathcal{T}_{\mathcal{D}}| \leq n$; the *for*-loop $(* \ 1 \ *)$ enforces the processing of all sublists, i.e., maximal q sublists since a sublist L_{Si} includes at least two dependent tasks. Thus, Algorithm 6.2 terminates.
2. Considering the q sublists $\{L_{S1}, \ldots, L_{Sq}\}$ containing k dependent tasks with a finite number of operations to be done during execution. The complexity of a task's algorithm is also considered to be 1. Then the complexity results in $O(kq)$.

□

Gantt Diagram Presentation

The screen print of the schedule facilitates the evaluation of the scheduling results. In addition to the timing of the robot tasks, the Gantt diagram also reflects possible transputer idle times.

Algorithm 6.3 (Gantt diagram representation)
Graphical presentation of the results.
begin
Input: output file *allocate.pro* and list of the precedence relations
consider the given number of transputers with its task lists L_{p_i}:
for (all transputers $p_i \in \mathcal{P}$) $(* \ 1 \ *)$
regard the task processing times τ_i and the precedence relation $\prec_{\mathcal{A}}$ to insert idle times into the diagram:
search the list of precedence relations
if $(t_a \prec t_i)$ **then**
for (all predecessor of t_i) $(* \ 2 \ *)$
search all predecessors of t_i to determine $\tau_{idle} = \sum \tau_i$ of a processor
end for (idle time determination)
end if (predecessor search)
Output: presentation of the timing of a processor
end for (idle times of all tasks)
end. (Gantt diagram presentation)

Theorem 6.3 Algorithm 6.3 terminates for every determined schedule given by the file entries.

Proof
The algorithm terminates if the *for*-loops (* 1 *) and (* 2 *) terminate. The *for*-loop (* 2 *) terminates after estimating the idle times, i.e., the execution of this loop is limited through the finite set $\mathcal{T}$ of robot tasks to solve the given problem. It is obvious that the *for*-loop (* 1 *) terminates as the set of $\mathcal{P}$ of processors is finite. Thus, Algorithm 6.3 terminates.

□

The implementation of the algorithm is realized in Prolog. The declarative character of the heuristics facilitates the problem solving in logic programming.

6.2.3 Quality of the Algorithm

In order to evaluate the heuristic scheduling algorithm, a quality measure is defined comparing the scheduling result with an optimal schedule of a given problem.

Definition 6.4 The ratio of the schedule and the value of an optimal schedule:

$$A(P_S) = \frac{S(P_S)}{O_{PT}(P_S)} \tag{6.1}$$

where:

$A(P_S)$	accuracy of the algorithm
P_S	scheduling problem to be solved
$S(P_S)$	result of a schedule
$O_{PT}(P_S)$	an optimal value of the considered schedule

is called the accuracy of a scheduling problem. The closer the value $A(P_S)$ is to 1, the better the heuristic algorithm performs. The difficulty of the accuracy determination is to estimate an optimal schedule $O_{PT}(P_S)$ of a given scheduling problem P_S. In case of more simple examples presented in a section later in this work, an optimal schedule can be estimated by the user considering the precedence constraints.

6.3 Scheduling Environment of PROLoop

The PROLoop environment provides a user-based and a system-supported scheduling technique [34]. The concept of each methodology is pointed out.

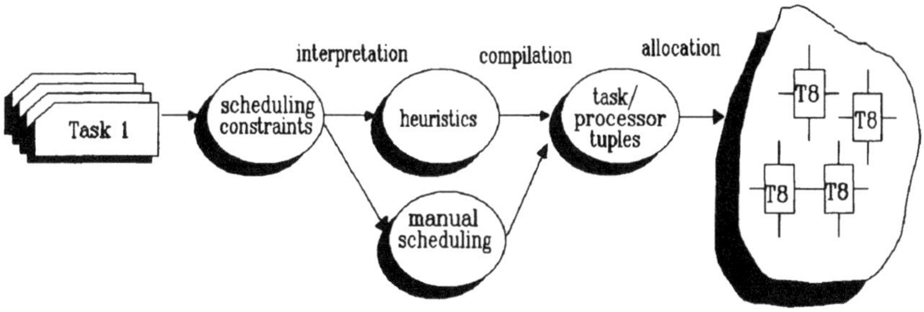

Figure 6.2: Scheduling techniques of PROLoop

6.3.1 User-Based Scheduling Methodology

The user-based scheduling maps objects and methods through predicates to the transputers realizing a particular schedule. This methodology also supports precedence constraints. Independent robot tasks can be scheduled using the predicate:

allocate (<Name>, <Processor>)

where:

<Name>	identifier of an element to be scheduled
<Processor>	a specified processor p_i a task t_j should be mapped to

Dependent robot tasks can be mapped to the same processor by means of the predicate:

collocate (<List>, <Processor>)

where:

<List>	elements to be mapped to the same processor
<Processor>	a specified processor p_i

If no processor is specified, the system determines automatically a processor.

The Precompiler for Task Allocation

After specification, the configuration conditions are interpreted through a precompiler implemented in PROLoop. To prevent delays, the interpretation of the input file is invoked explicitly before executing the application. The precompiler creates an output file storing the determined configuration in terms of:

at (<Task>, <Processor>)

where:

<Task>	task t_j to be assigned to a processor p_i
<Processor>	a processor p_i the task t_j should be assigned to

The assignment of the robot tasks to the processors is caused by the defined operators (see Chapter 4). For this purpose, the file entries are converted into CS-Prolog predicates such as *new(Goal, Name, Start, End, Processor)* [97] enabling the task distribution to the transputers.

6.3.2 A System-Supported Heuristic Scheduling Technique

Consider a robot application consisting of the tasks $t_1, t_2, \ldots, t_n$ with their execution times $\tau_1, \tau_2, \ldots, \tau_n$. In order to schedule the robot tasks, the user specifies the scheduling constraints (if existing), the number of available transputers and their initial state, as well as the robot tasks with their processing times. The file format and the required file entries are:

[<Task_1,...,Task_n>]
[[<Task_i,...,Task_l>],[<Task_o,...,Task_q>],...,
[<Task_x,...,Task_z>]]
[<Processor_1,...,Processor_n>]
<Initial State>
<(Task_i, Task_n)>
⋮
<(Task_x, Task_y)>

where:

[<Task_1,...,Task_n>]	list with data-independent robot tasks
[<Task_i,...,Task_l>]	sublists with data-dependent tasks
[<Processor_1,...,Processor_n>]	available processors with their initial load
<Initial State>	initial state of the schedule
<(Task_i, Task_n)>	precedence relation between Task_i and Task_n

Example 6.3 Input file of a robot application consisting of 12 tasks. To clearly represent the file entries, the robot tasks are only denoted by a *t* and a number.

$[t1/4, t2/10, t3/11, t4/5, t5/3, t6/20, t7/11]$
$[[t8/4, t9/10], [t10/9, t11/8, t12/6]]$
$[p\_1/0, p\_2/0, p\_3/0]$
0
$(t1, t4)$
$(t1, t5)$
$(t2, t4)$
$(t2, t5)$
$(t3, t5)$
$(t3, t6)$
$(t3, t7)$
$(t3, t9)$
$(t9, t12)$
end_of_file

The first file entry includes a list of data-independent robot tasks. The data-dependent robot tasks are given by the sublists as second entry of the input file. The tasks of each sublist will be assigned to the same processor in order to avoid great communication costs between distinct processors. Three processors (they are counted in ascending order) are deployed to solve the problem with their initial load at begin of the schedule. The next entry describes the initial state of the schedule. In this case, the schedule length is zero at the beginning. The following entries specify the precedence relations between the robot tasks, and the entry *end_of_file* concludes the input file.

The constructed output of the algorithm contains tuples specifying a robot task and a processor the task should be assigned to. The output is written into a file called *allocate.pro*.

6.4 Scheduling Applications

The examples of this section demonstrate the feasibility of the scheduling algorithm varying the number of transputers and the precedence relations. The schedule determination time τ_{det} and the amount of used inferences (e.g. in terms of unifications/matchings in Prolog in order to solve goals) are measured. In order to facilitate the presentation, the robot tasks are only denoted by a t and a corresponding index.

6.4.1 Robot Tasks of the Scheduling Examples

The following robot tasks are (multiply) mapped by means of the heuristic robot task scheduler. The task names are substituted by abbreviations such as $t1$ in order to clearly represent the Gantt charts of Section 6.4. Note that all referenced positions are known by the robot systems.

The different robot tasks describe material handling and sensor data processing and are comparable to those of Chapter 7. In order to enable the static scheduling of the robot tasks, average motion times of robot arm movements have to be assessed. Table 6.1 includes measurements of execution times to estimate the timing of robot operations (especially motions as they are more important and take much more execution time than the remaining activities) considering different motion lengths and velocities. The estimation is based on PROLoop instructions and is the basis for the execution time assessment of robot motions regarding the robot task scheduling.

Table 6.1: Average motion time of a robot regarding distinct distances

motion	velocity					average
	1	3	5	7	9	
long	81 s	22 s	9 s	5 s	4 s	24 s
intermediate	58 s	15 s	6 s	4 s	3 s	17 s
short	23 s	6 s	4 s	3 s	2 s	8 s

Similarly, the sensor data processing has been studied using the available sensors and the corresponding data base in PROLoop.

6.4.2 Scheduling Examples

Example 6.4 The following robot application consists of seven tasks $(t_1, \ldots, t_7)$ and the corresponding assumed task execution times specified in time units. The precedence relations between the tasks are given by the precedence graph of Figure 6.3.

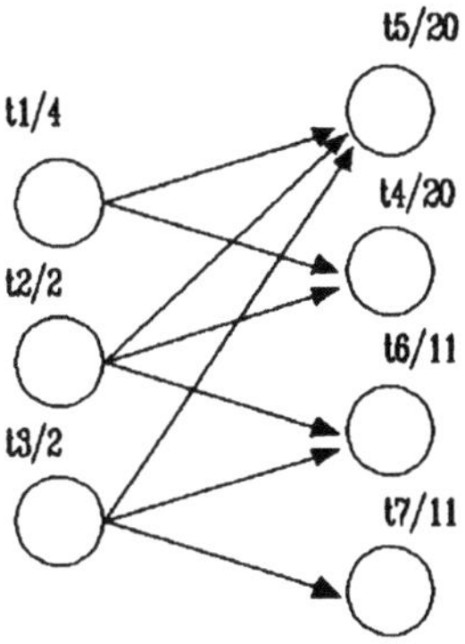

Figure 6.3: Precedence graph of Example 6.4

Table 6.2 includes the task schedule regarding two, three, four, and five processors (transputers).

Table 6.2: Schedule of $t_1, \ldots, t_7$ of Example 6.4

# Processors	Processor	Task List	$\tau_{\sigma_{det}}$	# Inferences
2	p1 p2	$[t_2, t_1, t_7, t_5]$ $[t_3, t_6, t_4]$	2.78 s	66161
3	p1 p2 p3	$[t_3, t_7, t_6]$ $[t_2, t_5]$ $[t_1, t_4]$	9.2 s	195522
4	p1 p2 p3 p4	$[t_2, t_4]$ $[t_6]$ $[t_1, t_7]$ $[t_3, t_5]$	7.62 s	168093
5	p1 p2 p3 p4 p5	$[t_2, t_4]$ $[t_1]$ $[t_6]$ $[t_7]$ $[t_3, t_5]$	62.68 s	1128694

Two Transputers

Figure 6.4 presents the timing of the schedule $\langle I2| \prec_{\mathcal{A}}, \tau_i | \tau_{\sigma,min} \rangle$ resulting in a minimized schedule length of 37 time units, i.e., $\frac{P_S}{O_{PT}} = 1$. The outcome can be proved easily for this simple example. The problem solving takes 2.78 s and needs 66161 inferences.

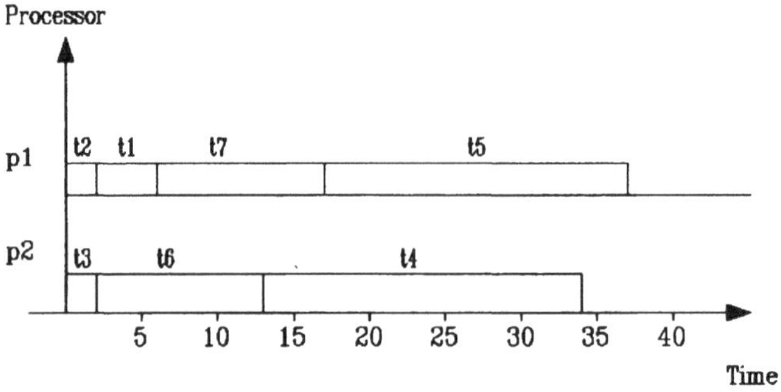

Figure 6.4: Timing of the robot tasks using two transputers

Three Transputers

The Gantt chart of Figure 6.5 represents the timing of the seven robot tasks applying three transputers. As in the previous case, the schedule is optimal taking 24 time units to be executed. However, the amount of inferences and the schedule determination time $\tau_{\sigma_{det}}$ increase significantly.

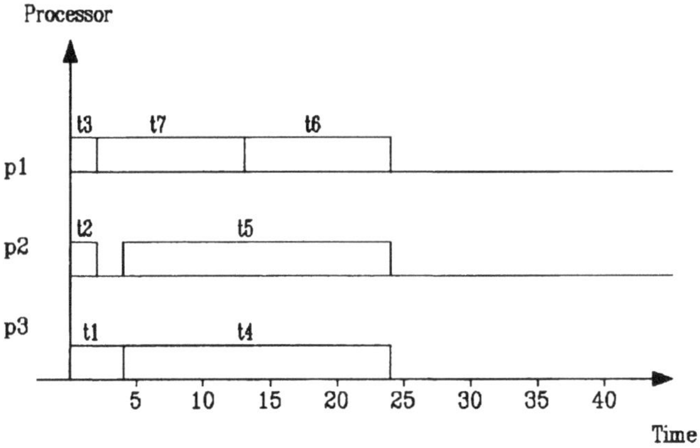

Figure 6.5: Timing of the robot tasks using three transputers

Four and Five Transputers

The $\langle \mathcal{P}, 4 | \prec_{\mathcal{A}}, \tau_i | \tau_{\sigma,min} \rangle$ schedule is based on four transputers. Figure 6.6 shows the timing of the robot tasks also depicting the shortening of the processing time of the program down to the optimized length of 24 time units. Although the complexity of the problem increases, the schedule determination time $\tau_{\sigma_{det}}$ and the number of inferences decrease in comparison with

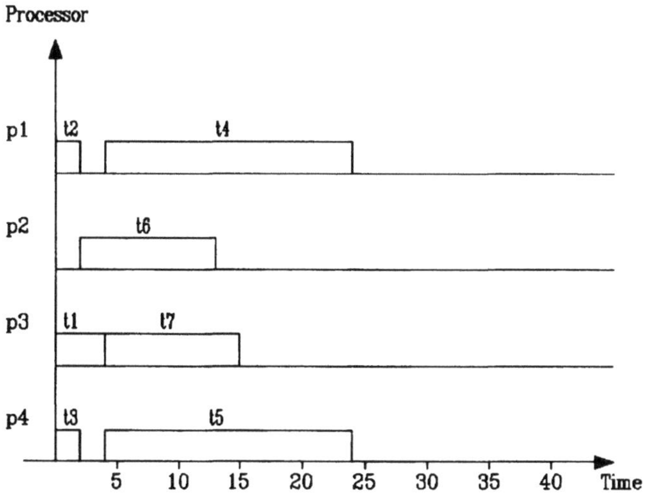

Figure 6.6: Timing of the robot tasks using four transputers

the previous schedule. Nevertheless, the schedule length τ_σ cannot additionally be shortened.

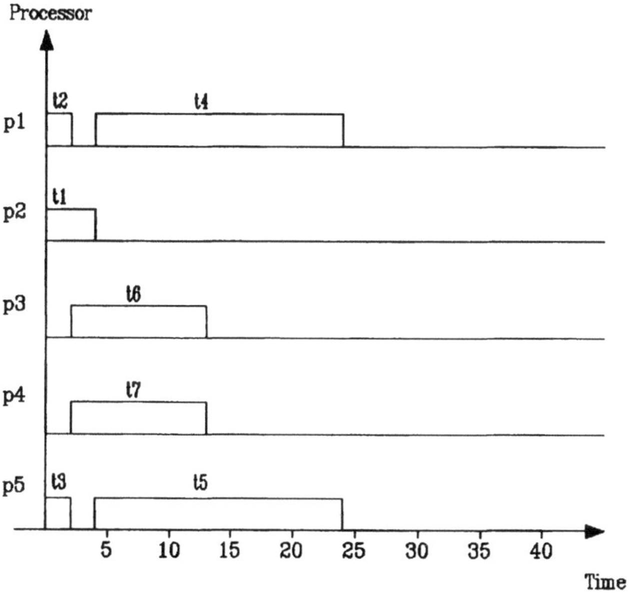

Figure 6.7: Timing of the robot tasks using five transputers

Hence, the use of more than three transputers is more inefficient since the additional hardware does not yield a shorter schedule length. Figure 6.7 underlies the result. The amount of inferences and the schedule determination time τ_{det} increase in a great extent.

In order to demonstrate the different influence of varying the precedence relation, the next example uses the same tasks with changed precedence relations between them. This example additionally demonstrates that heuristic scheduling cannot guarantee an optimal schedule, e.g. a minimized schedule length.

Example 6.5 Consider the robot tasks $t_1, \ldots, t_7$ with the corresponding execution times (in time units) and the precedence relations between the tasks presented in Figure 6.8.

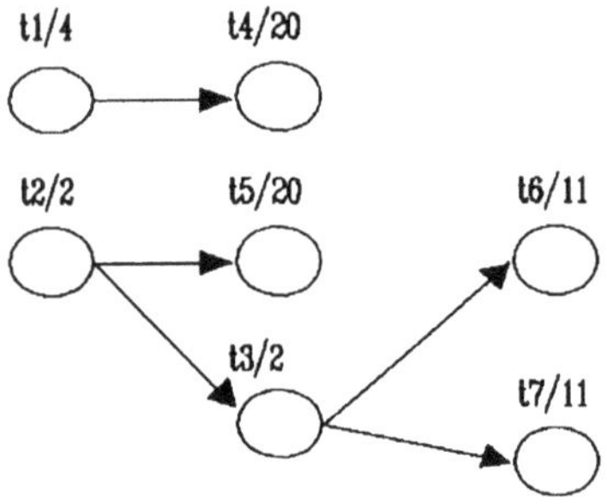

Figure 6.8: Precedence graph of Example 6.5

Table 6.3 reflects the changed tasks lists of the transputers, the schedule determination time $\tau_{\sigma_{det}}$ and the amount of inferences. In comparison to the previous example, the precedence relations between the given tasks weaken, i.e., especially, the structure of the precedence graph regarding the tasks t_4, t_5, and t_6 simplifies.

Table 6.3: Schedule results of Example 6.5

# Processors	Processor	Task List	$\tau_{\sigma_{det}}$	# Inferences
2	p1	$[t_1, t_4, t_7]$	0.38 s	10778
	p2	$[t_2, t_3, t_7, t_6]$		
3	p1	$[t_1, t_6]$	13.05 s	242148
	p2	$[t_3, t_5]$		
	p3	$[t_2, t_4, t_7]$		
4	p1	$[t_4]$	9.67 s	207249
	p2	$[t_3, t_5]$		
	p3	$[t_1, t_7]$		
	p4	$[t_2, t_6]$		
5	p1	$[t_3, t_5]$	49.93 s	849205
	p2	$[t_4]$		
	p3	$[t_6]$		
	p4	$[t_2]$		
	p5	$[t_1, t_7]$		

Two Transputers

Figure 6.9 illustrates the mapping of the tasks to two transputers yielding the schedule length τ_σ of 44 time units.

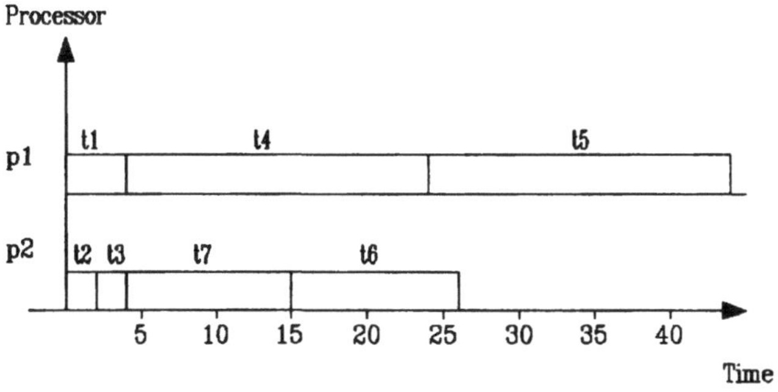

Figure 6.9: Timing of the robot tasks using two transputers

To minimize τ_σ, the task t_5 has to be assigned to transputer p_2 instead of task t_6 or task t_7 in order to shorten τ_σ from 44 time units down to 35 time units. Hence, the accuracy of the algorithm for this problem results in 0.79. The schedule determination time and the number of inferences decrease in comparison with the previous schedule attempt.

Three Transputers

The task mapping to three transputers also yields a suboptimal solution.

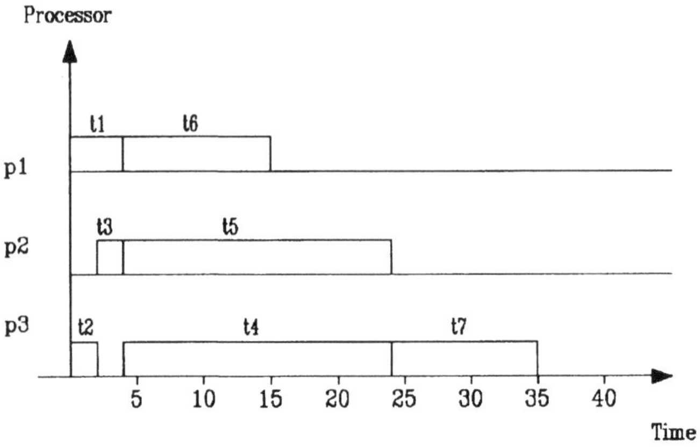

Figure 6.10: Timing of the robot tasks using three transputers

The assignment of task t_7 to processor p_1 would shorten the schedule length τ_σ from 35 time units to 26 time units. Thus, the accuracy of the algorithm for this problem falls off to 0.74.

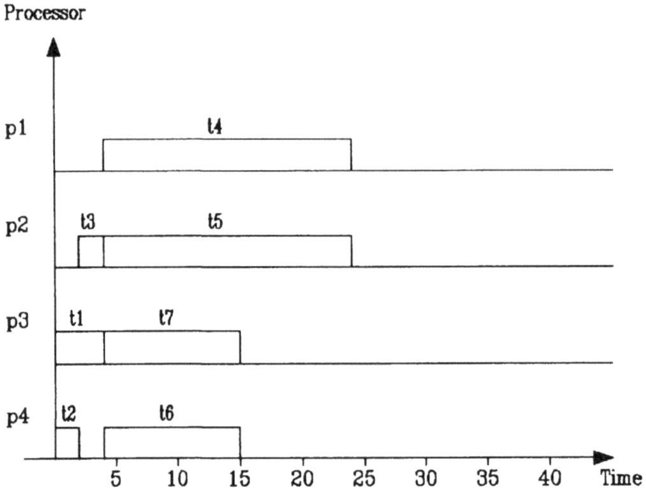

Figure 6.11: Timing of the robot tasks using four transputers

Four Transputers

Considering four transputers, the schedule length τ_σ can be minimized taking 24 time units to be executed (Figure 6.11), i.e., this schedule is optimal for the given problem. Further, the schedule demonstrates a typical behaviour of heuristics: although the number of transputers increases the amount of inferences falls off and, therefore, $\tau_{\sigma_{det}}$ can be shortened (see also Example 6.4).

Five Transputers

The solution of the $\langle I5| \prec_{\mathcal{A}}, \tau_i | \tau_{\sigma,min}\rangle$ problem (Figure 6.12) also takes 24 time units and represents an optimal schedule. Although the number of available transputers rises, τ_σ cannot be shortened. The precedence relations of this problem prevent a more efficient mapping of the tasks. The efficiency decreases, and $\tau_{\sigma det}$ increases in a high degree.

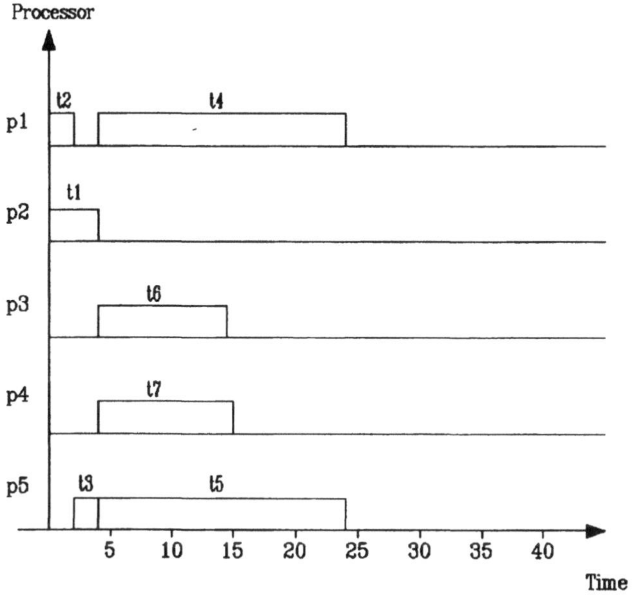

Figure 6.12: Timing of the robot tasks using five transputers

In order to analyze the behaviour of the scheduling algorithm for a greater number of tasks, the following experiment deploys ten dependent robot tasks.

Example 6.6 Consider a robot application consisting of the tasks $t_1, \ldots, t_{10}$ with their execution times specified in time units. Figure 6.13 presents the precedence relations.

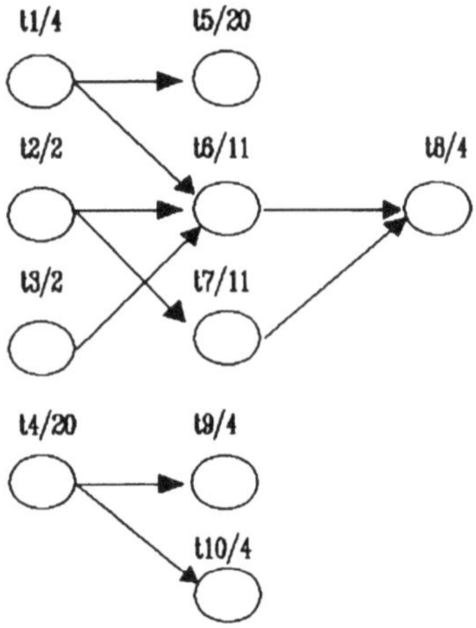

Figure 6.13: Precedence graph of Example 6.6

Table 6.4 includes the scheduling results according to a variable number of transputers and the schedule determination times $\tau_{\sigma_{det}}$.

Table 6.4: Task schedule of Example 6.6

# Processors	Processor	Task List	$\tau_{\sigma_{det}}$	# Inferences
2	p1 p2	$[t_2, t_3, t_5, t_7, t_{10}]$ $[t_1, t_4, t_6, t_9, t_8]$	0.26 s	7555
3	p1 p2 p3	$[t_2, t_3, t_6, t_7, t_8]$ $[t_1, t_5, t_{10}]$ $[t_4, t_9]$	147.43 s	3096030
4	p1 p2 p3 p4	$[t_4]$ $[t_3, t_5]$ $[t_1, t_7]$ $[t_2, t_6]$	9.67 s	207249
5	p1 p2 p3 p4 p5	$[t_3, t_5]$ $[t_4]$ $[t_6]$ $[t_2]$ $[t_1, t_7]$	49.93 s	849205

Two Transputers

Figure 6.14 represents the timing of the robot tasks deploying two transputers.

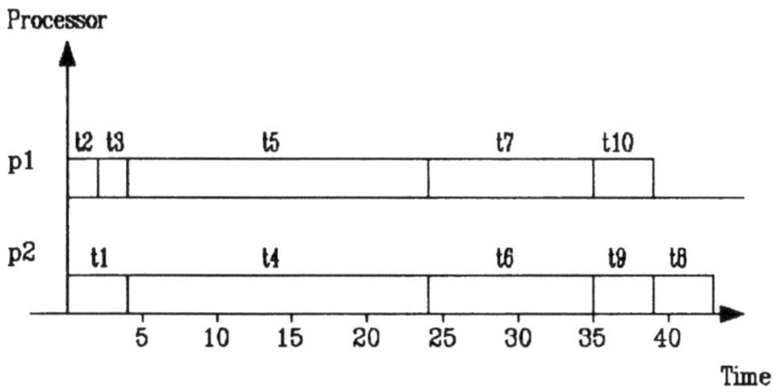

Figure 6.14: Timing of the robot tasks using two transputers

The solution is influenced by the precedence constraints and results in a minimized schedule length $\tau_{\sigma,min}$ of 43 time units. The algorithm maps the tasks in 0.26 s needing 7555 inferences.

Three Transputers

The solution of the $\langle \mathcal{P}, 3| \prec_{\mathcal{A}} |\tau_{\sigma,min}\rangle$ problem is also optimal, shortening $\tau_{\sigma,min}$ from 43 to 30 time units.

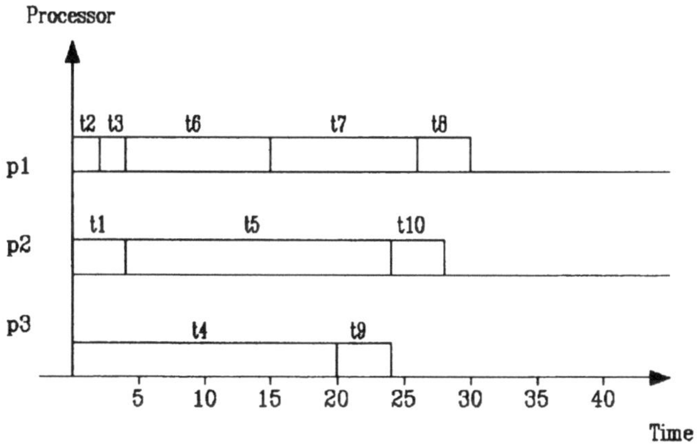

Figure 6.15: Timing of the robot tasks using three transputers

However, the amount of inferences rises extremely, and the estimation of the schedule takes more than 140 s. The reason is that the problem is inhomogeneous to the applied heuristics, i.e., this example clearly underlines that heuristics generally have another behaviour than analytical algorithms with e.g. monotonous growth.

Four Transputer

The task mapping to four transputers additionally shortens the schedule length and results in $\tau_{\sigma,min} = 24$ time units. Note that the schedule determination time $\tau_{\sigma_{det}}$ falls off to 9.7 s. Moreover, the mapping process yields a balanced transputer load. Figure 6.16 illustrates the schedule.

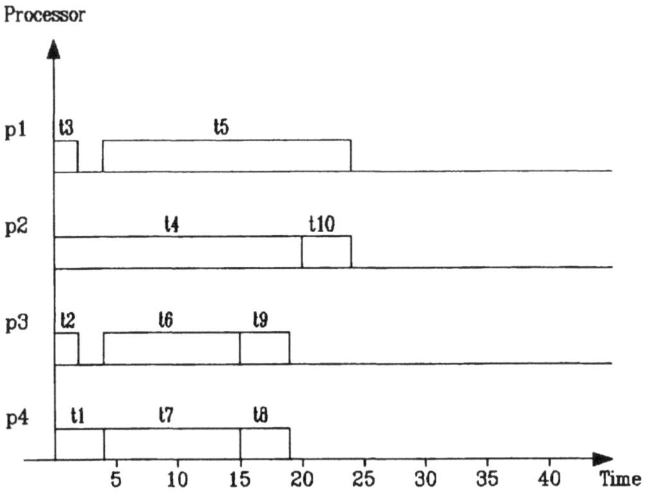

Figure 6.16: Timing of the robot tasks using four transputers

Five Transputers

The $\langle \mathcal{P}, 5| \prec_{\mathcal{A}} |\tau_{\sigma,min}\rangle$ schedule also results in a schedule length of 24 time units. Merely, the task allocation to the transputers is different to the previous approach and leads to an unbalanced transputer load of p_2.

To sum up, this problem can be efficiently scheduled by the defined heuristics deploying four transputers. The additional use of the fifth transputer cannot decrease the schedule length τ_σ.

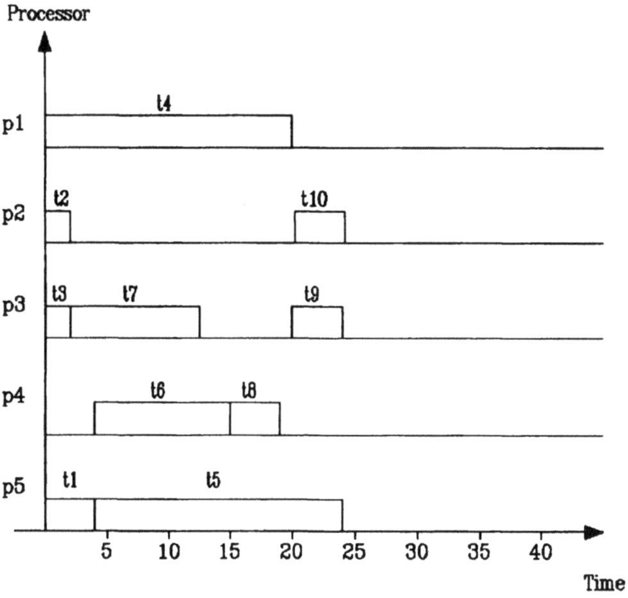

Figure 6.17: Timing of the robot tasks using five transputers

Chapter 7
Performance Analysis

Performance aspects of concurrent robot applications is the subject of this chapter. In order to determine the performance potential, the first section surveys performance influencing criteria and describes the analysis process. The following sections analyze the performance level factors. A summary of the results concludes this chapter.

7.1 Performance Assessment

The following explanations about the performance assessment include basic notations and the definitions of performance influencing criteria used in this work to discuss the performance level of robot applications [11, 9, 10]. Further, the representation of performance measurements of material handling tasks and the description of the performance analysis procedure concludes this section.

7.1.1 Basic Notions

The performance level of the robot applications is defined to be the speedup S_p. The speedup results in the ratio of the application execution time τ_1 applying a single processor and the application execution time τ_n running on n processors:

$$S_p = \frac{\tau_1}{\tau_n} \tag{7.1}$$

The efficiency E of robot applications is the ratio of the measured speedup S_p and the number of used processors n:

$$E = \frac{S_p}{n} \tag{7.2}$$

Definition 7.1 The *interface transformation time* T_{post} arises if a robot command of the robot-oriented programming language (the postprocessor) is interpreted by the robot control unit, e.g., the time for determination of joint coordinates and generation of their control signals.

Definition 7.2 The *robot operation time* T_{robot} consists of the time T_{mech} to execute robot instructions by the robot mechanics and the translation time T_{int}. The execution time T_{mech} depends on the specified speed and acceleration of the joint drives:

$$T_{robot} = T_{mech} + T_{post} \tag{7.3}$$

where:

T_{robot}	execution time to perform the robot instructions using the low-level robot programming language of the manufacturer
T_{mech}	time needed by the robot mechanics to perform commands
T_{post}	translation time of the postprocessor

Definition 7.3 The translation time T_{trans} is the delay arising through the translation of the logic/object-oriented robot statements, i.e., the time interval caused through execution of the robot instructions using PROLoop, $T_{PROLoop}$, the translation time of the CS-Prolog implementation, $T_{CS-Prolog}$:

$$T_{trans} = T_{PROLoop} + T_{CS-Prolog} \tag{7.4}$$

where:

T_{trans}	translation time of the object-oriented robot commands
$T_{PROLoop}$	translation time of the object oriented add-on
$T_{CS-Prolog}$	translation time of CS-Prolog

Definition 7.4 The *total execution time* T_{ex} represents the time interval between input of the robot instruction and abandoning the execution of the robot operation. Thus, the execution time consists of the translation time of the programming environment T_{trans}, the communication time T_{com}, and the robot instruction run time T_{robot}:

$$T_{ex} = T_{robot} + T_{trans} + T_{com} \tag{7.5}$$

where:

T_{ex}	total execution time of robot commands
T_{robot}	execution time using the manufacturer language
T_{trans}	translation time of the programming environment
T_{com}	communication time

Definition 7.5 The *execution factor* E_f is the ratio of the execution of the robot instruction using PROLoop and the robot controlling by the robot-oriented programming language:

$$E_f = \frac{T_{ex}}{T_{robot}} \tag{7.6}$$

where:

E_f	execution factor
T_{ex}	total execution time of robot commands
T_{robot}	execution time using the manufacturer language

The execution factor E_f specifies the quality of the robot programming methodology by PROLoop, i.e., the execution factor evaluates how efficient a given robot problem can be solved by PROLoop. The evaluation is based on the run time T_{robot} solving the same problem by means of the manufacturer language. The closer the value of E_f to 1, the better PROLoop performs.

7.1.2 Performance Measurements of Robot Applications

Before the performance affecting factors are discussed, this paragraph surveys the performance potential of typical robot applications as represented in detail through Chapter 5.

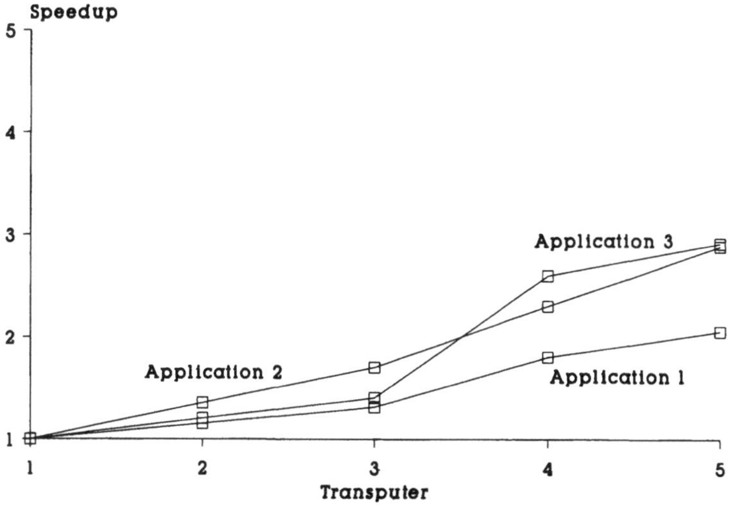

Figure 7.1: Speedup of material handling tasks [34]

Figure 7.1 demonstrates the performance level using several transputers shortening the run time.

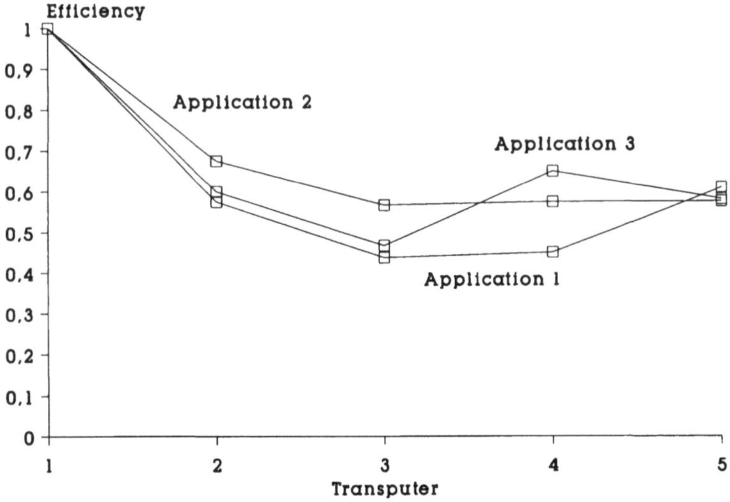

Figure 7.2: Efficiency of material handling tasks

Figure 7.2 illustrates the corresponding efficiency values deploying up to five transputers. The influence to the performance level is discussed in the following considering the mentioned criteria.

7.1.3 Performance Affecting Criteria

The performance level is an important criterion of the concurrent robot applications. Hence, it is essential to analyze the performance influencing factors, i.e., the user may expect an increase or a decrease of the performance potential when varying these factors.

The performance study of this work concentrates on the influence of following criteria assuming the performance level is mainly affected by:

- the translation times of sequential and concurrent robot applications determining the
  - system delays caused by Prolog system;
  - delays caused through the object-oriented add-on;
  - the postprocessor translation time;
- the allocation of objects and methods as discussed in the previous chapter;
- the performance of CS-Prolog;
- the amount of communication and the communication mode;

- the dependency between variation of the class structure and the execution times of the robot applications.

The justification of these assumptions is based on following measurements:

- the execution times of sequential robot applications programmed in a robot-oriented programming language, in CS-Prolog and in PROLoop.

  First, the different programming systems are specified which are used to program the robots. The simplest programming technique presents the robot-oriented programming language given by the manufacturer. Robot programs written in this language support the determination of the translation times caused through Prolog and PROLoop. Typical instructions of these systems are:
  - postprocessor commands as to *mo (move)*, *nt (nest)*, *og (origin)*, etc.
  - CS-Prolog commands:
    * robot-oriented commands as to *dbi_transline*, *io_send*, *io_line* realizing the communication between the transputer system and the robots;
    * CS PROLOG commands as *new*, *wait_for*, *send*, *cpu_time*;
  - PROLoop statements:
    * PROLoop commands as to *is_parent*, *subclss_of*, etc. enabling the access to the object-oriented database;
    * robot commands like
      move_to(robbi1,39,40,C);
    * sensor commands like
      take, *store*, *if_code_then*, etc. for sensor data processing;
- communication times arising through data transfer between various processors applying synchronous and asynchronous communication;
- run times of benchmarks to evaluate the performance potential of the CS-Prolog implementation. The execution times are then compared with other transputer-based concurrent Prolog versions;
- execution times of robot programs to evaluate the dependency between the execution times of robot applications and the variation of the class structure.

7.2 System Translation Times

The estimation of the translation times is performed in several steps:

- measurement of the execution times of sequentially performed robot applications to determine the translation time of such a program,

- investigation of translation times of single robot instructions in order to analyze the translation time T_{post}. This time can only be estimated in this manner because the time interval between the begin and the termination of the translation of a command by the postprocessor cannot be determined precisely for a sequence of commands. The analysis considers the translation time of frequently and rarely deployed robot instructions. Using the measurements, it is possible to infer about the delay of a robot program consisting of n of instructions, $n > 1$. Commands including a coordinate transformation additionally affect T_{post} through the low-level performance of the Z80 processor of the involved robot systems. This affect is demonstrated later in the performance discussion;
- execution of the test programs concurrently to investigate the translation interval of concurrent processed instructions.

7.2.1 Determination of the Translation Times

The analysis of the translation times $T_{PROLoop}$ and $T_{CS-Prolog}$ considers typical robot applications as shown in Chapter 5. The robot programs are written in the object-oriented notation and consist of "pure" robot instructions to determine the translation time. First, the test programs with increasing length have been performed sequentially applying the language of the manufacturer to determine T_{robot}. Subsequently, the test applications (denoted as application A1, A2, A3) have been performed concurrently.

Translation of Sequential Programs

The sequential execution of the test applications documents Table 7.1, and Figure 7.3 summarizes the execution times of the test applications.

Table 7.1: Measurements of the considered applications

Time	A1	A2	A3
T_{ex}	15.28 s	28.26 s	43.11 s
$T_{CS-Prolog}$	4.19 s	7.4 s	13.36 s
$T_{PROLoop}$	4.98 s	11.17 s	14.35 s

In case of a sequential execution, PROLoop causes greater execution times than CS-Prolog application, because the object-oriented add-on requires an additional translation time. The translation time T_{post} of the programs is neglected because of the lack to determine this delay for a sequence of robot commands. Instead, T_{robot} is measured.

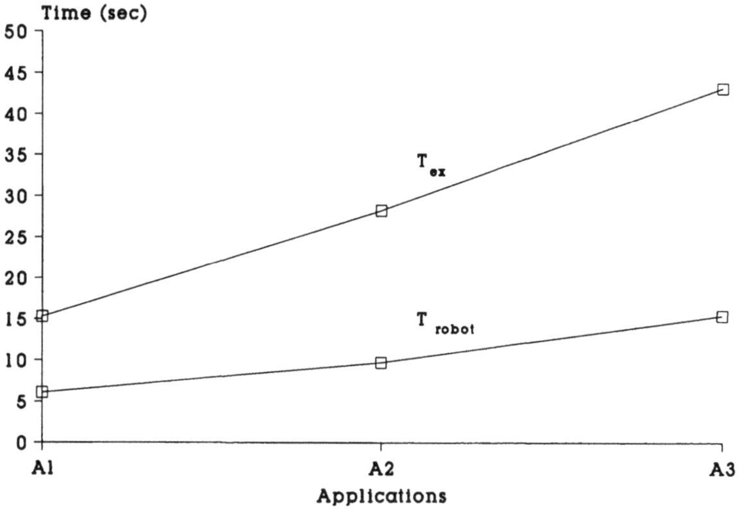

Figure 7.3: Test program execution times

The translation times taken by each system presents Figure 7.4 demonstrating the difference between each system.

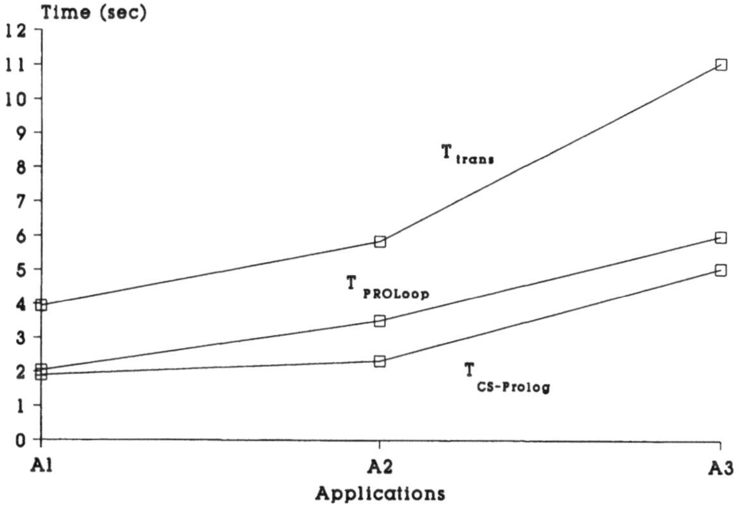

Figure 7.4: Translation times

The logic/object-oriented robot programming offers significant benefits but the run time behaviour of these applications falls off in a degree that real-time requirements may be violated. To meet these requirements, another experiment treats with the simultaneous execution of the programs achieving their concurrent translation utilizing synchronous and asynchronous message passing.

Concurrent Translation of Commands

The concurrent execution of the test programs is supported by the transputer network aiming to compensate the translation time deploying parallel processing.

Table 7.2: Concurrent execution of the test programs

	A1	A2	A3
T_{ex}	7.45 s	11.87 s	20.66 s

Table 7.2 includes the corresponding measurements, and Figure 7.5 presents the comparison between the sequential and concurrent execution of the robot test programs utilizing PROLoop.

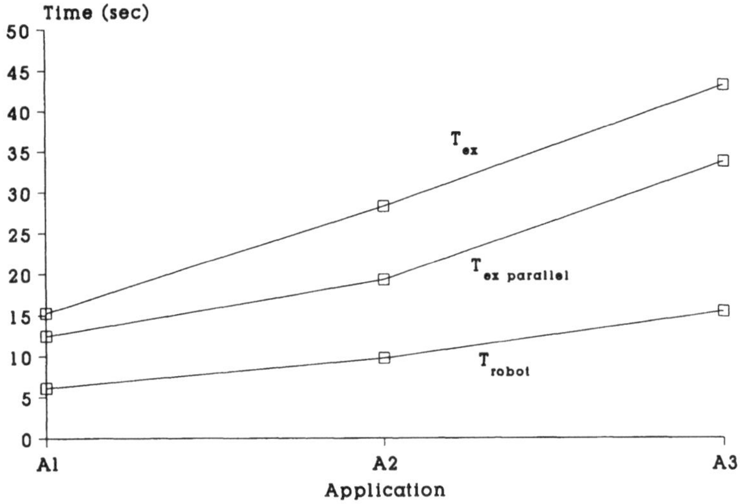

Figure 7.5: Sequential/concurrent execution of the robot test programs

The execution times of the concurrent test programs decrease but are longer than using the robot-oriented language. Diagram 7.6 illustrates the execution factor.

Although the parallel execution takes a greater execution time than the direct robot controlling by the postprocessor (T_{robot}), this robot programming methodology is efficient because of the benefits provided by Prolog

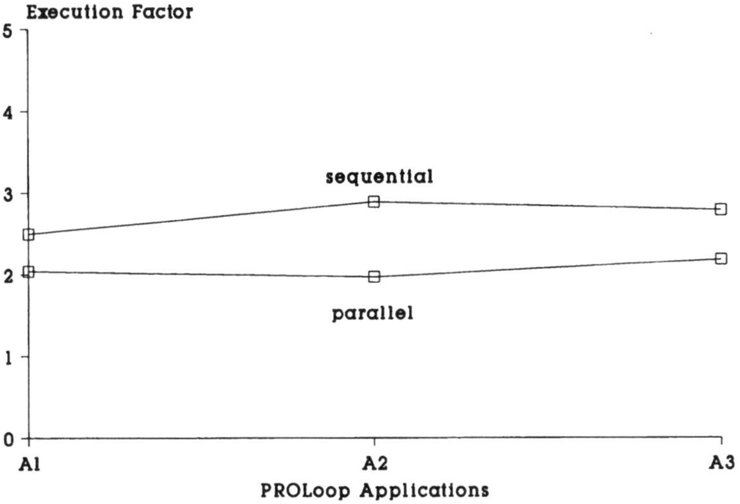

Figure 7.6: Execution factor of sequential/concurrent execution

and object-orientation (see Section 2.2). Further, this experiment demonstrates that the concurrent translation of robot programs only increase the performance level in a small degree, i.e., in order to significantly rise the performance potential, it is essential to concentrate the parallel processing on concurrent activities (see Chapter 2, Chapter 5) for solving robot tasks compensating Prolog and PROLoop-caused translation times.

7.2.2 Postprocessor Translation Time

In order to evaluate the postprocessor translation time, different single robot commands are performed.

Table 7.3: Analyzed robot instructions

nt	move nest
og	origin (a reference position)
dp	decrement position
ip	increment position
sp	speed
pl	position load
mc	move to a position in Cartesian coordinates
ms	move straight through a specified number of intermediate points
go/gc	grip/open close

The translation time T_{post} results in the difference between the total execution time T_{robot} and T_{mech} of the robot mechanics. Some of the often used robot commands presents Table 7.3.

Table 7.4 includes the delay of each statement. The different commands cause various delays. Simple commands like *nest*, *origin*, *decrement*, *increment* cause less delays because no arguments have to be considered. Complex motion commands (e.g. move continuously, move straight) require extensive computations (e.g. interpolations) and generate the great delays. Unfortunately, motion instructions are the most frequently applied robot operations.

Table 7.4: Postprocessor delays

Commands	Postprocessor
nt	184.5 ms
og	224.4 ms
dp	256.8 ms
sp	282.2 ms
pl	867.4 ms
go/gc	170 ms
mc	1374 ms
ms	computation time ca. 2.4 s for 100 intermediate points

In case of a motion command in Cartesian coordinates, Table 7.5 shows the postprocessor delay T_{post} representing another potential to increase the efficiency of robot applications.

Table 7.5: Measurements of a backward transformation

T_{ex}	T_{robot}	T_{post}
2314 ms	960 ms	1354 ms

The postprocessor delay T_{post} is mainly caused through computations like:

- coordinate transformation from Cartesian coordinates to joint coordinates;
- determining of intermediate positions by dividing the distance of travel and position angle between two positions. The Z80 processor needs approximately 2.4 s to compute 100 intermediate points [95].

The computation of the desired joint coordinates of the target position or the computing of the intermediate points represents a significant load of the Z80-based processor of the drive unit. In order to demonstrate the computation cost, the required arithmetical operations are presented in terms of kinematics equations given below.

7.2.3 Introduction to Manipulator Kinematics

Figure 7.7 illustrates the configuration of a manipulator in three dimensions. The manipulator has four degrees of freedom:

- Φ_w specifies the rotation of about the z axis;
- Φ_s describes the rotation of the shoulder. This rotation is perpendicular to the z axis;
- Φ_e describes the rotation of the elbow. This rotation is parallel to the rotation of the shoulder;
- Φ_p specifies the rotation of the wrist pitch.

This configuration does not consider the roll angle of the wrist which presents the fifth degree of the used robots. Figure 7.7 illustrates their construction.

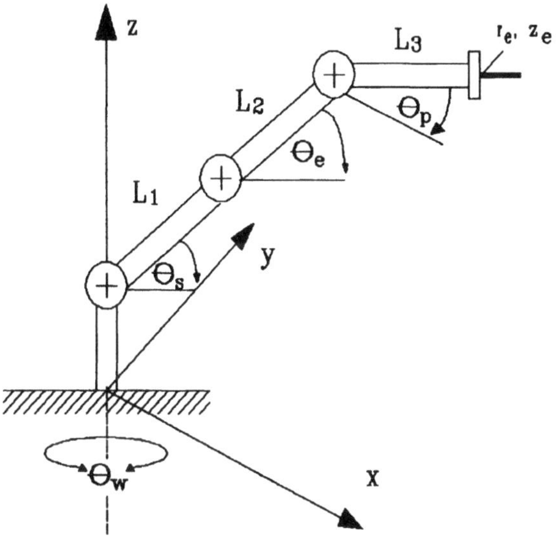

Figure 7.7: Model of the robots

The position determination of the used robot systems by means of the reverse transformation is based on a complex system of equation [55] computed by the transputers. For this reason only the results are presented. The complete derivation can be found in [55, 101].

The position determination is performed in several steps. First, the shoulder turning angle is estimated by means of the equations:

$$r_e = L_1 \cos(\Phi_s) + L_2 \cos(\Phi_s + \Phi_e) + L_3 \cos(\Phi_s + \Phi_e + \Phi_p) \quad (7.7)$$

$$z_e = L_1 \sin(\Phi_s) + L_2 \sin(\Phi_s + \Phi_e) + L_3 \sin(\Phi_s + \Phi_e + \Phi_p) \quad (7.8)$$

$$\psi = \Phi_s + \Phi_e + \Phi_p \quad (7.9)$$

To facilitate the computations, x and y are substituted for $r_e = \sqrt{x^2 + y^2}$ to estimate the tool center point. Thus, the derivation of the equations results in the shoulder turning angle Φ_s:

$$\Phi_{s_{1/2}} = +\arccos\left(v \pm \sqrt{v^2 - u}\right) \quad (7.10)$$

$$\Phi_{s_{3/4}} = -\arccos\left(v \pm \sqrt{v^2 - u}\right) \quad (7.11)$$

where:

$$v = -\frac{(L_2 \cos(\Phi_p) + L_3)^2 + {L_2}^2 \sin^2(\Phi_p) - {L_1}^2 - {r_e}^2 - {z_e}^2}{2L_1} \cdot \frac{r_e}{{r_e}^2 + {z_e}^2} \quad (7.12)$$

$$u = \frac{((L_2 \cos(\Phi_p) + L_3)^2 + {L_2}^2 \sin^2(\Phi_p) - {L_1}^2 - {r_e}^2 - {z_e}^2)^2 - 4{L_1}^2{z_e}^2}{4{L_1}^2({r_e}^2 + {z_e}^2)} \quad (7.13)$$

The determination of the shoulder turning angle yields four eligible values whose usability must be checked by the Equations 7.7 - 7.9.

After determination of a shoulder turning angle Φ_s, the corresponding elbow turning angle Φ_e, the wrist pitch rotation angle Φ_p, and the wrist turning angle Φ_w are computed. For the estimation of the angles these coordinate basic origin is moved to the elbow joint reducing the amount of computations [55] and denoted by O_n. The transformation is based on the equations:

$$O_n = (r_1, z_1) \quad (7.14)$$

$$r_1 = r_e - L_1 \cos(\Phi_s) \quad (7.15)$$

$$z_1 = z_e - L_1 \sin(\Phi_s) \quad (7.16)$$

The transformed coordination basic origin O_n leads to the equations determining the desired angles:

$$r_e = L_2 \cos(\Phi_z) + L_3 \cos(\Phi_z + \Phi_p) \quad (7.17)$$

$$z_e = L_2 \sin(\Phi_z) + L_3 \sin(\Phi_z + \Phi_p) \quad (7.18)$$

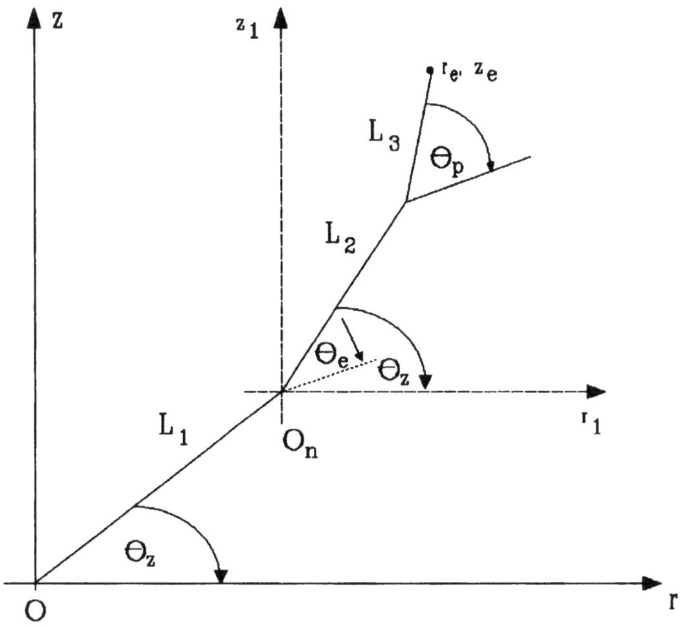

Figure 7.8: Coordinate transformation

The angle Φ_z, the wrist turning angle, the wrist pitch angle Φ_p, and the elbow turning angle Φ_e are given as:

$$\Phi_p = \arccos\left(\frac{{r_e}^2 + {z_e}^2 - {L_2}^2 - {L_3}^2}{2L_2L_3}\right) \tag{7.19}$$

$$\Phi_z = \arctan\left(\frac{z_e(L_2 + L_3\cos(\Phi_p) - r_eL_3\sin(\Phi_p))}{r_e(L_2 + L_3\cos(\Phi_p) - z_eL_3\sin(\Phi_p))}\right) \tag{7.20}$$

$$\Phi_e = \Phi_z - \Phi_s \tag{7.21}$$

$$\Phi_w = \arccos\left(\frac{y}{r}\right) \tag{7.22}$$

The computed angles can be transmitted to the drive units in order to initiate the corresponding robot motion. Algorithm 7.1 reflects the required computations.

The reverse coordinate transformation can be supported by parallel processing through the simultaneous computation of the four shoulder turning angles, the concurrent computation of the wrist turning angle, the wrist pitch angle, and the elbow turning angle or through concurrent solution of the equations.

Algorithm 7.1 (reverse coordinate transformation)
The transputer-based reverse coordinate transformation converts the coordinates of the destination position of a robot into joint coordinates, i.e. positive or negative angle increments the robot joints must be turned to arrive at the desired position

begin
Input: World coordinates of the destination position $\omega_{p_i,j}$
if ($\omega_{p_i,j} \in \Omega_{p_i}$)
    determination of Φ_e, Φ_p, Φ_w and Φ_z:
    par
        for (all angles $\Phi_{s_i}, 0 < i \leq 4$)
            begin
                computation of Φ_{s_i}
                verification of Φ_{s_i}, i.e. the value of the angle is in the valid shoulder angle scope of the robot
            end
        end for (shoulder angle estimation)
        coordinate transformation to get O_n
        computation of Φ_e, Φ_p, Φ_w and Φ_z
    end par (reverse coordinate determination)
    Output: joint increments and decrements to be turned by each axis
else
    break coordinate transformation
    Output: error message
end. (algorithm reverse coordinate transformation)

Theorem 7.1 Algorithm 7.1 terminates for each world coordinates of a destination position $\omega_{p_i,j}$.

Proof Consider the *for*-loop of Algorithm 7.1 computing Φ_{s_i}. It is obvious that this loop terminates after estimating all values of the shoulder angle using Equations 7.10 - 7.11. Further, unsufficient world coordinates lead to an immediate break of the algorithm.

□

To speedup the backward transformation, the corresponding equations are implemented in C (the parallel 3L-C compiler) and computed by means of transputers as demonstrated in Table 7.6 and shown in Figure 7.9. The Z80 processor of the used robot drive units takes much more computation time for this task than the transputer system.

The support of the multi-transputer for the coordinate transformation additionally speeds up the computation. Table 7.6 reflects the speedup values

Table 7.6: Backward transformation of a motion

Z80 processor	transputer (T800 G25)			
	sequential	concurrent		
		# transputer	computation time	speedup
1374 *ms*	129.7 *ms*	2	86.5 *ms*	1.49
		3	54.1 *ms*	2.3
		4	44.2 *ms*	2.93
		5	37.1 *ms*	3.5

which are graphically presented in Figure 7.10. The computation (as part of the translation) of the postprocessor commands by external hardware is circumstantial since the data (e.g. of the finial position of a motion) must be readout by the external hardware and the transformed data must be returned to the drive unit(s). An acceptable solution for this problem is to replace the Z80 processor system through e.g. a transputer-based system [51] or another multi-processor [71, 78] or to choose an alternative more efficient robot system.

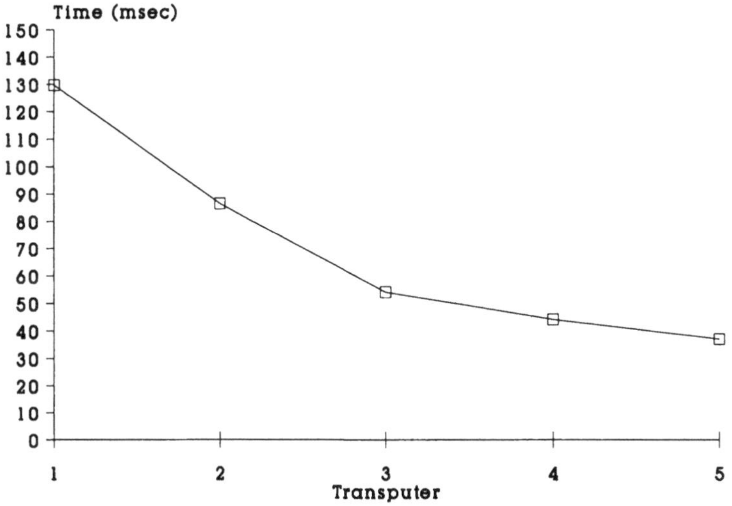

Figure 7.9: Parallel processing of the backward transformation

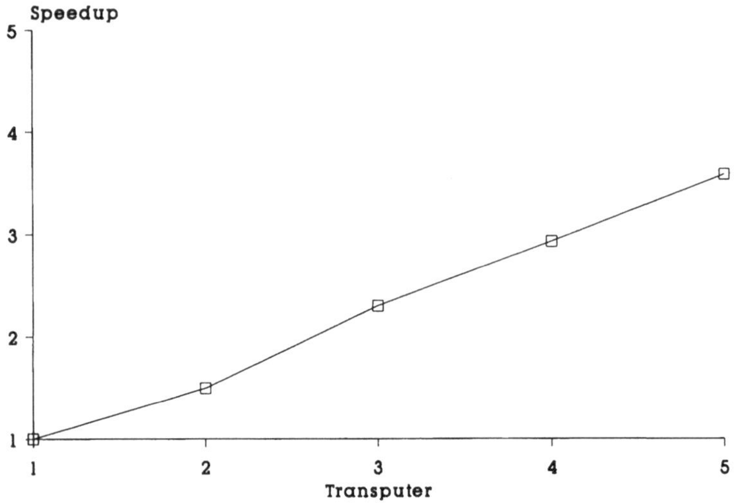

Figure 7.10: Speedup of the backward transformation

7.2.4 Performance of CS-Prolog

In order to evaluate the delay T_{trans}, it is essential to analyze the performance of the CS-Prolog environment i.e., the time taken to execute a CS-Prolog program. For this purpose, benchmarks are implemented in CS-Prolog and the benchmark run times are compared with benchmark run times implemented in comparable systems.

List Processing in CS-Prolog

Generally, the performance of a Prolog implementation is measured in lips (list instructions per second) frequently applying the naive_reverse benchmark.

Program 7.1

$$naive\_reverse([A|X], Z) :- naive\_reverse(X, Y), append(Y, [A], Z).$$
$$naive\_reverse([], []).$$
$$append([A|X], Y, [A|Z]) :- append(X, Y, Z).$$
$$append([], L, L).$$

Considering the naive_reverse benchmark, list operations are executed sequentially and concurrently with a variable number of list elements (integer values) deploying synchronous and asynchronous data transfer.

Table 7.7: List processing times in CS-Prolog

# list elements	10	30	60	90	100
sequential	94 *ms*	524 *ms*	1955 *ms*	4281 *ms*	5160 *ms*
asynchronous	165.8 *ms*	383.1 *ms*	1055 *ms*	2231 *ms*	2684 *ms*
synchronous	527 *ms*	808 *ms*	1698 *ms*	3069 *ms*	3242 *ms*

Figure 7.11 and Figure 7.12 summarize the measurements, indicating that the sequential and parallel execution of the benchmark causes different execution times to process Prolog lists.

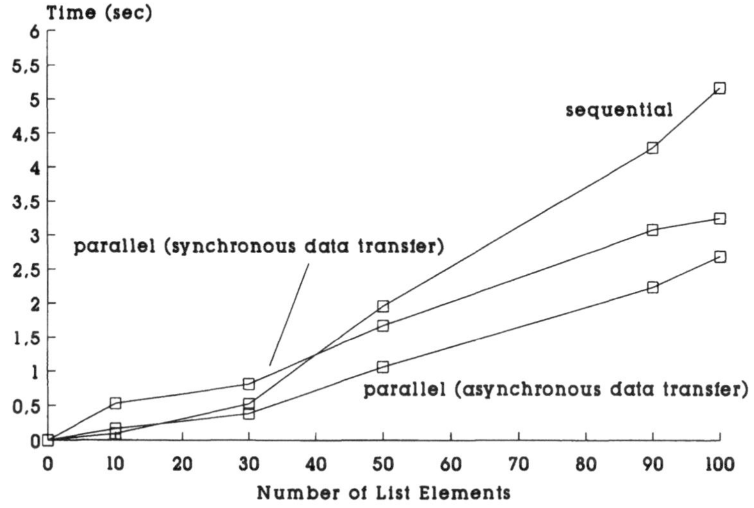

Figure 7.11: Processing times of a list in CS-Prolog

Parallel list processing applying asynchronous and synchronous communication is more efficient using lists with more than 20 resp. 40 list elements. In case of lists with less elements, the communication costs (e.g. startup time) affect the processing time of a list element more significantly.

Table 7.8: List processing times/list element

# list elements	10	30	60	90	100
sequential	9.4 *ms*	17.5 *ms*	32.58 *ms*	47.56 *ms*	51.6 *ms*
asynchronous	16.58 *ms*	12.77 *ms*	17.58 *ms*	24.78 *ms*	26.84 *ms*
synchronous	52.7 *ms*	26.93 *ms*	28.3 *ms*	34.1 *ms*	32.42 *ms*

Deploying synchronous communication, list processing is less efficient, because synchronous data transfer requires a bi-directional communication between the communicating processes. The impact of the communication costs and the data transfer modes is discussed later in this chapter.

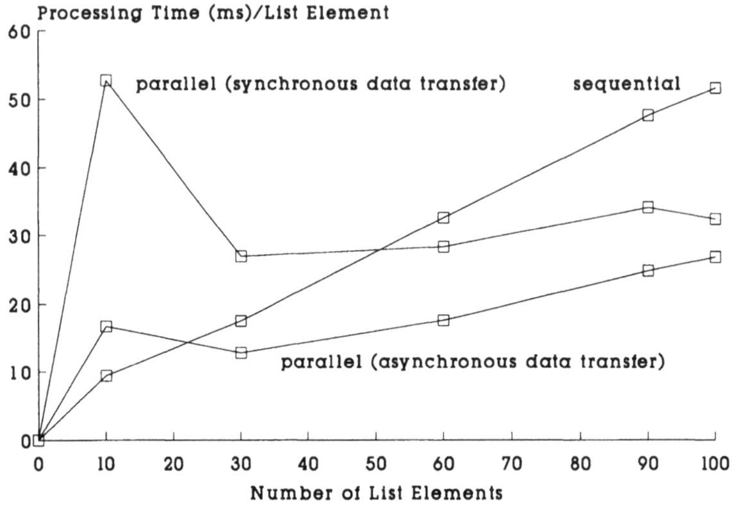

Figure 7.12: Processing time/list element

Comparison of the Results with other Prolog Systems

To evaluate the results of the list processing, it is necessary to compare the benchmark run times of CS-Prolog with similar Prolog versions also implemented on transputer systems providing identical processing features. In case of sequential list operations with 30 elements, a comparison between various non-commercial concurrent Prolog implementations becomes possible (see [72]). In a former study, Kacsuk analyzed OPERA Prolog, Padmavati

Table 7.9: Comparison between some transputer-based Prolog implementations

WAM Prolog	63 *ms*
Concurrent Prolog	129.2 *ms*
Padvamati Prolog	212 *ms*
Opera Prolog	399.79 *ms*
CS-Prolog	524 *ms*

Prolog, Concurrent Prolog and WAM Prolog using the same benchmark and the same processing environment (T800-G25).

The comparison of the measurements with Kacsuk's study [72] shows Table 7.9 demonstrating that list operations in CS-Prolog are substantially slower than in other implementations. Unfortunately, Kacsuk referenced the results of these Prolog implementations only using lists including 30 elements. A detailed performance analysis requires the variation of the number of list elements applying sequential and concurrent list processing (see above). Moreover, all the mentioned systems are still under development and not commercially available. Thus, detailed information about these systems cannot be found, and a comparison between the involved systems is only possible for this special case of list processing. Although, it is assumed that CS-Prolog is substantially slower than the other systems. As a consequence, this environment itself affects the translation times $T_{CS-Prolog}$ and $T_{PROLoop}$.

7.3 Object and Method Allocation

The performance measurements of the example applications (material handling tasks) of Chapter 6 demonstrate that the achievable speedup and efficiency depends also on the allocation of the distributable entities. Especially, precedence constraints may decrease the performance potential in a high degree. Chapter 6 introduced a scheduling technique that allows manual, user-based and system-supported scheduling aiming to find an efficient allocation. Because of the detailed scheduling study of Chapter 6, the following sections mainly concentrate on the other introduced criteria and their affect on the performance level.

7.4 Communication Cost

The next study in the performance analysis deals with the communication behaviour of asynchronous and synchronous data transfer deploying CS-Prolog constructs.

7.4.1 Analytical Communication Model

The following theoretical discussion treats with an analytical communication model in order to demonstrate the influence of communication in dependence on the number of transferred messages and their different message lengths as well as the message transfer modes and the message startup time.

The analytical model distinguishes communication caused by parallelism between and within objects on the level on which communication is done: in interobject communication (IOC) and interprocessor communication (IPC). IOC arises if the communicating objects are residing on the same processors. If the communicating objects are additionally resided on different processors, a more special form of IOC rises: the IPC.

To represent communication in the analytical model, communication-oriented parameters are introduced describing IOC and IPC. For this purpose, each component of communication may be considered as an arrangement which can be specified as matrices.

Definition 7.6 In general, interobject communication is realized through the volume matrix $\underline{V}$:

$$\underline{V} = \{v_{i,j}\}, i = 1, \ldots, n, j = 1, \ldots, n$$

where $v_{i,j}$ represents the volume of data sent from object o_i to object o_j. If $v_{i,j} = 0$, then object o_i does not communicate with object o_j.

Definition 7.7 The distributed processing environment is based on an interconnection network. The processor interconnection is represented by the distance matrix $\underline{D}$ on the set of processors:

$$\underline{D} = \{d_{k,l}\}, k = 1, \ldots, p, l = 1, \ldots, p$$

where p is the number of processors. The distance $d_{k,l}$ is a measure of the communication cost between processor p_k and processor p_l, i.e., the value $d_{j,l}$ is the approximate communication cost of an unit size message between these processors. If two processors are not connected, then $d_{k,l} = \infty$. By allowing $d_{k,k}$ to be nonzero, IOC can be represented. This is very important for the model since in practice, it seems to be realistic that object-oriented application will include more elements than a processor network nodes. So several objects must be resided on the same processor which are of course also allowed to communicate with each other. Realizing the distribution of elements, an assignment matrix $\underline{A}$ is defined as follows:

Definition 7.8 In order to present the static allocation of objects to processors an assignment matrix $\underline{A}$ is given as a binary matrix

$$a_{i,k} = \begin{cases} 1 & \text{if object } o_i \text{ is assigned to processor } p_k \\ 0 & \text{otherwise} \end{cases}$$

Now, the communication cost can be derived as a function of IOC, IPC, the number of processors, and the number of distributing elements:

$$C(P_S) = f(IPC(P_S), p, d_{i,j}, IOC)$$

In consideration of the matrices $\underline{A}$, $\underline{D}$, and $\underline{V}$, the communication cost of a given schedule P_S results in:

$$C(P_S) = \sum_{i=1}^{n}\sum_{j=1}^{p}\sum_{i=1}^{n}\sum_{j=1}^{p} v_{i,k} \cdot d_{j,l} \cdot a_{i,j} \cdot a_{k,l} \tag{7.23}$$

where:

$C(P_S)$	communication cost of schedule P_S
$v_{i,k} \cdot d_{j,l}$	communication delay to send data of total size $v_{i,k}$ from processor p_j to p_l
$a_{i,j}$, $a_{k,l}$	assignment indices

Thus, the term $v_{i,k} \cdot d_{j,l}$ sums the communication delays across all other objects that must communicate with object o_i. It represents IPC cost.

Example 7.1 Figure 7.13 illustrates a simple example configuration to demonstrate the IPC- and IOC cost assessment. The example configuration consists of five objects that are located on two transputers. According to Definition 7.6, the volume matrix $\underline{V}$ specifies the volume of data sent between object o_1, o_2, o_3, o_4, and o_5. Further, the distance matrix $\underline{D}$ presents the communication cost between processors p_1 and p_2. For simplification, it is additionally assumed, that all cost are known as soon as the volume of transferred data. Moreover, it should be excluded that any object sends a message to itself. Figure 7.13 surveys the scheme of this arrangement.
Considering Equation 7.23, $C(P_S)$ results in following expression:

$$C(P_S) = \sum_{i=1}^{5}\sum_{j=1}^{2}\sum_{i=1}^{5}\sum_{j=1}^{2} v_{i,k} \cdot d_{j,l} \cdot a_{i,j} \cdot a_{k,l} \tag{7.24}$$

and the matrices yield:

$$\underline{V} = \begin{vmatrix} 0 & v_{1,2} & v_{1,3} & 0 & v_{1,5} \\ v_{2,1} & 0 & 0 & 0 & v_{2,5} \\ v_{3,1} & 0 & 0 & v_{3,4} & 0 \\ 0 & 0 & v_{4,3} & 0 & v_{4,5} \\ v_{5,1} & v_{5,2} & 0 & v_{5,4} & 0 \end{vmatrix} \tag{7.25}$$

The distance matrix includes the values for the processor interconnection network cost:

$$\underline{D} = \begin{vmatrix} d_{1,1} & d_{1,2} \\ d_{2,1} & d_{2,2} \end{vmatrix} \tag{7.26}$$

and the assignment matrix specifies the allocation of each object to the processor network:

$$\underline{A} = \begin{vmatrix} 1 & 0 \\ 1 & 0 \\ 0 & 1 \\ 0 & 1 \\ 1 & 0 \end{vmatrix} \tag{7.27}$$

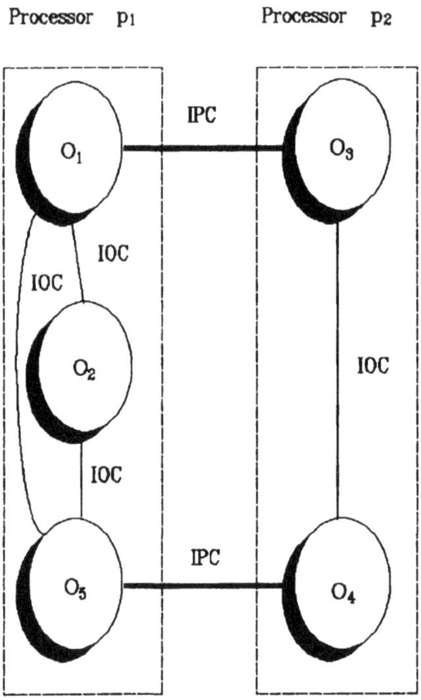

Figure 7.13: IOC and IPC of Example 7.1

The summation results in the communication cost $C(P_S)$:

$$\begin{aligned} C(P_S) = \; & v_{1,2}d_{1,1}a_{1,1}a_{2,1} + v_{1,3}d_{1,2}a_{1,1}a_{3,2} + v_{1,5}d_{1,1}a_{1,1}a_{5,1} \\ + \; & v_{2,1}d_{1,1}a_{2,1}a_{1,1} + v_{2,5}d_{1,1}a_{2,1}a_{5,1} + v_{3,1}d_{2,1}a_{3,2}a_{1,1} \\ + \; & v_{3,4}d_{2,2}a_{3,2}a_{4,2} + v_{4,3}d_{2,2}a_{4,2}a_{3,2} + v_{4,5}d_{2,1}a_{4,2}a_{5,1} \\ + \; & v_{5,1}d_{1,1}a_{5,1}a_{1,1} + v_{5,2}d_{1,1}a_{5,1}a_{2,1} + v_{5,4}d_{1,2}a_{5,1}a_{4,2} \end{aligned} \tag{7.28}$$

Under assumption that the values $a_{i,j}$ of the assignment matrix are binary in nature, the expression simplifies to the sum of the communication delays to send the specified data of the given volumes objects residing on processor p_1 or on processor p_2, and to objects that are located on the same processor:

$$\begin{aligned} C(P_S) = {} & v_{1,2}d_{1,1} + v_{1,3}d_{1,2} + v_{1,5}d_{1,1} + v_{2,1}d_{1,1} \\ & + v_{2,5}d_{1,1} + v_{3,1}d_{2,1} + v_{3,4}d_{2,2} + v_{4,3}d_{2,2} \\ & + v_{4,5}d_{2,1} + v_{5,1}d_{1,1} + v_{5,2}d_{1,1} + v_{5,4}d_{1,2} \end{aligned} \tag{7.29}$$

Thus, Equation 7.28 resp. Equation 7.29 determine the IOC and IPC cost.

Example 7.2 The special case of a multi-processor system only consisting of a single operational processor (p_1) merely enables "pure" IOC because IPC cannot arise. Nevertheless, the system performance will also decrease since there is no support of parallelism. Assuming the conditions of Example 7.1, C(A) is now only influenced through the data transfer between the five objects located on p_1. Further assuming, that $d_{1,1}$ is nonzero, $C(P_S)$ can be specified in a simple way. The volume matrix does not change since the amount of communication between all objects is constant. The assignment matrix results in:

$$\underline{A} = \begin{vmatrix} 1 \\ 1 \\ 1 \\ 1 \\ 1 \end{vmatrix} \tag{7.30}$$

Equation 7.31 estimates the communication cost:

$$C(P_S) = d_{1,1} \sum_{i=1}^{5} \sum_{k=1}^{5} v_{i,k} \cdot a_{i,1} \cdot a_{k,1} \tag{7.31}$$

$C(P_S)$ can be described as:

$$\begin{aligned} C(P_S) = d_{1,1} \; (& v_{1,2}a_{1,1}a_{2,1} + v_{1,3}a_{1,1}a_{3,1} + v_{1,5}a_{1,1}a_{5,1} \\ + & v_{2,1}a_{2,1}a_{1,1} + v_{2,5}a_{2,1}a_{5,1} + v_{3,1}a_{3,1}a_{1,1} \\ + & v_{3,4}a_{3,1}a_{4,1} + v_{4,3}a_{4,1}a_{3,1} + v_{4,5}a_{4,1}a_{5,1} \\ + & v_{5,1}a_{5,1}a_{1,1} + v_{5,2}a_{5,1}a_{2,1} + v_{5,4}a_{5,1}a_{4,1}) \end{aligned} \tag{7.32}$$

Considering the binary values of the assignment matrix $\underline{A}$, Equation 7.32 reduces to:

$$C(P_S) = d_{1,1} \quad (v1,2 + v1,2 + v1,2 + v1,2 + v1,2 + v1,2 \\ + v1,2 + v1,2 + v1,2 + v1,2 + v1,2 + v1,2)$$

Nevertheless, it is extremely difficult to determine a length of an arbitrary message during program execution. Thus, the performance measurements according to the communication influence concentrate on a more general evaluation of message lengths. Therefore, this analysis considers the essential the more criterion of the transfer modes and the startup time and estimates only the data transfer rate for longer and shorter messages. The experiments below investigate these characteristics in detail.

7.4.2 Data Transfer Modes

Asynchronous data transfer enables the communicating processes to continue their work without communicating any more, i.e., an asynchronous communication requires no response of the receiving process.

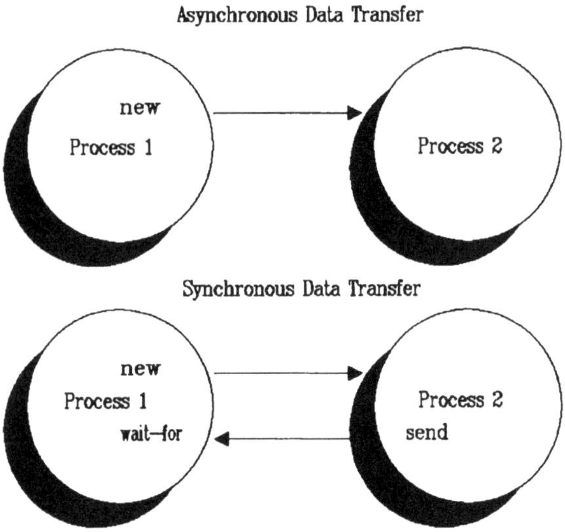

Figure 7.14: Data transfer modes

The synchronous data transfer consists of messages and their corresponding response as shown in Figure 7.14. The response of the message is achieved by the *send* instruction and its synchronization is supported by the *wait_for* command. The introduced operators are based on these various data transfer modes.

To estimate the communication costs of the synchronous and asynchronous data transfer mode, the communication times are measured using messages with variable length.

Table 7.10: Communication times and communication time/byte in CS-Prolog

transferred bytes	synchronous		asynchronous	
10	29 ms	2.9 ms	16 ms	1.6 ms
100	240 ms	2.4 ms	130 ms	1.3 ms
200	380 ms	1.9 ms	120 ms	600 μs
400	480 ms	1.2 ms	100 ms	250 μs
500	475 ms	950 μs	60 ms	120 μs
600	460 ms	766 μs	66 ms	110 μs
700	355 ms	507 μs	73.5 ms	105μs
1000	500 ms	500 μs	100 ms	100 μs
10000	4900 ms	490 μs	950 ms	95 μs

Figure 7.15 represents the results transferring messages up to 10000 bytes.

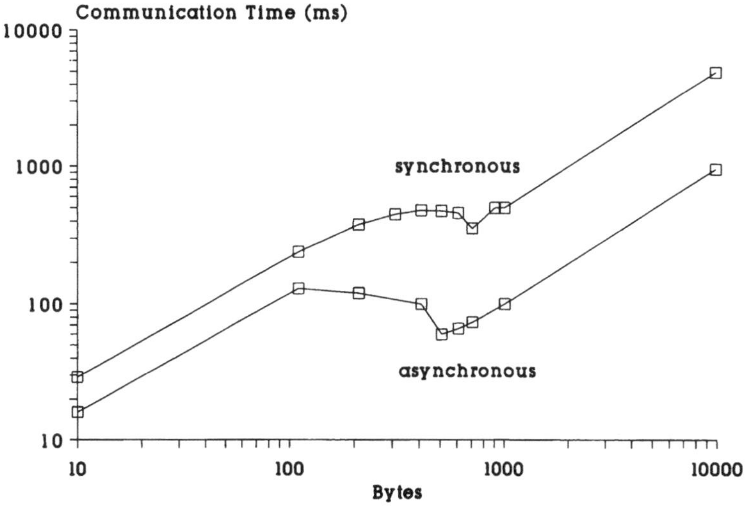

Figure 7.15: Communication times in CS-Prolog

Figure 7.16 shows the communication times taken for transferring a single byte.

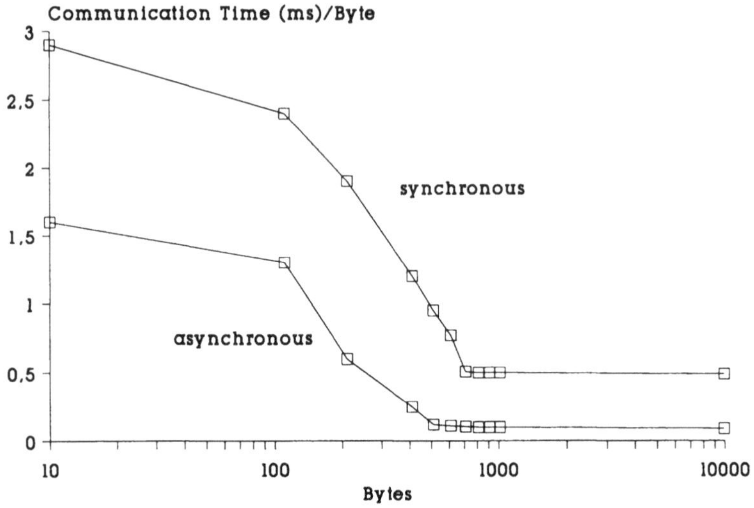

Figure 7.16: Communication times/byte in CS-Prolog

Messages including more than 700 bytes yield an average communication time of

- 0.1 ms/byte using asynchronous
- 0.5 ms/byte using synchronous

communication mode. Messages less than 700 bytes cause longer communication times to transfer a byte. In this case, the communication time is affected significantly through the startup time. As a consequence, the transfer of messages including less than 700 bytes is more inefficient, i.e., the performance potential decreases sending numerous of these messages. Following, the startup time is investigated in detail.

7.4.3 Startup Time Estimation

The initialization of the underlying hardware (e.g. link interfaces) and the activation of the software functions for a data transfer take a special amount of time: the startup time T_l [66, 65]. The initialization has only to be performed once for each communication. Thus, the startup time is independent of the message length.

The determination of the startup time is based on following equation presenting the dependency on communication time and average data transfer time:

$$T_{com} = T_l + NT_c \tag{7.33}$$

where:

T_{com}	communication time
T_l	data transfer startup time
N	number of bytes to be sent
T_c	average transfer time/byte

The transmission rate is assumed to be 0.8 MByte/s [68, 67], i.e., a byte is transferred in 1.25 μs. Hence, the startup time T_l results in the difference between the communication time T_{com} and the average transfer time T_c for a given number of transferred bytes.

Figure 7.17 illustrates the difference between the physical data transfer time T_c and the communication time T_{com} transferring messages with variable length. The transfer time T_c is 1000 times shorter than the communication time.

Table 7.11: Communication, transfer and startup time

bytes	$T_{com_{syn}}$	$T_{com_{asyn}}$	T_c	$T_{l_{syn}}$	$T_{l_{asyn}}$
10	29 ms	16 ms	12.5 μs	28.98 ms	15.98 ms
100	240 ms	130 ms	125 μs	239.875 ms	129.875 ms
200	380 ms	120 ms	250 μs	379.75 ms	119.75 ms
400	480 ms	100 ms	500 μs	479.5 ms	99.5 ms
500	475 ms	60 ms	625 μs	474.375 ms	59.375 ms
600	460 ms	66 ms	750 μs	459.25 ms	65.25 ms
700	355 ms	73.5 ms	875 μs	354.125 ms	72.625 ms
1000	500 ms	100 ms	1.25 ms	498.75 ms	98.75 ms
10000	4900 ms	950 ms	12.5 ms	4887.5 ms	937.5 ms

Figure 7.18 presents the decrease of the ratio $\frac{T_l}{T_c}$ considering synchronous and asynchronous communication with its corresponding average data transfer rate.

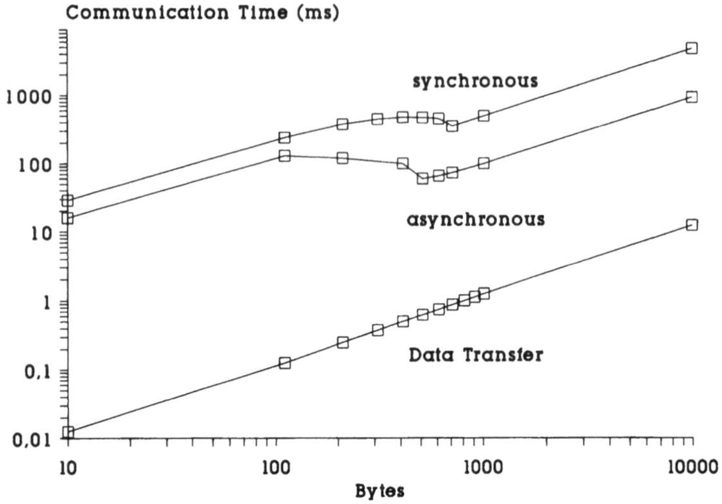

Figure 7.17: Communication time and data transfer time

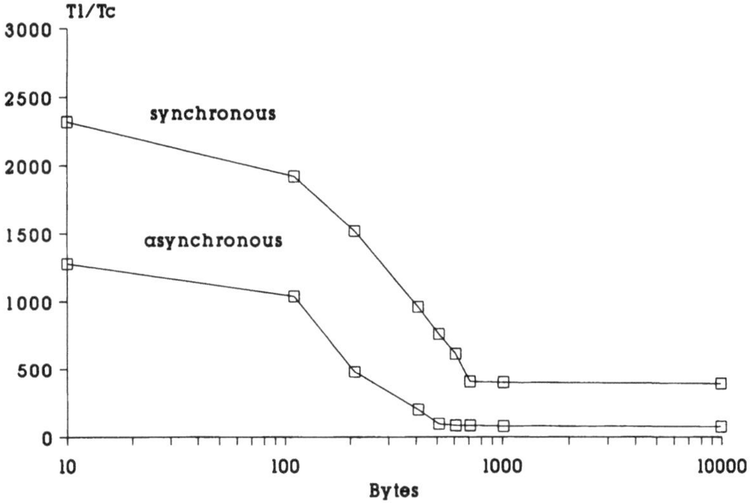

Figure 7.18: The ratio $\frac{T_l}{T_c}$

7.5 Effect of Class Hierarchy Variation

An important question arises in object-oriented systems in how far the selected class hierarchy may influence the run time behaviour of robot applications. In order to determine this influence, another experiment varies the class structure through:

- changing the class depth;
- changing the class width.

The reduction and enlargement of the class hierarchy according to the number of subclasses is performed in consideration that the properties of object-orientation (e.g. inheritance) are preserved.

7.5.1 Robot Tasks for Class Structure Variation

The applications below are deployed to demonstrate the affect of class structure variation as well as for general estimation of the performance potential. The programs are varied according to the experiment, e.g. using different message passing operators or distinct application lengths.

Program 7.2

```
% Instance creation:

object_data :<<: [create(sensor, 2)].
arm         :<<: [create(robot_1, 0)].
arm         :<<: [create(robot_2, 1)].


% Robot statements:

task_1 :- [move_to(123, O),
           move_straight(120, 30, O),
           move_straight(123, 30, C)].

task_2 :- [move_to(133, O),
           move_straight(130, 30, O),
           move_straight(133, 30, C)].

task_3 :- [read_code,
           convert_code,
           get_val(term, Term),
           write(Term), nl].
```

```
demo_1 :- robot_1 :<<: [task_1],
          robot_2 :<<: [task_2],
          sensor :<<: [task_3].

task_4 :- [move_to(253, C),
          move_straight(251, 30, C),
          move_straight(253, 30, O)].

task_5 :- [move_to(293, C),
          move_straight(291, 30, C),
          move_straight(293, 30, O)].

task_6 :- [read_code,
          convert_code,
          get_val(term, Term),
          write(Term), nl].

demo_2 :- robot_1 :<<: [task_1, task_4],
          robot_2 :<<: [task_2, task_5],
          sensor :<<: [task_3, task_6].

task_7 :- [move_to(572, O),
          move_straight(570, 30, O),
          move_straight(572, 30, C)].

task_8 :- [move_to(532, O),
          move_straight(530, 30, O),
          move_straight(532, 30, C)].

task_9 :- [read_code,
          convert_code,
          get_val(term, Term),
          write(Term), nl].

demo_3 :- robot_1 :<<: [task_1, task_4, task_7],
          robot_2 :<<: [task_2, task_5, task_8],
          sensor :<<: [task_3, task_6, task_9].

task_10 :-[lock_sec(c1),
          move_to(542, C),
          move_straight(541, 30, C),
          move_straight(542, 30, O),
```

```
                  security_point(robot_1, 590),
                  unlock_sec(cl)]).

task_11 : -[lock_sec(cl),
                  move_to(552, C),
                  move_straight(551, 30, C),
                  move_straight(552, 30, O),
                  security_point(robot_2, 595),
                  unlock_sec(cl)].

task_12 : -[read_code,
                  convert_code,
                  get_val(term, Term),
                  write(Term), nl].

demo_4 : - robot_1 :<<: [task_1, task_4, task_7, task_10],
                  robot_2 :<<: [task_2, task_5, task_8, task_11],
                  sensor :<<: [task_3, task_6, task_9, task_12].
```

7.5.2 Class Depth Variation

The first experiment varies the class depth. The robot test applications (sensor-supported material handling tasks with increasing length) denoted as TP1, TP2, TP3 are executed sequentially and concurrently deploying synchronous and asynchronous message passing.

Table 7.12: Execution times with changing class depth

execution	class depth	TP1	TP2	TP3
sequential	reduced	29.92 s	63.93 s	104.55 s
	current	36.17 s	64.49 s	105.47 s
	enlarged	31.43 s	66.74 s	106.77 s
synchronous	reduced	24.53 s	51.7 s	83.3 s
	current	25.07 s	51.84 s	83.56 s
	enlarged	25.31 s	52.14 s	84.26 s
synchronous/ asynchronous	reduced	19.53 s	43.81 s	70.11 s
	current	20.07 s	44.03 s	70.89 s
	enlarged	20.41 s	44.13 s	71.17 s

First, the applications are performed by means of synchronous message passing (PAR_{II}-operator). Subsequently, the test program execution is supported by a combination of synchronous and asynchronous message passing

(PAR_{II} and PAR_{III}-operator). Table 7.12 reflects the measurements. Diagram 7.19 presents the results of the measurements. The diagram shows that the applications using the synchronous message passing take more run time than the applications based on the combination of synchronous and asynchronous message passing. The higher degree of parallel processing additionally shortens the execution time of the applications.

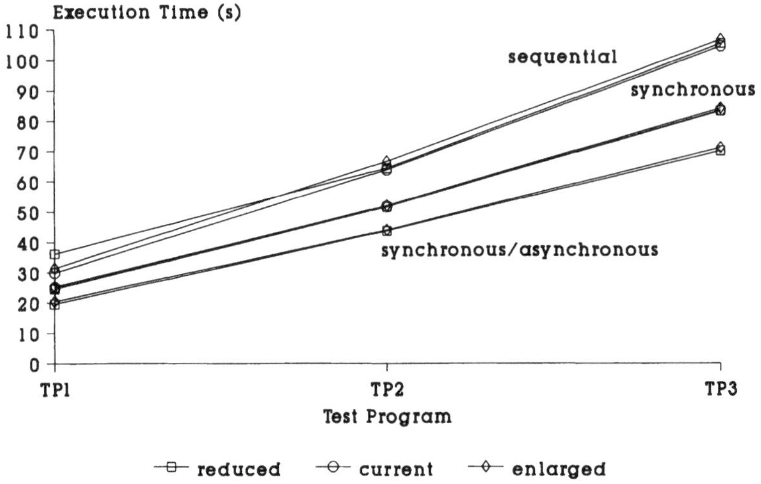

Figure 7.19: Application execution times changing the class depth

The enlargement of the class depth causes greater communication costs between the involved objects indicated through greater application run times. Hence, the reduction of the class depth yields shorter execution times. The communication costs decrease when some subclasses are fused.

Table 7.13: Maximal differences

message mode	TP1	TP2	TP3
sequential	1.51 s	2.81 s	2.22 s
synchronous	0.78 s	0.44 s	0.96 s
synchronous/asynchronous	0.88 s	0.32 s	1.06 s

Nevertheless, the measurements demonstrate that a variation of the class depth influences only the application execution time in a small degree compared with the original run times. Moreover, the affect of class depth variation according to the concurrently performed test programs is negligible.

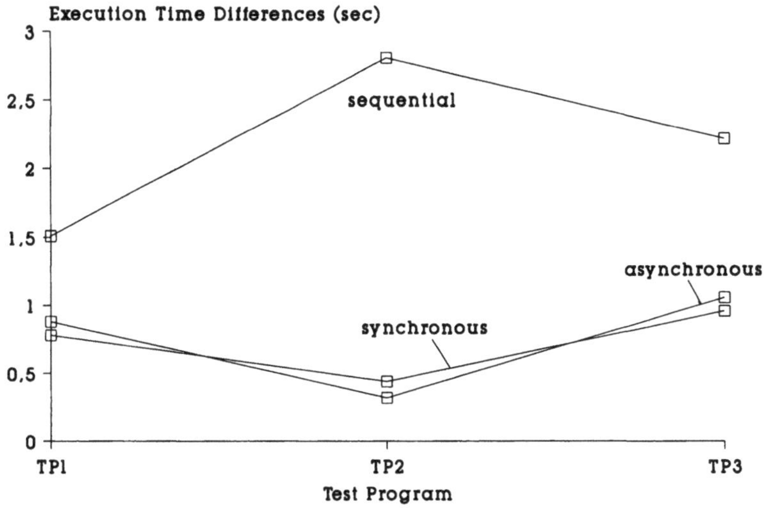

Figure 7.20: Execution time differences

Graphic 7.20 represents the execution time differences of the test applications given in Table 7.13.

7.5.3 Class Width Variation

In order to analyze the run time affect of test applications regarding the variation of the class width, the programs are performed in the same environment under the same conditions as in the previous experiment. Table 7.14 reflects the measurements of the execution times.

Table 7.14: Maximal differences

execution	class width	TP1	TP2	TP3
sequential	reduced	34.68 s	63.13 s	104.36 s
	current	36.17 s	64.49 s	105.47 s
	enlarged	39.94 s	70.21 s	118.07 s
synchronous	reduced	21.29 s	47.38 s	79.22 s
	current	25.07 s	51.84 s	83.56 s
	enlarged	28.11 s	56.31 s	89.41 s
synchronous/ asynchronous	reduced	19.1 s	41.01 s	65.78 s
	current	20.05 s	44.03 s	70.88 s
	enlarged	22.48 s	48.71 s	75.9 s

The class width variation affects the application run time in a higher degree than the class depth variation. The reason for this behaviour is connected with the decrease of inheritance. The enlargement of the class width shallows the class hierarchy. Instead of inheriting methods and class variables, the extension of the class width now demands additional message passing to achieve the same results. Hence, the communication costs increase causing a growth of the execution times. The run time differences between the enlargement and the reduction of the class width (Table 7.14) are significantly greater than in the previous experiment.

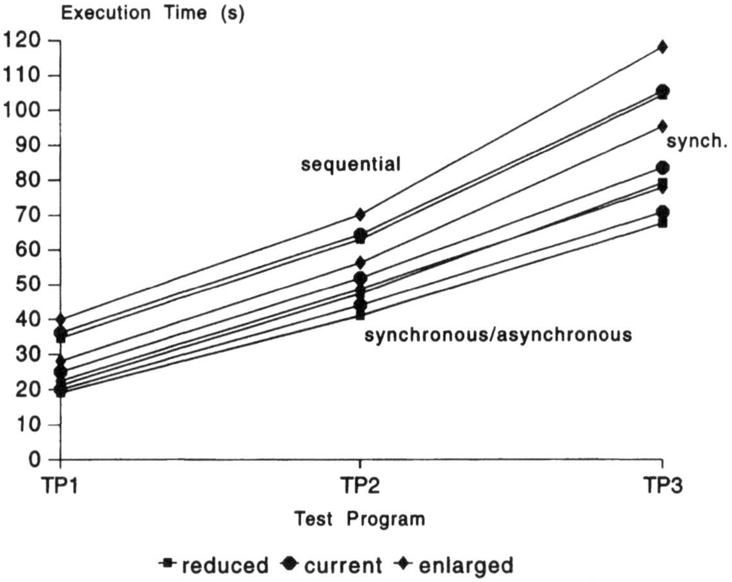

Figure 7.21: Application execution times changing the class width

Figure 7.21 represents graphically the results. The run time measurements of the reduced class width are similar to those reducing the class depth. However, the execution time differences increase as shown in Table 7.15 and indicated by Figure 7.22.

Table 7.15: Execution time differences

message mode	TP1	TP2	TP3
sequential	5.26 s	7.08 s	13.71 s
synchronous	6.82 s	8.92 s	16.19 s
synchronous/asynchronous	3.38 s	7.7 s	10.12 s

To sum up the results of both class variations, the enlargement and reduction of the class depth affect the execution times of robot applications insignificantly. The class width enlargement limits the inheritance mechanism and causes greater execution times.

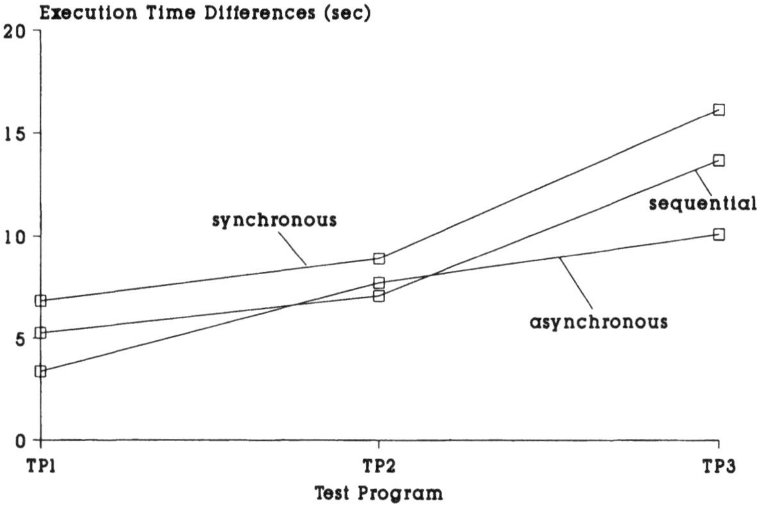

Figure 7.22: Execution time differences

7.6 Parallelism Characterization of Robot Applications

When robot programs are designed and executed as concurrent applications on the multi-transputer, the total processing time required is only one aspect to characterize a parallel application. A more complete characterization of the parallelism can be achieved through other techniques such as the derivation of the parallelism profile and its corresponding shape [125]. This profile indicates the number of processors in use by the application and can be determined through experiments or using methodologies described in [52, 56, 70, 75, 80, 91]. This approach applies Gantt-diagrams for this purpose. By means of the parallelism profile, the processor loads are graphically presented enabling the determination of the average parallelism factor.

Definition 7.9 The average parallelism factor *APF* specifies the average parallelism arising during execution of the robot application using a finite set $\mathcal{P}$ of available processors. Considering, that the execution of the robot application deploying $|\mathcal{P}| = p$ processors takes τ_p the average parallelism factor is defined to be:

$$APF = \frac{1}{\tau_p}\frac{1}{p}\sum_{i=1}^{p} p_i \cdot \tau_i \tag{7.34}$$

where:

- τ_p application execution time using a single processor
- p number of processors
- p_i number of active processors executing a fraction of the application
- τ_i time taken to execute a fraction of the application

In contrast to the efficiency which results in the ratio of the speedup and the number of processors $E = \frac{S_p}{p}$, the APF considers separately each processor state offering the possibility to predict the increase or the decrease of the APF changing the program allocation.

Example 7.3 A simple robot application moving the arm to different positions is given below. The program consists of four tasks executed by means of five transputers $(p_1, p_2, \ldots, p_5)$ configured to a farm topology. Transputer p_1 -the master transputer- controls a data base including kinematical, geometrical, or hardware-oriented information and the hardware interfaces; the remaining ones perform the required robot operations.

Program 7.3

```
move(arm, [], self) :- self :<>: [get_val(pos_nr_1, Pos1),
                                  test_pos_nr,
                                  get_val(grip_stat, GS),
                                  test_grip_stat,
                       port :<<:[interface,
                                  write_robot(mo, [Pos1, GS], self].

move(arm, [], self) :- self :<>: [get_val(pos_nr_2, Pos2),
                                  test_pos_nr,
                                  get_val(grip_stat, GS),
                                  test_grip_stat,
                       port :<<:[interface,
                                  write_robot(mo, [Pos2, GS], self].
```

```
move(arm, [], self) : - self :<>: [get_val(pos_nr_3, Pos3),
                                   test_pos_nr,
                                   get_val(grip_stat, GS),
                                   test_grip_stat,
                        port :<<:[interface,
                                   write_robot(mo, [Pos3, GS], self].

move(arm, [], self) : - self :<>: [get_val(pos_nr_4, Pos4),
                                   test_pos_nr,
                                   get_val(grip_stat, GS),
                                   test_grip_stat,
                        port :<<:[interface,
                                   write_robot(mo, [Pos4, GS], self].
```

Executing this simple robot program, following instructions have to be performed:

- T_1 allocation command of the master transputer
- T_2 method "set_val"
- T_3 data base search of the master transputer
- T_4 method "get_val"
- T_5 method "test_pos_nr"
- T_6 interface access
- T_7 method to send the robot instruction using the interface command "write_robot"

The execution times are given by Table 7.16.

Table 7.16: Execution times using several processors

1 processor	2 processors	3 processors	4 processors	5 processors
41.9 s	36.9 s	23.9 s	18.4 s	14 s

The allocation of the tasks to several processors and their concurrent processing may shorten the processing time from 41.9 s to 14 s.

Table 7.17: Speedup using several Processors

1 processor	2 processors	3 processors	4 processors	5 processors
1	1,1	1,7	2,2	3

Deploying equation (7.1), the speedups are computed and presented by Table 7.17 as well as illustrated by Figure 7.23.

The difference between the theoretical speedups ($S_p = p$) and the computed ones is caused e.g. through communication because communication (see above) may create delays which effect the efficiency of a parallel application or by waiting periods regarding precedence constraints.

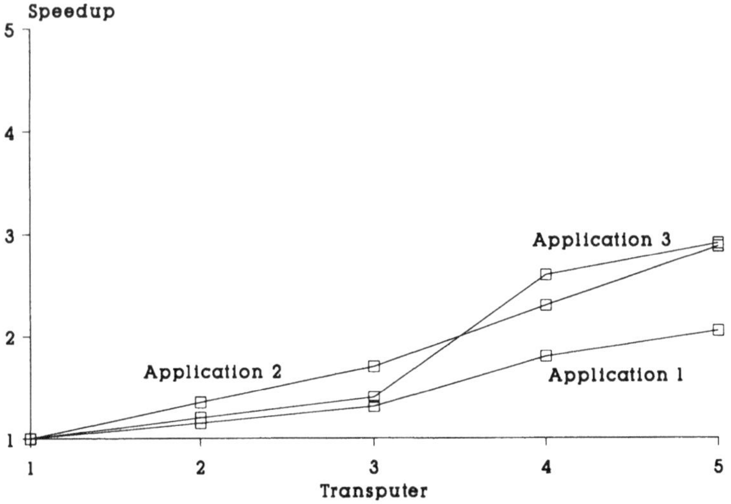

Figure 7.23: Speedup of Example 7.3

Figure 7.24 shows the Gantt-diagram presenting the timing of the robot tasks using five processors assuming that the task processing times are known.

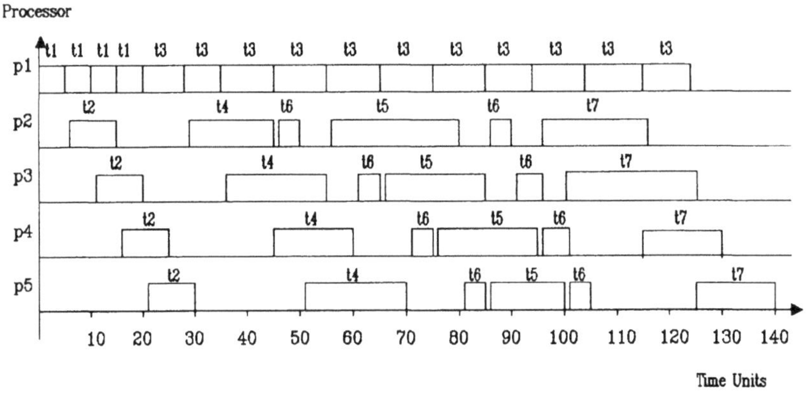

Figure 7.24: Timing of the program applying five transputers

To enable an easy realization of the graphs (Gantt-diagram, parallelism profile, parallelism shape), the scope of the representation is enlarged, i.e., one second $\triangleq$ 10 time units.

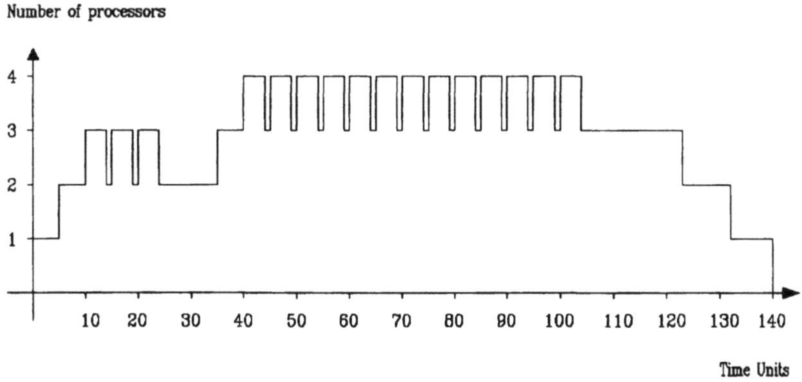

Figure 7.25: Parallelism profile of the robot application

The parallelism profile is rearranged preserving the time spent at each degree of parallelism to form the shape of the application. Figure 7.26 illustrates this shape depicting the number of active processors during the application's timing.

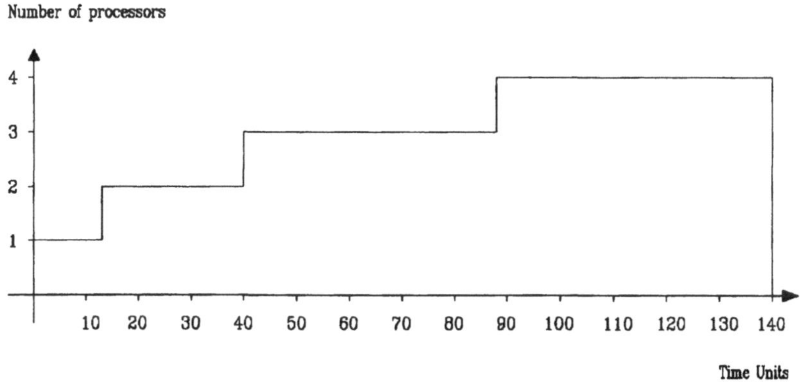

Figure 7.26: Corresponding shape of the robot application

The rearrangement of the parallelism profile changes neither the execution time nor the processor efficiency. To achieve a nondecreasing order ($p_{i-1} \leq p_i$) several stages with identical processor work loads are merged into one stage simply by adding the corresponding work loads. This procedure begins with processor p_1. Subsequently, the determination of the APF is very simple only summing each processor state:

$$APF = \frac{1}{140} \cdot \frac{1}{5}(12 + 2 \cdot 27 + 3 \cdot 48 + 4 \cdot 52) = 0.60 \qquad (7.35)$$

7.7 Results of the Performance Analysis

The first experiment analyzed the execution times of sequential robot programs using CS-Prolog, PROLoop and a robot-oriented programming language given by the manufacturer. Because of the object-oriented add-on, the PROLoop applications took longer execution times than the programs written in the other languages. The test programs deploying the language of the manufacturer caused the shortest execution times. Since this language supports neither the implicit robot programming nor concurrent processing this programming language cannot support this work.

The concurrent execution of robot applications by means of PROLoop led to a considerable decrease of the run times. Moreover, the run times of the applications could be shortened considerablely through simultaneous computing of operations for robot control.

Another experiment analyzed the influence of communication. The asynchronous communication is more efficient than synchronous communication since no response of the message is necessary. Moreover, the investigation of the start up time demonstrated that the communication time is essentially affected by this component. Especially, the sending numerous short messages may decrease the performance potential in a higher degree.

The study of concurrent Prolog systems resulted in great run time differences of benchmarks. The CS-Prolog implementation is more inefficient than the other systems. Thus, CS-Prolog also caused a decrease of the performance behaviour of the robot programming environment.

The variation of the class structure yielded different execution time changes. The variation of the class depth influenced the execution times only in a small degree whereas the class width variation is more inefficient. Particularly, the class width enlargement limits the inheritance mechanism and therefore more communication is necessary to perform the same robot program. The run times increased to a great extent.

The parallelism characterization models a parallel processing system as a sequence of stages, each of which requires a certain integral number of processors for a certain interval of time. Deploying this methodology, it is possible to find the optimal system operating point and the optimal number of processors to use in the parallel processing system such that performance is maximized.

Chapter 8
Conclusions

This chapter summarizes the results and discusses some promising directions for further research and development extending the robot controlling attempt presented in this book.

8.1 Results of the Book

Current industrial robot tasks require flexible and powerful programming methodologies. For the execution of these tasks, several robots and other involved manufacturing devices have to cooperate with each other within the manufacturing environment, i.e., they have to be coordinated in time and space. Apart from the overhead for this coordination, complex multi-robot control and application tasks often demand comprehensive computations which cause long execution times. To meet real-time conditions, the robot programming system should provide concurrent, distributed processing.

Commercially available robot programming languages such as SRL, PASRO, SIGLA, RAIL, VAL, or HELP are used for several years to control industrial robots deploying explicit programming techniques, based on imperative high-level languages. Only a few of these languages support concurrency and none of them allow declarative programming, providing techniques to implicitly derive suitable robot commands from the specified task descriptions (e.g. for planning tasks). Moreover, existing robot programming languages hardly support the programming of different robot types or the programming of additional devices in the robot cell (e.g. complex sensors) in a uniform environment. Thus, each device has to be programmed by its own host usually applying different programming languages and/or programming techniques (e.g. interactive, teach-in). This local control requires greater hardware costs and also greater programming effort. To remove this lack, a global control of the manufacturing cell should be aimed also considering the above mentioned decentralization.

This book describes a robot programming approach adopting the notation of object-orientation in logic programming to efficiently exploit the merits of concurrent, implicit and distributed programming in a global way, especially deploying the emerging transputer technology. The results can be summarized as follows:

- **Concurrent Processing for Robot Control**
  The emphasis of the book lays on concurrent processing. Concurrency increases not only the efficiency of robot applications but also facilitates the global control of the robot environment. In order to provide concurrency, following criteria are met by this approach:
  - **Definition and implementation of message passing operators**
    The object-oriented characteristic of the robot programming approach supports concurrent processing by means of relevant message passing modes. For this, distinct message passing operators are defined and specified using Hoare's formalism of CSP (Communicating Sequential Processes) and are experimentally implemented into the PROLoop environment (PROLoop as the acronym of "Prolog-based language for object-oriented programming). The message passing operators realize concurrency between objects, taking also concurrency of methods into account.
  - **Specification of suitable scheduling heuristics and their realization for robot task scheduling**
    In order to efficiently utilize concurrency, the introduced robot programming environment additionally supplies several scheduling techniques to map robot tasks to available transputers.

    The system-supported robot task scheduler maps the robot tasks by means of scheduling constraints presented as heuristics in Prolog. The power of heuristics may significantly reduce the combinatorical complexity of the scheduling problem caused through the proliferation of alternatives. Further, the PROLoop strategy is guided by the fact that a heuristic scheduling algorithm cannot guarantee an optimal schedule for each scheduling problem. The robot programming system therefore also enables manual scheduling by the user. The programmer makes the decisions for granularity and partitioning, and the system allocates the specified schedule to the processors.
  - **Definition of appropriate performance criteria and the demonstration of the performance potential of robot tasks**
    The analysis of the performance characteristic of different robot tasks demonstrates the feasibility of the robot programming approach. Typical multi-robot control tasks are implemented in an experimental environment presenting the efficiency of concurrent robot operations.

The analysis is based on various criteria which are defined in this book assuming to cause the influence of the performance level.

- **Global Control of the Robot Working Cell**
  The concurrency mechanisms of the robot programming environment facilitate the global control of the robot working cell. The feature of object-orientation to realize decentralization through distributed objects presents an appropriate basis for a uniform control of the manufacturing cell. Moreover, the integration of distinct postprocessors by defining additional classes and the concurrent activation of their instances support the global cell control in a great extent. The coordination of the involved machines is realized through the semaphore technique ensuring collision-free operations and through the evaluation of sensor data.
- **Implicit Robot Programming**
  The robot programming environment supports implicit robot programming using Prolog. Prolog's benefits stem from its declarativeness enabling precise mathematical characterizations of relationships between robot programs and their results. However, the topic of this book concentrates on concurrent processing for robot controlling. Implicit robot programming and its corresponding problems is the subject of other works involved in the robot programming project also using the PRO-Loop system.

8.2 Outlook on Future Work

The remaining problems briefly mentioned in the previous chapters are the subject of future research:

- **Increase of the Programming Support by means of Planning**
  The integration of planning capabilities [116, 122] into the programming environment is an important step since planning facilitates the robot programming significantly. At present, other works treats with planning aspects extending this environment;
- **Improvement of the Performance Potential**
  The performance study demonstrated the effect of special factors influencing the performance level. Hence, the future work has to concentrate on these criteria distinguishing the reason of the influence:
  - software influence. Especially considering CS-Prolog, it is necessary to deploy another concurrent, more efficient transputer-based Prolog system to shorten the execution times of Prolog applications. However, the limited supply of suitable Prolog systems complicates the switch extremely. Thus, this lack requires either the improvement

of the CS-Prolog system or the development of a dedicated concurrent Prolog environment for robot controlling. Further, alternative high-level languages such as C or Pascal should be applied to create the object-oriented robot programming system offering both advantages: realizing planning tasks by logic programming and influencing the performance potential of robot applications efficiently. For this, an interface has to be developed to access the (external) logic programming system solving planning tasks and passing the results to the calling objects of the robot programming environment;

- hardware influence. The applied robot system causes significant delays to translate the postprocessor instructions. The elimination of this shortcoming demands a more efficient transformation of the postprocessor instructions, e.g. by means of a transputer-based postprocessor replacing the given Z80-based one.

Bibliography

[1] 3L Ltd, Peel House, Ladywell, Livingston EH54 6AG, Scotland. *Parallel C User Guide*, version 2.1.1 edition, October 1989.

[2] G. A. Agha. *Object-Oriented Concurrent Programming*, chapter Actors: A Model of Concurrent Computation in Distributed Systems, pages 13–34. The MIT Press, Cambridge, Massachsetts, 1987.

[3] I. Aleksander and H. Farreny. *Decision and Intelligence.* Kogan Page Ltd., London, 1987.

[4] A. P. Ambler, H. G. Barrow, and R. J. Popplestone. A Versatile System for Computer-Controlled Assembly. *Artificial Intelligence*, (1975)(6):129–156, 1975.

[5] B. Anderson. Object-Oriented Programming. *Microprocessors and Microsystems*, 12(8), October 1988.

[6] Anorad Corporation, Smiththown, N. Y., USA. *ANOMATIC CONTROLLER -II: Operation and Programming Manual for the Computer Numeric Controller*, December 1979.

[7] Automatix Inc., Burlington, Massachusetts. *RAIL Reference Manual. Autovision*, 1982.

[8] Automatix Inc., Burlington, Massachusetts, USA. *RAIL Software Reference Manual. Robovision and Cybervision*, 1982.

[9] F. Belli, R. Crişan, and A. Pollmann. An Approach to Performance Assessment of Concurrent and Distributed Logic/Object-Oriented Multi-Robot Control. In M. Tanik, editor, *ESDA'94 — The Second Biennial European Joint Conference on Engineering Systems Design and Analysis, Proceedings of the 1994 Engineering Systems Design and Analysis Conference, Volume 5*, pages 443–452, University of London, London, UK, July 1994.

[10] F. Belli, R. Crişan, and A. Pollmann. An Approach to Performance Assessment of Concurrent and Distributed Logic/Object-Oriented Multi-Robot Control. In F. Anger, editor, *Proceedings of the Seventh International Conference on Industrial & Engineering Applications of Artificial Intelligence & Expert Syustems*, pages 293–304, 820 Town Center Drive, Langhorne, PA 19047, 1994. IEA/AIE-94, Austin, Texas, Gordon and Breach Publishers, Inc.

[11] F. Belli, R. Crişan, and A. Pollmann. Logic/Object-Oriented Control of a Multi-Robot Manufacturing Cell and its Performance. In *Proceedings of Computers in Engineering Symposium within the Energy-Sources Technology Conference & Exhibition, Session Software Systems in Engineering*, pages 93–103, New Orleans, Lousiana, USA, January 1994. The American Society of Mechanical Engineers, ASME.

[12] F. Belli and J. Dreyer. Systems Modelling and Simulation of Predicate/Transition Nets and Logic Programming. In F. Anger, editor, *The 7th International Conference on Industrial & Engineering Applications of Artificial Intelligence & Expert Systems*, pages 465–474, 820 Town Center Drive, Langhorne, PA 19047, 1994. IEA/AIE-94, Austin, Texas, Gordon and Breach Publishers, Inc.

[13] F. Belli, O. Jack, and A. Pollmann. Analyse und Konstruktion komplexer Systeme mit Prädikaten-/Transitionsnetzen und Prolog—Ansatz und Fallstudie. In W. Reisig G. Scheschonk, editor, *Petri-Netze im Einsatz für Entwurf und Entwicklung von Informationssystemen*, pages 152–164, Berlin, Heidelberg, September 1993. GI, Springer Verlag.

[14] F. Belli and A. Pollmann. A Production Environment for Object-Oriented Concurrent Programming in Prolog. In M. Tanik, editor, *ESDA'94 — The Second Biennial European Joint Conference on Engineering Systems Design and Analysis, Proceedings of the 1994 Engineering Systems Design and Analysis Conference, Volume 5*, pages 317–326, University of London, London, UK, July 1994.

[15] F. Belli and A. Pollmann. Concurrent and Distributed Programming in Prolog. In *Proceedings of Computers in Engineering Symposium within the Energy-Sources Technology Conference & Exhibition, Session Software Systems in Engineering ASME'94*, pages 111–121, New Orleans, USA, January 1994. The American Society of Mechanical Engineers.

[16] D. Ben-Arieh. Concurrent Modeling and Simulation of Multi-Robot Systems. *Robotics & Computer-Integrated Manufacturing*, 8(1):67–73, 1991.

[17] G. Blair. *Object-Oriented Languages, Systems and Applications.* Pitman Publishing, London, 1991.

[18] J. Błazewicz et al. *Scheduling in Computer and Manufacturing Systems.* Springer Verlag, Berlin, Heidelberg, 1993.

[19] Ch. Blume. *Konzeptionierung eines Programmiersystems für Industrieroboter.* VDI Verlag, Düsseldorf, 1987.

[20] Ch. Blume and W. Jakob. *Programming Languages for Industrial Robots.* Springer Verlag, Berlin, 1986.

[21] Ch. Blume, W. Jakob, and J. Favaro. *PasRo.* Springer Verlag, Berlin, 1987.

[22] S. Bonner and K. G. Shin. A Comparative Study of Robot Languages. *IEEE Transactions on Computer*, pages 82–96, 1982.

[23] J. P. Briot and A. Yonezawa. Inheritance and Synchronozation in Concurrent OOP. In *ECOOP'87: European Conference on Object-Oriented Programming*, pages 33–40, Berlin, Heidelberg, 1987. Springer Verlag.

[24] T. J. Bublick. *Robot Applications in Finishing and Painting*, chapter Finishing Coating and Painting, pages 1249–1263. John Wiley & Sons, New York, USA, 1985.

[25] K. Clark and J. Gregory. PARLOG: Parallel Programming in Logic. *Report DOC/84*, 1984.

[26] W. F. Clocksin and C. S. Mellish. *Programming in Prolog.* Springer Verlag, Heidelberg, 1984.

[27] E. G. Coffman and R. L. Graham. Optimal Scheduling for Two-Processor Systems. *Acta Informatica*, (1972)(1):200–213, 1972.

[28] J. Conery and D. Kibler. AND-Parallelism and Nondeterminism in Logic Programs. *Newe Generation Computing*, 3, 1985.

[29] P. Corsini. A Parallel PROLOG Interpreter for Multitude Systems. In *International Conference on Parallel Processing and Applications*, L'Aquila, Italy, September 1987.

[30] P. Corsini. The Parallel Interpretation of Logic Programs in Distributed Architectures. *Computer Journal*, 32(1), 1989.

[31] P. Corsini, G. Frosini, and L. Rizzo. Implementing a Parallel PROLOG Interpreter by Using OCCAM and Transputer. *Microprocessors and Microsystems*, 13(4), May 1989.

[32] I. Cox and H. Narain. Concurrent Programming and Robotics. *The International Journal of Robotics Research*, 8(2), April 1989.

[33] T. Csakvary. Planning Robot Applications in Assembly. In *Proceedings of the 2nd International Conference on Assembly Automation*, pages 201–210, Brighton, U.K., May 1981.

[34] C. Czirr. Möglichkeiten der Parallelverarbeitung durch logisch objektorientierte Programmierung zur Robotersteuerung. Master's thesis, Universität Paderborn, Fachbereich Elektrotechnik, Fachgebiet Angewandte Datentechnik, Paderborn, 1992.

[35] P. Dadam and R. Dillmann. Objekt-orientierte Datenhaltung für die Robotersteuerung. Interner Bericht 26/86, Fakultät für Informatik der Universität Karlsruhe, Karlsruhe, 1986.

[36] J. A. Darringer and M. W. Blasgen. MARPLE: A High Level Language for Research in Mechanical Assembly. Report RC 5606, IBM T. J. Watson Research Center, Yorktown Heights, N. Y., USA, September 1975.

[37] Data Logic Optic Electronics GmbH, Daimlerstraße 2, Erkenbrechtsweiler. *Bedienungshandbuch Decoder DP 600 und CCD-Kamera TC 200*, 1990.

[38] D. DeGroot. Restricted AND-Parallelism. In *Proceedings of the International Conference on Fith Generation Computer Systems 1984*, North Holland, 1984. Elsevier.

[39] Digital Electronic Automation, Turin, Italy. *Guide to HELP-Language*, 1981.

[40] R. Dillmann and M. Huck. *Informationsverarbeitung in der Robotik.* Springer Verlag, Berlin, 1991.

[41] T. P. Dobry. Design Decision Influencing the Microarchitecture. In *Proceedings 17th International Symposium on Microarchitecture*, October 1984.

[42] Y. Dotan and D. Ben-Arieh. Modeling Flexible Manufacturing Systems: The Concurrent Logic Programming Appraoch. *IEEE Transactions on Automation*, 7(1):135–148, 1991.

[43] J. Du, J. Leung, and G. H. Young. Scheduling Chain-Structured Tasks to Minimize Makespan and Mean Flow Time. *Information and Computation*, (1991)(92):219–236, 1991.

[44] J. Du and J. Y-T. Leung. Scheduling tree-structured tasks on two processors to minimize schedule length. *SIAM Journal of Discrete Mathematics*, (2):176–196, 1989.

[45] H. El-Rewini and T. G. Lewis. Scheduling Parallel Program Tasks onto Arbitrary Target Machines. *Journal of Parallel and Distributed Computing*, (9):138–153, 1990.

[46] R. C. Evans. Software System for a Computer Controlled Manipulator. Report RC 6210, IBM T. J. Watson Research Center, Yorktown Heights, N.Y., USA, September 1979.

[47] E. Freund, H. Heck, and K. Kreft. OSIRIS — Ein objektorientiertes System zur impliziten Roboterprogrammierung und Simulation. *Robotersysteme*, 6(4):185–192, 1990.

[48] B. Frommherz. *Ein Roboteraktionsplanungssystem.* Springer Verlag, Berlin, 1990.

[49] I. Futo and P. Kacsuk. CS-PROLOG on Multitransputer Systems. *Microprocessor and Microsystems*, 13(2), March 1989.

[50] M. R. Garey and D. S. Johnson. *Computers and Intractability — A Guide to the Theory of NP-Completeness.* A Series of Books in the Mathematical Science. W. H. Freeman and Company, San Francisco, 1979.

[51] S. Geffin and B. Furht. Transputer-based Dataflow Multiprocessor for Robot Arm Control. *Microprocessors and Microsystems*, 13(3):219–226, April 1989.

[52] E. Gelenbe. *Multiprocessor Performance.* John Wiley, New York, 1989.

[53] W. M. Gentleman. Message Passing Between Sequential Processes: The Reply Primitive and the Administrator Concept. *Software Practice and Experience*, 1(11):435–466, 1981.

[54] J. C. Gonzalez, M. H. Williams, and I. E. Aitchison. Evaluation of the Effectiveness of Prolog for a CAD Application. *IEEE Transactions on Computer Graphics and Applications*, 4(2):67–75, March 1984.

[55] M. P. Groover, M. Weiss, and R. N. Nagel. *Industrial Robotics: Technology Programming and Applications.* McGraw Hill Company, New York, 1986.

[56] U. Herzog. Leistungsbewertung und Modellbildung für Parallelrechner. *Informationstechnik it*, 31(1):31–38, 1989.

[57] C. A. R. Hoare. *Communicating Sequential Processes.* Prentice Hall, Englewood Cliffs, New Jersey, 1985.

[58] K. R. Honchell. *Machine Loading Application Cases*, chapter 10, pages 994–997. John Wiley & Sons, New York, 1985.

[59] T. B. Huynh. Erweiterung des Roboterprogrammiersystems PROBot um aufgabenorientierte Klassen und deren Methoden. Master's thesis, Universität Paderborn, Fachbereich Elektrotechnik, Fachgebiet Angewandte Datentechnik, Paderborn, September 1992.

[60] IBM Corporation, Boca Raton, Florida, USA. *AML — A Manufacturing Language. Concepts*, 1982.

[61] IBM Corporation, Boca Raton, Florida, USA. *AML — A Manufacturing Language. Reference*, 1983.

[62] IBM Corporation, Boca Raton, Florida, USA. *AML/Entry, Version 4, User's Guide*, 1984.

[63] S. Inaba. *Applications of Robots in Assembly Cells*, chapter 11, pages 1117–1129. John Wiley & Sons, New York, USA, 1985.

[64] *OPS: Occam Programming System & TDS: Transputer Development System.* INMOS Ltd., Prentice Hall, Bristol, UK, 1985.

[65] *The Transputer Applications Notebook - Architecture and Software.* INMOS Ltd., Bristol, UK, 1989.

[66] *The Transputer Applications Notebook - Systems and Performance.* INMOS Ltd., Bristol, UK, 1989.

[67] *The Transputer Databook.* INMOS Ltd., Bristol, UK, 1989.

[68] Transputer Technical Notes. Technical report, INMOS Ltd., Prentice Hall, 1989.

[69] *The T9000 Transputer Products Overview Manual.* INMOS Data Book Series. INMOS Ltd., Bristol, UK, 1991.

[70] B. Jereb and L. Pipan. Measuring Parallelism in Algorithms. *Microprocessing and Microprogramming*, 34:49–52, 1992.

[71] G. Jimenez et al. RISC-based Architecture for Multiple Robot Systems. *Microprocessors and Microsystems*, 16(4):177–185, April 1992.

[72] P. Kacsuk. *Execution Models of Prolog for Parallel Computers*. Research Monographs in Parallel and Distributed Computing. Pitman, London, 1990.

[73] P. Kacsuk and M. J. Wise. *Implementations of Distributed Prolog*. Wiley Professional Computing. John Wiley & Sons, New York, 1992.

[74] D. G. Kafura and K. H. Lee. Inheritance in Actor Based Concurrent Object-Oriented Languages. *The Computer Journal*, 32(4):297–304, 1989.

[75] A. Kapelnikov, R. R. Muntz, and M. D. Ercegovac. A Modeling Methodology for the Analysis of Concurrent Systrems and Computations. *Journal of Parallel and Distributed Computing*, 6:568–597, 1989.

[76] R. M. Karp. *Complexity of Computer Computations*, chapter Reducibility among combinatorical problems, pages 85–103. Plenum Press, New York, 1972.

[77] M. Kaufmann. Objekt-orientierte Sensordatenverarbeitung in der Roboterprogrammierumgebung PROBot. Master's thesis, Universität Paderborn, Fachbereich Elektrotechnik, Fachgebiet Angewandte Datentechnik, Paderborn, September 1992.

[78] N. Kirćanski et al. Multiprocessor Control System for Industrial Robots. *Robotics & Computer-Integrated Manufacturing*, 8(2):77–86, 1991.

[79] A. Krawinkel. Erweiterung von CS-PROLOG zur Anbindung eines Transputersystems an einen Industrieroboter. Master's thesis, Universität Paderborn, Fachgebiet Elektrotechnik, Fachgebiet Angewandte Datentechnik, Paderborn, 1991.

[80] M. Kumar. Measuring Parallelism in Computation Intensiv Scientific/Engineering Applications. *IEEE Transactions on Computers*, 37(9):1088–1097, 1988.

[81] C. Laurgeau and M. Parent. *Logic and Programming*, volume 5 of *Robot Technology*. Kogan Page Ltd., London, 1984.

[82] J. K. Lenstra and A. H. G. Rinnooy Kan. Complexity of Scheduling under Precedence Constraints. *Operations Research*, 26(1):22–35, January 1978.

[83] P. Levi. *Planen für autonome Montageroboter*. Springer Verlag, Berlin, Heidelberg, 1988.

[84] P. Levi and L. Vaija. Sensoren für Roboter. *Robotersysteme*, (3):1–15, 1987.

[85] L. I. Lieberman and M. A. Wesley. AUTOPASS: An Automatic Programming System for Computer Controlled Mechanical Assembly. *IBM Journal Research and Development*, 21(4):321–333, July 1977.

[86] T. Lozano-Perez. Robot programming. In *Proceedings of the IEEE Vol71, No 7*, pages 821–841, San Francisco, USA, July 1983. IEEE Society Press.

[87] T. Lozano-Perez and P. H. Winston. LAMA: A Language for Automatic mechanical assembly. In *Proceedings of the 5th International Joint Conference on Artificial Intelligence*, pages 710–716, Massachusetts, USA, August 1975. MIT, Massachusetts, USA.

[88] E. Lusk et al. The Aurora OR-Parallel Prolog System. In *International Conference on Fifth Generation Computer Systems*, pages 819–830, Berlin, Heidelberg, November 1988. Springer Verlag.

[89] F. B. May, A. R. Kaye, and S. A. Mahmoud. Control and Communications for Multiple, Cooperating Robots. *Robotics & Computer-Integrated Manufacturing*, 6(1):37–53, 1989.

[90] McDonnell Douglas, U.S.A. *Manufacturing Control Language User's Manual*, January 1982.

[91] D. A. Menasce and L.A. Barroso. A Methodology for Performance Evaluation of Parallel Applications on Multiprocessors. *Journal of Parallel and Distributed Computing*, 14:1–14, 1992.

[92] B. Meyer. *Object-Oriented Software Construction*. Prentice Hall, New York, 1988.

[93] J. D. Meyer. *An Overview of Fabrication and Processing Applications*, chapter 8, pages 807–821. John Wiley & Sons, New York, USA, 1985.

[94] *Operation Manual for Cincinnati Milacron T3 Industrial Robot*. Cincinnati , USA, 1980.

[95] Mitsubishi Coorporation Europe GmbH, Ratingen. *Handbuch Industrie-Roboter RV-M1*, 1990.

[96] S. Mujtaba and R. Goldman. *AL User's Manual.* Stanford University, Palo Alto, California, USA, 1979.

[97] MULTILOGIC COMPUTING Ltd., Budapest. *CS-PROILOG, Version 3.2*, 1990.

[98] K. Nakajima, J. Y-T. Leung, and S. L. Hakimi. Optimal two processor scheduling of tree precedence concstrained tasks with two execution times. *Performance Evaluation*, 1(1):320–330, 1981.

[99] J. Nentwich. Logisch/objekt-orientierte Programmierung zur Robotersteuerung — Konzeption einer Rechner-Roboterschnittstelle und ihre Implementierung. Master's thesis, Universität Paderborn, Fachbereich Elektrotechnik, Fachgebiet Angewandte Datentechnik, Paderborn, 1991.

[100] N. J. Nilsson. *Principles of Artifical Intelligence.* Springer Verlag, Berlin, New York, 1980.

[101] S. Nof. *Handbook of Industrial Robotics.* John Wiley & Sons, New York, 1985.

[102] U. Olschewski. *Robotermontagesysteme — Aufgabenorientierte Off-Line Programmierung.* Verlag TÜV Rheinland, Köln, 1990.

[103] M. Otto. *Objektorientierte Modellierung mechatronischer Systeme am Beispiel geregelter Roboter.* VDI-Verlag, Düsseldorf, 1995.

[104] W. T. Park. The SRI Robot Programming System (RPS): An Executive Summary. Technical report, SRI International, March 1981.

[105] D. L. Parnas. On the Criteria to be Used in Decomposing Systems into Modules. *Communications on the ACM*, 15(12), December 1972.

[106] Parsytec GmbH, Aachen. *MultiCluster Series, Hardware Documentation*, June 1989.

[107] R. J. Popplestone, A. P. Ambler, and I. M. Bellos. An Interpreter for a Language for Describing Assemblies. *Artificial Intelligence*, (1980)(14):79–107, 1980.

[108] D. Pountain. Parallelizing Prolog. *BYTE*, 2, 1988.

[109] K. Preiss and O. Shai. Process Planning by Logic Programming. *Robotics & Computer-Integrated Manufacturing*, 5(1):1–10, 1989.

[110] C. C. Price and M. A. Salama. Scheduling of Precedence-Constrained Tasks on Multiprocessors. *The Computer Journal*, 33(3):219–229, 1990.

[111] K. Ramamritham, J. A. Stankovic, and P. F. Shiah. Efficient Scheduling Algorithms for Real-Time Multiprocessor Systems. *IEEE Transactions on Parallel and Distributed Systems*, 1(2):184–194, April 1990.

[112] K. Rathmill. *Robotic Assembly*. International Trends in Manufacturing Technology. Springer Verlag, Berlin, Heidelberg, 1985.

[113] W. Reisig. *Petrinetze - Eine Einführung*. Springer Verlag, Berlin, 1982.

[114] W. Reisig. *Systementwurf mit Netzen*. Springer Verlag, Berlin, 1985.

[115] W. Round. Applications of Topology to Semantics of Communicating Processes. Technical report, Computer Science and Engineering Devision, University of Michigan, 1988.

[116] S. Safurin. Robotersteuerung mittels eines logisch-objektorientierten, transputerbasierten Planungssystems. Master's thesis, Universität Paderborn, Fachbereich Elektrotechnik, Fachgebiet Angewandte Datentechnik, 1995.

[117] R. Salmon. SIGLA — The Olivetti Sigma Robot Programming Language. In *8th ISIR*, Stuttgart, 1978.

[118] V. Sarkar. *Partitioning and Scheduling Parallel Programs for Multiprocessors*. Research Monographs in Parallel and Distributed Computing. Pitman, London, U.K., 1989.

[119] A. Schill. Verteilte objektorientierte Systeme: Grundlagen und Erweiterungen. *Informatik Spektrum: Forschung und Entwicklung*, pages 14–27, 1991.

[120] A. Schmidt and F. Belli. An Extension of PROLOG for Object-Oriented Programming in Logic. In *Proceedings of the Third International Conference on Industrial & Engineerings Applications of Artificial Intelligence & Expert Systems*, Charleston, South Carolina, 1990.

[121] St. Schulze-Kremer. CS-PROLOG: Parallel Programming in Logic with Transputers. Technical report, Brainware GmbH, Berlin, 1990.

[122] S. Schurig. Planen kollisionsfreier Bahnen mit Logikprogrammierung. Technical Report 1994/7, Fachbereich Elektrotechnik, Fachgebiet Angewandte Datentechnik, Universität Paderborn, 1994.

[123] B. Schwinn. Parallelität und intelligentes Backtracking in logischen Programmen. *Informationstechnik it*, 31(4), 1989.

[124] M. Sciaky. *Robots in Spot Welding*, chapter Welding, pages 899–913. John Wiley & Sons, New York, USA, 1985.

[125] K. C. Sevcik. Characterizations of Parallelism in Applications and their Use in Scheduling. *Performance Evaluation Review*, 17(1), 1989.

[126] E. Shapiro. Concurrent Logic Languages are Truly Object-Oriented. *IEEE Transactions on Software Engineering*, (3):11, 1993.

[127] E. Y. Shapiro. A Subset of Concurrent Prolog and its Interpreter. Technical Report TR003, Department of Computer Science, The Weizmann Institute of Science, Rehovot, Israel, 1983.

[128] E. Y. Shapiro. An OR-Parallel Execution Algorithm for Prolog and its FCP Implementation. Technical report, Department of Computer Science, The Weizmann Institute of Science, Rehovot, Israel, 1987.

[129] R. Shaw. Real-Time State Machines. *IEEE Transactions on Software Engineering*, 18(9), September 1992.

[130] P. C. Sheu and R. L. Kashyap. Programming Robot Systems with Knowledge. *Robotics & Computer-Integrated Manufacturing*, 4(3):359–367, 1988.

[131] K. G. Shin and M. E. Epstein. Communication Primitives for a Distributed Multi-Robot System. In *Procedings of the IEEE International Conference on Robotics and Automation*, pages 910–917, San Fransisco, March, 25-28 1985. IEEE, IEEE Society Press.

[132] K. G. Shin, M. E. Epstein, and R. A. Volz. A Module Architecture for an Integrated Multi-Robot System. In *Proceedings of the Eighteenth Annual Hawaii International Conference on System Science*, pages 120–129, January 1985.

[133] K. G. Shin, G. P. Vukkadala, and N. D. McKay. Development of an Explicit Robot Control Language. In *Proceedings Compsac 82*, Chicago, Illinois, USA, November 1982.

[134] B. Shirazi and A. R. Hurson. Special Issue on Scheduling and Load Balancing. *Journal of Parallel and Distributed Computing*, (16):271–275, 1992.

[135] B. Shirazi and M. Wang. Analysis and Evaluation of Heuristic Methods for Static Task Scheduling. *Journal of Parallel and Distributed Computing*, (10):222–232, 1990.

[136] R. K. Shyamasundar. Proof-Systems for Communication Complexity of CSP Programs. In *Proceedings of the International Conference on Parallel Processing and Applications*, pages 87–98, L'Aquila, Italy, 1987.

[137] G. C. Sih and E. A. Lee. A Compile-Time Scheduling Heuristic for Interconnection-Constrained Heterogeneous Processor Architectures. *IEEE Transactions on Parallel and Distributed Systems*, 4(2):175–187, February 1993.

[138] B. S. Smith. Welding and Robotics: The New World of Robotic Arc Welding. *Iron Age*, 226(25):1–30, March 1983.

[139] B. Sokora. What Can't Robot Languages Do? In *Proceedings of the 13th International Symposium on Industrial Robots*, pages 1–8, 1983.

[140] J. A. Solworth. Programming Language Constructs for Highly Parallel Operations on Lists. Report, Department of EECS, University of Illinois, 1989.

[141] H. Stoyan and H. Wedekind. *Objektorientierte Soft- und Hardwarearchitekturen*. Teubner Verlag, Stuttgart, 1983.

[142] K. Takasa. A Structural Approach to Robot Programming and Teaching. *IEEE Transactions on Systems Manufacturing and Cybernetics*, SMC-11(4):274–289, April 1981.

[143] K. Trachos. CHiPP — A Class Hierarchy for Data Structures Used in Parallel Programs. In *Parallelrechner-Grundlagen und Anwendungen*, pages 188–197. TAT'94, IOS Press Ohmsha, Tokyo, 1994.

[144] K. Trachos and E. Maehle. A Class Hierarchy Emulating Virtual Shared Objects on Message Passing Systems. Technical report, Fachgebiet Datentechnik, Universität Paderborn, June 1994.

[145] K. Ueda. *Guarded Horn Clauses*. Springer Verlag, Berlin, 1986.

[146] Unimation Robotics Inc., Danbury, Connetticut. *User,s Guide to VAL. A Robot Programming and Control System*, 1980.

[147] Unimation Robotics Inc., Danbury, Connetticut, USA. *User's Guide to VAL II — A Robot Programming Language and Control System*, 1983.

[148] R. A. Volz. Distributed Systems Integration Tools for Robotics. In *Proceedings of the Symposium on Factory Automation and Robotics*, pages 23–25, New York, USA, 1985. Courtant Institute of Mathematical Science, New York University.

[149] P. Wegener. Dimensions of Object-Based Language Design. In *OOPSLA'87: Conference on Object-Oriented Programming, Systems, Languages, and Applications*, pages 168–182, Berlin, Heidelberg, 1987. Springer Verlag.

[150] J. A. White. Robots—A Materials Handling Alternative. *Modern Materials Handling*, 37(6):25, May 1982.

[151] D. E. Whitney. Quasi-Static Assembly of Compliantly Supported Rigid Parts. *Transactions of ASME Journal of Dynamic System Measurement and Control*, 104(1):65–77, 1982.

[152] M. J. Wise. *Prolog Multiprocessors*. Prentice Hall Inc, Englewood Cliffs, New Jersey, 1986.

[153] D. Wloka. *Robotersysteme*, volume 3. Springer Verlag, Berlin, Heidelberg, 1992.

[154] A. Yonezawa and M. Tokoro. *Object-Oriented Concurrent Programming*. The MIT Press, Cambridge, Massachusetts, 1987.

[155] M. J. Zeestraten. *Scheduling Flexible Manufacturing Systems*. Thesis Delft. CIP-Data Koninklije Bibliotheek, Den Haag, 1990.

Part IV

Appendices

Appendix A
General Properties of CS-Prolog

This appendix briefly introduces the foundations of logic programming and surveys general characteristics of the CS-Prolog system.

A.1 A Survey of Logic Programming

This section briefly introduces the foundations of logic programming. Detailed information can be found in [26, 81, 108].

A.1.1 Programming in Prolog

A Prolog program is a database made up of a collection of logical clauses (Horn clauses), either facts or rules. A clause has the form:

$$A : -B, C, \ldots, N.$$

and can be read as "A is true if B and C and ... N are true". A is called the clause head and $B, C, \ldots, N$ the clause body. If a clause has an empty body, it is called *unit clause* or a *fact*; otherwise, it is called a *rule*. Each member of a clause is called a *predicate* defining the kind of relation between its arguments. A predicate has a name or *functor*, and a sequence of arguments. The arguments of a predicate can be constants, variables, or structures, i.e., compound arguments made up of a functor and some arguments.

The user can interrogate the Prolog database by posing queries. A query has the form

$$? - V, W, \ldots, Z.$$

and can be read as "are $V, W, \ldots,$ and Z satisfied for some values of the variables in them". The Prolog engine tries to answer the question by solving all predicates (also called *goals*) sequentially in the query. Doing this, the database is searched for a clause whose head can be matched with the first goal. The matching process possibly assigns a value to some variables in the goal and in the matching clause (this process is called *unification*), then the truth of the goal must be proved by verification of each goal in the clause body. When a goal is matched against a fact, the goal is satisfied and the Prolog engine can try to satisfy the next goal. If a goal cannot be satisfied with the current values of the variables, a new solution for the previous goal is searched, and the new goal is tried to be solved again. This process is called *backtracking*.

A.1.2 Example Applications

In order to demonstrate the Prolog mechanisms, several Prolog programs are given below.

Example A.1 The first Prolog program describes the parts of a robot. A query is posed to find which parts are common to a robot arm and the shoulder:

Program A.1

```
part_of_robot_arm(grip).                                  % *1*
part_of_robot_arm(joint).                                 % *2*
part_of_robot_body(waist).                                % *3*
part_of_robot_body(base).                                 % *4*
part_of_robot_shoulder(joint).                            % *5*
part_of_robot_shoulder(shoulder_cover).                   % *6*
part_of(robot_arm, X) :- part_of(robot_arm(X)).           % *7*
part_of(robot_body, Y) :- part_of(robot_body(Y)).         % *8*
part_of(robot_shoulder, Z) :- part_of(Z).                 % *9*

?- part_of(robot_arm, A), part_of(robot_shoulder, A).
```

In response to the query, a solution is first searched to solve the goal *part_of(robot_arm, X)*. By consulting the database, the matching of the goal with the head of Rule 7 is possible by binding the variable A to variable X. Then, the body of Rule 7 must be solved. Rule 1 is found and the goal is satisfied with $X = grip$. As A is bound to X, the original goal is also satisfied for $A = grip$. Now the second goal in the query must be solved. Using Rule 9, Z is bound to grip (the value of A) and an attempt is made to solve the body of Rule 9 which becomes *part_of_robot_shoulder(grip)*. As no rule in the database can now be matched with the current goal, the second goal cannot be satisfied with the current value for A. Then, the Prolog engine backtracks, i.e., it tries to find another solution for the first goal. The binding of X created by Rule 1 is removed, and the next matching rule is searched. From Rule 2, $X = joint$ is found, and another attempt is made to satisfy the second goal in the query. Again, Rule 9 can be used, and Z is now bound to *joint*. Now Rule 6 can be matched with the current goal. As no more goals are present in the query, a solution has been found with $A = joint$. No other solutions exist. These steps can be represented graphically with a search tree illustrated in Figure A.1.

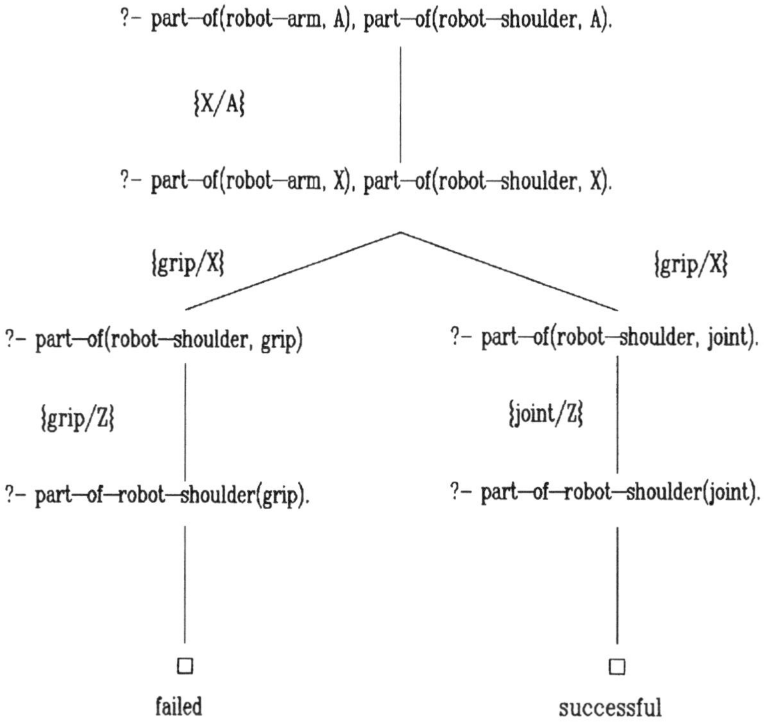

Figure A.1: SLD-tree of the example

The mathematical background for Prolog is the procedure of logical resolution. Initially, the negated form of the goal to be proved is added to the database. In the next step, any propositions, whose negated form are also contained in the database, are removed together. Finally, when no further contradictory pairs can be found, there is either an empty or a non-empty set of propositions. In the first case, resolution was successful and the original (negated) form is logically incompatible with the existing database. Therefore, the initial (positive) goal is proved. Otherwise, it is false. Resolution is said to be refutation complete and correct.

Example A.2 The second Prolog application deals with robot task scheduling the introduced work deploys for assignment and allocation of robot jobs to the multi-transputer system.

Program A.2

```
:-consult(bf).

% initial goal                                              (* 1 *)

bestfirst :-
    start(Task, NTask),
    ins_idles(Task, NTask, [], Sched, 0/0, Totals),
    user_yesno(Gant),
    output(Sched, Totals, Gant).

user_yesno(X) :-
    nl,
    repeat,
    write('Do you wish graphical output? (y/n)'),
    get_single_char(Ans),
    nl, nl,
    (   [Ans] = "y", X = 1
    ;   [Ans] = "Y", X = 1
    ;   [Ans] = "n", X = 0
    ;   [Ans] = "N", X = 0
    ),
    !.

% graphical output                                          (* 2 *)

output([], _, 0) :-
    nl,
    write('Allocation table written on allocate.pro.').

output([Head|Tail], _, 0) :-
    write(Head),
    nl,
    output(Tail, _, 0).
output(Schedule, P/K, 1) :-
```

```
    (   P >= 5,
        write('Graphical output impossible. Too many processors.'),
        nl,
        nl,
        output(Schedule, _, 0)
    ;   K >= 68,
        write('Graphical output impossible. Schedule too long.'),
        nl,
        nl,
        output(Schedule, _, 0)
    ;   K =< 34,
        gant(Schedule, 1)
    ;   gant(Schedule, 0)
    ).

gant(Schedule, Mode) :-
    output(Schedule, _, 0),
    nl,
    nl,
    write('Processors'),
    nl,
    write('^'),
    nl,
    gant1(Schedule, Mode).

gant1([], Mode) :- gant_ruler(Mode).
gant1([Head * _|Tail], Mode) :-
    prepare(Head, Mode, [], Sol, 0),
    (   Sol = [],
        Ver = Head,
        write('|'),
        nl,
        write(' ')
    ;   rev(Sol, [[]/0 * 0], Weu),
        write('|'),
        gant_text(Weu),
        nl, write(' '),
        deselect(Head, Sol, Small),
        Ver = Small
    ),
    append([[]/0], Head, Seu),
    append(Seu, [idle/0], Heu),
```

```
    single_sched(Heu, Mode, Ver),
    nl,
    write('|'),
    append(Head, [[]/0], Keu),
    ruler(Keu, Mode, 0, 0),
    nl,
    gant1(Tail, Mode).
```

% *preparation of the lists L_σ including the robot tasks* (* *3* *)

```
prepare([], _, V, V, _).
prepare([T1/Z1|Tail], Mode, List, Sol, Rest) :-
    Time is Rest + Z1,
    (   T1 = idle,
        prepare(Tail, Mode, List, Sol, Time)
    ;   atom_length(T1, Len),
        scale(Mode, Z1, Scale),
        (   Scale >= Len,
            prepare(Tail, Mode, List, Sol, Time)
        ;   Scale < Len,
            scale(Mode, Rest, Scale1),
            prepare(Tail, Mode, [T1/Scale1 * Scale1|List], Sol, Time)
        )
    ).

scale(Mode, K, Rest) :-
    (   Mode = 1,
        Pscale is (K * 2) - 1
    ;   Pscale is K - 1
    ),
    (Pscale < 0,
        Rest = 0
    ;   Rest = Pscale
    ).

rev([], L, L).
rev([H|T], Prev, Rev) :- rev(T, [H|Prev], Rev).
```

% *Gantt diagram denotation and presentation* (* *4* *)

```
deselect(V, [], V).
deselect(List, [T/_* _|Tail], Sol) :-
```

```
    append(K, [T/_|R], List),
    append(K, R, App),
    deselect(App, Tail, Sol).

gant_text([T1/Z1 * A, T2/_ * B|Tail]) :-
    tab(Z1),
    write(T1),
    atom_length(T1, X),
    Stretch is B-A-X,
    (   T2 = []
    ;   Stretch > 0,
        gant_text([T2/Stretch * B|Tail])
    ;   Stretch =< 0,
        NStretch is B-Stretch+1,
        gant_text([T2/1 * NStretch|Tail])
    ).

single_sched([idle/0|[]], _, _).
single_sched([A/_, B/K2|T], Mode, Sched) :-
    (A = [],
        (   B = idle,
            put(124),
             mode_put(Mode, 32, K2, [], _)
        ;   put(124),
            mode_put(Mode, 045, K2, B, Sched)
        )
    ;   B = idle,
        put(124),
        mode_put(Mode, 32, K2, [], _)
    ;   A = idle,
        put(124),
        mode_put(Mode, 045, K2, B, Sched)
    ;   put(124),
        mode_put(Mode, 045, K2, B, Sched)
    ),
    single_sched([B/K2|T], Mode, Sched).

mode_put(Mode, Char, K, B, List) :-
    (   B = [],
        (   Mode = 1,
        N is (K * 2) - 1,
            n_put(Char, N)
```

```
          ;   N is K - 1,
              n_put(Char, N)
          )
      ;   +member(B/_, List),
          (Mode = 1,
              N is (K * 2) - 1,
              n_put(Char, N)
          ;   N is K - 1,
              n_put(Char, N)
          )
      ;   atom_length(B, X),
          (   Mode = 1,
              N is (K * 2) - 1,
              G is ((N - X)//2),
              n_put(Char, G),
              write(B),
              M is N - G - X,
              n_put(Char, M)
          ;   N isK - 1,
              G is ((N - X)//2),
              n_put(Char, G),
              write(B),
              M is N - G - X,
              n_put(Char, M)
          )
      ).

n_put(_, N) : -N =< 0.
n_put(Char, N) : -
    put(Char),
    M is N - 1,
    n_put(Char, M).

ruler([[]/0], 1, _, 34) : -write('-- > t').
ruler([[]/0], 0, _, 68) : -write('-- > t').
ruler([H/K|Tail], Mode, X, Time) : -
    (   Mode = 1,
        put(045)
    ;   Mode = 0
    ),
    T is Time + 1,
    S is X + 1,
```

```
    R is T mod 2,
    (   S = K,
        (   R = 0,
            put(043),
            ruler(Tail, Mode, 0, T)
        ;   put(043),
        ruler(Tail, Mode, 0, T)
        )
    ;   R = 0,
        put(045),
        ruler([H/K|Tail], Mode, S, T)
    ;   put(045),
        ruler([H/K|Tail], Mode, S, T)
    ).

gant_ruler(1) :-
    write('246810121416182022242628303234').
gant_ruler(0) :-
    write('48121620242832364044485256606468').

% insertion of execution times of robot tasks and idle times        (* 5 *)

ins_idles([], _, V, V, W, W).
ins_idles([Head * _|Tail], Acc, Rest, Sched, P/Time, Total) :-
     append([[]/0|Head], [[]/0], List),
    ins_idle(List, Acc, [], [H/B|T]),
    append([H/B|T], [[]/0, []/0], Wi),
    twice(Wi, [], Ziel),
    N is P + 1,
    (   B > Time,
        ins_idles(Tail, Acc, [Ziel * B|Rest], Sched, N/B, Total)
    ;   ins_idles(Tail, Acc, [Ziel * B|Rest], Sched, N/Time, Total)
    ).
ins_idle([A/K1, B/K2|T], Task, Acc, Sched) :-
    (   B = [],
        Sched = Acc
    ;   A = [],
        prdcs([[B]], [], Prdcs),
    (   Prdcs = [],
            ins_idle([B/K2|T], Task, [B/K2|Acc], Sched)
        ;   search(Prdcs, Task, 0, Max),
            NMax isMax + K2,
```

```
        ins_idle([B/NMax|T], Task, [B/NMax, idle/Max|Acc], Sched)
        )
    ;   prdcs([[B]], [], Prdcs),
        (   Prdcs = [],
            NMax is K1 + K2,
            ins_idle([B/NMax|T], Task, [B/NMax|Acc], Sched)
        ;   search(Prdcs, Task, 0, Max),
        (   Max =< K1,
            NMax is K1 + K2,
            ins_idle([B/NMax|T], Task, [B/NMax|Acc], Sched)
        ;   NMax is Max + K2,
            ins_idle([B/NMax|T], Task, [B/NMax, idle/Max|Acc], Sched)
            )
        )
    ).
twice([[]/_, []/_], V, V).
twice([A/K1, B/K2|T], Acc, Task) :-
    Dif is K1 - K2,
    twice([B/K2|T], [A/Dif|Acc], Task).

% precedence relation determination                          (* 6 *)

prdcs([], V, V).
prdcs([[H|T]|Tail], Prev, Prdcs) :-
    pss(H, Pd),
    (   Pd == [],
        T == [],
        prdcs([], [], Prdcs)
    ;   Pd == [],
        prdcs(Tail, [[H|T]|Prev], Prdcs)
    ;   distr([H * Pd], Mal),
        combine(Mal, T, [], So),
        append(So, Tail, Win),
        prdcs(Win, Prev, Prdcs)
    ).

pss(Task, PdList) :-
    findall(prec(A, B), prec(A, B), List),
    inl(Task, [], PdList, List).

inl(_, Pds, Pds, []).
inl(Task, Tail, Pds, [prec(A, B)|T]) :-
```

```
    (   Task == B,
        inl(Task, [A|Tail], Pds, T)
    ;   inl(Task, Tail, Pds, T)
    ).

distr(Prdcs, Distr) :-
    distr1(Prdcs, [], Prdcs1),
    strip_off_collect(Prdcs1, [], Distr).

distr1([], Distr, Distr).
distr1([H|T], Tail, Distr) :-
    pairs(H, [], Pairs),
    distr1(T, [Pairs|Tail], Distr).

pairs(X * [], Tail, X * Tail).
pairs(X * [H|T], Tail, Sol) :-
    Time = [H, X],
    pairs(X * T, [Time|Tail], Sol).

strip_off_collect([], Stripped, Stripped).
strip_off_collect([_ * List|T], Tail, Stripped) :-
    append(List, Tail, NTail),
    strip_off_collect(T, NTail, Stripped).

combine([], _, V, V).
combine([H|T], List, Tail, Cmbs) :-
    append(H, List, NList),
    combine(T, List, [NList|Tail], Cmbs).

search([], _, V, V).
search([H|T], Task, PrvTime, MaxTime) :-
    sum_up(H, Task, 0, Time),
    (   Time > PrvTime,
        search(T, Task, Time, MaxTime)
    ;   search(T, Task, PrvTime, MaxTime)
    ).

% load balancing processing and file output                    (* 7 *)

sum_up([_], _, Time, Time).
sum_up([H|T], Task, PrvTime, Time) :-
    member(H/K, Task),
```

```
    TimeSum is K + PrvTime,
    sum_up(T, Task, TimeSum, Time).

start(Soln, UTask) :-
    scan(Task),
    scan(DepTask),
    unpack(Task, [], DepTask, Temp, UTask),
    scan(Proc),
    scan(Time),
    scan(Classes),
    classify(UTask, CTask, [], Classes),
    scan_prdcs,
    best(CTask * Proc * Time, Soln, Temp, UTask, _).

scan(Atom) :-
    see('schedule.in'),
    get_line(Line),
    name(Str, Line),
    term_to_atom(Atom, Str),
    see(user).

get_line(Line) :-
    get0(Next),
    (   Next =:= 10,
        !,
        Line = []
    ;   Line = [Next|Tail],
        get_line(Tail)
    ).

unpack(V, X, [], X, V).
unpack(Task, B, [H|T], Acc, NewTask) :-
    tot_dep_time(H, 0, _, L),
    place(L, Task, NTask),
    place([L|H], B, TList),
    unpack(NTask, TList, T, Acc, NewTask).

place(A, X, [A|X]).
```

```
tot_dep_time([],_,X,X).
tot_dep_time([A/B|T],K,_,Totals) :-
    Z is (B + K),
    tot_dep_time(T,Z,A/Z,Totals).

classify(V,V,_,[]).
classify([],V,V,_).
classify([H|T],CTasks,X,Classes) :-
    convert(H,[C],Classes),
    classify(T,CTasks,[C|X],Classes).

convert(_,[],[]).
convert(A/B,CTask,[J/G|Tail]) :-
    (   J == 0,
        CTask = [A/G]
    ;   B =< J,
        CTask = [A/G]
    ;   convert(A/B,CTask,Tail)
    ).

scan_prdcs :-
    see('schedule.in'),
    retractall(prec(_,_)),
    assert_precs,
    seen.

assert_precs :-
    repeat,
    get_line(List),
    name(X,List),
    (   X == end_of_file ->
        true
    ;   term_to_atom((A,B),X) ->
        assert(prec(A,B)),
        fail
    ;   write('Input file format error. Entry: '),
        write(X),
        abort
    ).
```

```
% robot task schedule determination                    (* 8 *)

best(Start, End, Acc, NTask, Small) :-
   biggest(Big),
   expand([], l(Start, 0/0), Big, _, yes, Solution),
   length(Solution, Exit),
   init(Solution, Begin),
   output_form(Solution, Exit, Begin, 1, Proc),
   remove(Proc, [], Rem),
   single(Rem, [], Small),
   reconvert(Rem, NTask, End, []),
   tell('allocate.pro'),
   alloc_table(End, 1, Acc),
   told.

init([_ * W * _|_], Begin) :- workload(W, [], Begin).

workload([], X, X).
workload([H|T], X, End) :-
   task_insert([H], X, L),
   workload(T, L, End).

task_insert([H/F], L, [[H/F] * F|L]).

reconvert([], _, V, V).
reconvert([Head|Tail], NTask, End, K) :-
   find(Head, NTask, Sol, []),
   single(Sol, [], NSol),
   complete(NSol, Num, 0),
   reconvert(Tail, NTask, End, [NSol * Num|K]).

single([], V, V).
single([H|T], K, NSol) :- single(T, [H|K], NSol).

find([] * _, _, V, V).
find([A/B|T] * X, [W/Z|Y], HH, L) :-
   (  A == W,
      find(T * X, Y, HH, [A/Z|L])
   ;  A == idle,
      find(T * X, [W/Z|Y], HH, L)
   ;  rotate([W/Z|Y], Lp), find([A/B|T] * X, Lp, HH, L)
   ).
```

```
complete([], V, V).
complete([_/B|T], Num, K) :-
    X is K + B,
    complete(T, Num, X).

% formatted output lists                                    (* 9 *)

output_form(_, V, W, V, W).
output_form(List, End, Begin, Y, Out) :-
    X is Y,
    nth_element(X, List, _ * E * _),
    Z is Y + 1,
    nth_element(Z, List, _ * B * _),
    check(B, E, Last/Zw),
    check(E, B, Prev/Zi), TisZw - Zi,
    change(Begin, Last/T, Sol),
    done(Sol, Prev/Zi, Done),
    W is (Y + 1),
    output_form(List, End, Done, W, Out).

nth_element(1, [H|_T], H).
nth_element(N, [_H|T], X) :-
    N1 is N - 1,
    nth_element(N1, T, X).

check([], [X], X).
check(_, [], idle/0).
check([AA|I], G, Task) :-
    remove_all(AA, G, Task1),
    check(I, Task1, Task).

remove_all(_, [], []).
remove_all(X, [X|Z], T) :- !, remove_all(X, Z, T).
remove_all(X, [H|Z], [H|T]) :- remove_all(X, Z, T).

change([[H/_|T] * U|A], H/W, [[H/W|T] * U|A]).
change([H|T], Z, Chg) :-
    rotate([H|T], Rot),
    change(Rot, Z, Chg).

rotate([H|T], X) :- append(T, [H], X).
```

```
done([L * B|A], X, [[X|L] * B|A]).

remove([], X, X).
remove([[_|X] * G|T], K, Rem) :- remove(T, [X * G|K], Rem).

alloc_table([], _, _).
alloc_table([H * _|W], D, Temp) :-
   assign(H, D, Temp),
   X is (D + 1),
   alloc_table(W, X, Temp).

assign([], _, _).
assign([H/_|T], W, Temp) :-
   (  H == idle,
      assign(T, W, Temp)
   ;  task_control(H, W, Temp, V),
      (  V == 1,
         assign(T, W, Temp)
      ;  write(at(H, W)),
      write('.'),
      nl,
      assign(T, W, Temp)
      )
   ).

task_control(_, _, [], 0).
task_control(X, W, [[H/_|T]|D], V) :-
   (  X == H,
      jet(T, W),
      V is 1
   ;  task_control(X, W, D, V)
   ).

jet([], _).
jet([H/_|T], W) :-
   write(at(H, W)),
   write('.'),
   nl,
   jet(T, W).
```

The program listing above can be separated into nine parts denoted by two stars and a number in ascending sequence.

- The first part of the program represents the initial goal (*bestfirst*) the user has to call starting the scheduling algorithm including all the functions that are described in the remaining parts below. The *start* predicate enables the processing of the robot tasks schedule together with the *insert_idle* clause; the *output* predicate realizes the graphical output of the schedule by means of Gantt diagrams;
- if the programmer selects the graphical screen print, the determined task schedule $S(P_S)$ is presented in terms of Gantt diagrams. For this purpose, the predicates *gantt* and *append* convert robot task lists L_σ including the robot tasks with their processing times into a corresponding graphical timing;
- the third part contains predicates like *prepare* or *scale* materializing the scaling of the Gantt diagram axis;
- the Gantt diagram format and the denotation is supported through predicates such as *gant_text*, *single_sched*, *mode_put*, or *ruler*. Different parameters enable the representation of various scopes varying between 32 and 64 time units deploying the *gant_ruler* predicate;
- the fifth part of the listing provides predicates like *ins_idles* or *prdcs* in order to compute the processor loads $[\![p_i]\!]$ of each processor by evaluating the processing times τ_i of the robot tasks. The idle times are estimated and taken into account during derivation of the processor load lists to get the correct timing of the tasks;
- the next program part handles the precedence relation considering the task-dependent relation $t_a \prec_\mathcal{A} t_b$, the data-dependent relation $t_a \prec_\mathcal{D} t_b$, and the independent precedence relation $t_a \not\prec_{\mathcal{A},\mathcal{D}} t_b$. For this, the predicates *pss*, *prdcs*, *inl*, and *distr* as well as *strip_off_collect* and *combine* for analyzing the precedence relations;
- the load balancing process and the file output of the computed schedule is subject of the seventh listing section. Further, the predicates *unpack* and *place* as well as *classify*, *convert*, and *tot_dep_time* substitute robot tasks $t_i, \ldots, t_n$ in the sublist through t_x and replace the substitution through t_x. The file operating predicates *scan* and *assert_precs* complete this part;
- the eighth part represents a particular function of the scheduling program: the best-first algorithm which is related to the A^*-algorithm of Nilsson [100]. This heuristical search strategy tries to find an optimal path in a search tree through estimation of the path length caused by the available and usable nodes in the tree always considering the destination node. To do this, the predicates *biggest*, *expand*, *length*, and *find* investigate the solution space to find the shortest path. The successful search is associated with the execution of special predicates like *workload*, *task_insert*, *reconvert*, *single*, and *complete* all together realizing the allocation of the robot tasks $t_k \rightsquigarrow p_i$ to the processors yielding their work load $[\![p_i]\!]$;

- finally, the program concludes with predicates converting and formatting the output of the best-first algorithm from the descending into an ascending sequence of the robot tasks. For this purpose, the predicate *output_form* occurs the rotation (*rotate*, *remove*, *change*, *done*) of the A^*-output lists. Subsequently, the lists are checked on idle times. The predicates *assign* and *task_control* generate the required output format in terms of task/processor tuples.

A.2 CS-Prolog - A Concurrent Prolog with Transputer Philosophy

The realization of the concurrent logic/object-oriented programming environment for robots is supported by a concurrent extension of Prolog [29, 30, 41, 152]. For a first study of this project, the CS-Prolog (Communicating Sequential Prolog) [97, 72, 49] has been chosen. CS-Prolog explicitly involves the concept of communicating sequential processes and is intended to be implemented on distributed, non-shared memory parallel computers, mainly transputer networks.

The design and implementation of CS-Prolog enables the same CS-Prolog program to be run on a single transputer and on multi-transputer. On a mono-processor, parallel execution is virtual and controlled by a scheduler; on a distributed architecture, the execution of processes on different processors is in parallel.

A CS-Prolog program consists of a set of communicating sequential Prolog programs executed in parallel or in quasi-parallel way on mono-processors. Each of the communicating Prolog program is an ordinary Prolog program without any restriction and implemented on the left-to-right, depth-first (LRDF) strategy of sequential Prolog programs.

A.3 The Language Concept of CS-Prolog

The basic notions of CS-Prolog are the same as in OCCAM [64]:

- process;
- communication;
- time.

Each process represents a Prolog goal to be resolved. An independent Prolog interpreter or compiler is assigned to each process to execute the goal of the process in parallel with other processes. These processes can communicate with each other by means of messages. A process can send a message to another process or a group of processes. Synchronization of the cooperative processes is achieved through the handling of messages. Execution of processes is suspended if a message is asked for but has yet to arrive, and the continuation of process execution can only be realized if an appropriate message arrives. The sender process can continue even if the addressed process is not ready to receive the message.

The process philosophy of CS-Prolog is based on a basic AND/OR-process model [121, 31] solving Prolog clauses. The OR-processes search the database to find all the clauses that solve a single goal; an AND-process solves the body of a clause, i.e., it solves all the goals in the clause body sequentially and backtracks when necessary. Processes are connected logically as shows in Figure 3.4.

An OR-process is started with the goal to be solved and a list of variable bindings. The process scans the database to find all the clauses whose heads can be unified with the goal. For each successful unification, an AND-son is created solving the body of the clause. As soon as an AND-process produces solutions, it sends them to the OR-father which in turn reorders the solutions received from all its sons, according to the standard depth first order of sequential Prolog. Before terminating, the OR-process sends a FAIL solution to its father.

The call parameters of an AND-process are the index of the clause whose body must be solved, and a set of variable bindings that have been generated during the unification of the head of the clause. The AND-process creates a son OR-process for the first goal in its clause body; as soon as a solution is received from the first son, the AND-process creates a new OR-son to solve the second goal, and so on until the last son sends back its first solution. The AND-process then composes the solution consisting of the partial solutions and sends it to its father. The solution from the last goal is then dropped, and the next one is used to build a new reply. When the last goal has no more solutions (a FAIL is received from a son), an AND-process backtracks. It gets a new solution (if one exists) from the previous son and generates a new process to solve the last goal with the new solution. Backtracking can cause the process to take more steps backwards, and finally, the process attempts to backtrack through the first goal. In case of a successful attempt, the process definitively fails and, after sending a FAIL-message to the OR-father, it terminates. A special case occurs when a fact has to be solved. In this case, the OR-process solves the fact directly without creating a son process.

In CS-Prolog, the only tool for process communication and synchronization is the message passing mechanism. Shared variables among concurrent processes are not allowed. Similarly, communication is prohibited via the

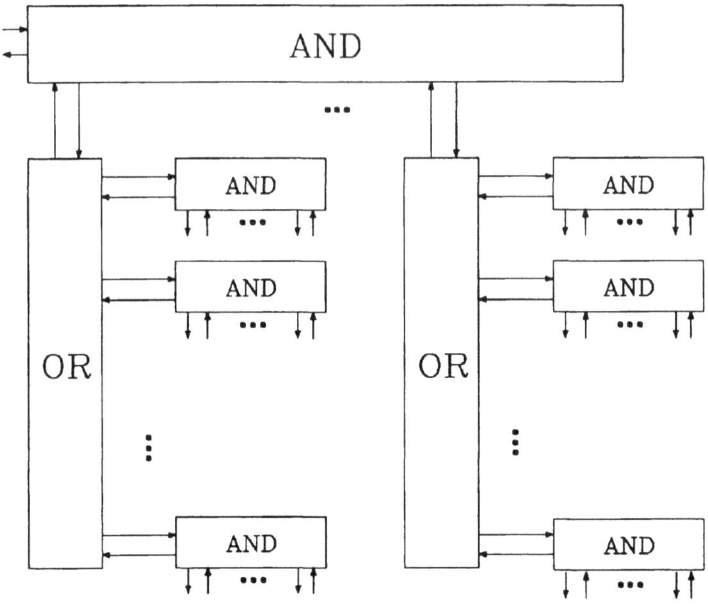

Figure A.2: AND/OR- process model of Section 3.3

access of dynamically created clauses (dynamical database). These features of CS- Prolog suggest a transputer network implementation. The process, communication and time concept of CS-Prolog is defined by means of a collection of built-in predicates. By means of examples, these concepts and some of the corresponding built-in predicates are explained in detail below.

A.3.1 Process and Communication Concept

The process and communication concept is based on a set of built-in predicates. The built-in predicate

$$new(G, N, T)$$

creates dynamically a new process for the goal G and the name N on the transputer T. The caller process continues to execute. All variables in N are unified with a constant differing from other constants of the program, in this way generating a unique inner name for the new process. If the variable T is missing, then the default is the current transputer where the caller process is running. In a mono-processor environment, the parameter T can be omitted and each processor is allocated on the same transputer. Similarly, if T identifies a missing transputer, then the new process is allocated on the current transputer. The transputers are identified by integers in the range of $(0, N)$, where $N+1$ is the number of transputers in the system, since the identifier number of the root transputer is always 0.

When the goal of a process has resolved according to the semantics of Prolog, then the process is terminated. The termination of the whole CS-Prolog program is achieved when all processes have terminated. Successfully terminated processes are deleted automatically. Other processes can be deleted by the built-in predicate

$$delete\_process(P).$$

All processes whose names can be unified with P are deleted. These processes are restored as a result of backtracking. The predicate

$$send(M, P_L)$$

is one of the built-in procedures realizing the communication concept. The caller process sends the message M to the processes in the processor list P_L. If P_L is an unbound variable, then all processes can receive the broadcast message. M must not include any uninstantiated variables for preventing a tentative communication via common shared variables.

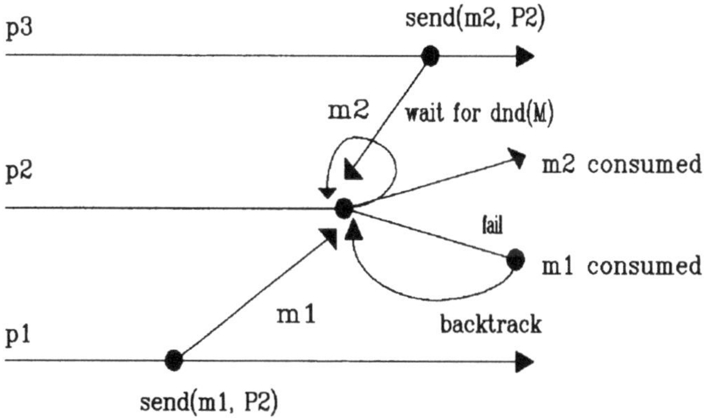

Figure A.3: Interprocess communication in CS-Prolog

If a $send(S, P_L)$ procedure had executed earlier and the caller process is on P_L and M unifiable with S, then the caller process continues to execute. Otherwise, the caller process is suspended. It can continue as soon as another process evaluates a $send(S, P_L)$ predicate, where M and S are unifiable, and the process is addressed by the sending predicate

$$wait\_for(M), wait\_for\_dnd(M)$$

The predicate *wait_for* is deterministic; it can receive only the first message. In contrast, *wait_for_dnd* is nondeterministic; in case of backtrack, it is able to pick up new messages sent by other sending procedures. The implementation of *wait_for_dnd* ensures that all possible solutions of the CS-Prolog program can be found by backtracking.

The principle of interprocess communication based on the nondeterministic *wait_for_dnd* predicate is depicted in Figure A.3. The sender processes P_1 and P_3 can continue their progress without delay after sending a message (asynchronous communication). The receiver process P_2 is suspended until a message arrives for it. When a unifiable message M_2 is received P_2 becomes active and continues the resolution of its goal. If the resolution fails by M_2, then P_2 backtracks to the *wait_for_dnd* call and retries the resolution by the other available message M_1.

A.3.2 The Time Concept

The time concept of CS-Prolog differs significantly from the OCCAM concept. Instead of using the global real-time concept, CS-Prolog applies the local virtual time, i.e., all processes can have their own local times, which might be different. As an example for the utilization of this concept, the initial value of the local time for a process can be given by the built-in procedure

$$new(G, N, S_T, E_T)$$

where S_T defines the initial value of the local time for the process N, and G should be resolved before the local time passes execution time E_T; otherwise G fails. The parameter S_T and E_T are optional and typically used for simulation.

The time concept is also important for message passing. Whenever a message is sent by the built-in predicate (*send*), the CS-Prolog distributor puts a time stamp on the message. The time stamp includes the local time of the sender process and is the tool for the implicit modification of the local time, i.e., if the local time T_1 of the receiver process is less than the time stamp T_2, then T_1 should be modified $T_1 = T_2$. If the local time T_1 of the receiver process is greater than or equal to the time stamp at the moment of the message reception, then there is no change in the local time of the receiver process. This concept of local time allows CS-Prolog to be used as a distributed simulation language. Independent execution of processes on different processors takes place, and the processes form the simulation model.

A.3.3 Mechanism of Parallelism

Conceptually, CS-Prolog is a two level language. At the higher level, the notion of process is available to describe parallel activities. At the lower level, the behaviour of each process is given by a Prolog program. The declarative semantics of Prolog is preserved within each process; meanwhile the process is able to receive and send information from/to its environment (other processes). The process level parallelism offered by CS-Prolog ensures a new type of parallelism, similarly to Hoare's concept of communicating sequential processes which is not realized in another Prolog-based languages. By means of this parallelism, both, the AND and OR-parallelism can be achieved. The granularity of parallelism can be controlled by the user encapsulating Prolog programs of different size into one process. The relationship between standard Prolog programs and CS-Prolog programs can be investigated from two points of view:

- transformation of existing Prolog programs into CS-Prolog;
- reconsidering the Prolog solution of a problem by using the process concept of CS-Prolog.

By definition, all standard Prolog programs are valid CS-Prolog programs. Exploitations of the simplest case of AND-parallelism can be achieved by means of a simple syntactical modification as shown below. The standard Prolog program is:

$$a : -b, c.$$

The equivalent parallel CS-Prolog program is:

$$a : -b\&c.$$

where & is an operator defined as:

$$\&(X, Y) : -new(X, \_, T1), new(Y, \_, T2).$$

where X and Y are ground terms.

A.4 Control Mechanisms in CS-Prolog Programs

The basic control mechanism of CS-Prolog is identical with the LRDF control strategy of sequential Prolog systems. The difference appears when the interpreter reaches a communication point. A communication point is a built-in procedure effecting the execution of other Prolog processes. Two types are available in CS-Prolog according to process generation and message sending. In both cases, the execution of the caller process continues without delay and as a result of these procedures parallel processes can start or continue on other transputers (distributed forward execution).

A.4.1 Distributed Forward Execution

The basic control mechanism of CS-Prolog is identical with the LRDF strategy of sequential Prolog systems. The difference appears when the interpreter reaches a so-called communication point, which is a CS-Prolog built-in predicate effecting the execution of other Prolog processes. Two types of communication points are available in CS-Prolog:

- *new*: creating a new process;
- *send*: sending a message to other processes.

In both cases, the execution of the caller process continues without delay and as a result of these procedures, parallel processes can start or resume on other transputers.

A.4.2 Distributed Backtracking

A major problem of CS-Prolog and other distributed Prolog languages is how to ensure the backtracking facility in a distributed environment. The main difference between the distributed forward execution and distributed backtracking is in the parallelism. While the former is parallel in nature, the latter is sequential. Distributed backtracking is performed sequentially and is controlled by one transputer until a new alternative can be found by one of the processes which ensures the parallel reactivation of the other processes.

In CS-Prolog, two kinds of backtrackings are distinguished finding alternative solutions or alternative routes in the search tree:

- local backtracking;
- global backtracking.

Backtracking between two communication points (e.g. new or send) is local and has no direct effect on the behaviour of other processes. Backtracking passing a communication point is global and immediately alters the behaviour of other processes. Similarly, two kinds of choice points can be distinguished:

- normal choice point;
- communication choice point.

The choice point created when a *wait_for_dnd* procedure is activated is the communication choice point. Based on the notions introduced, the algorithm of distributed backtracking is:

- if during backtracking a process passes a communication point, an anti-message is sent to the receiver processes, forcing backtracking for these processes. The backtracking of the original process continues to its last choice point. This mechanism is illustrated in Figure A.4;

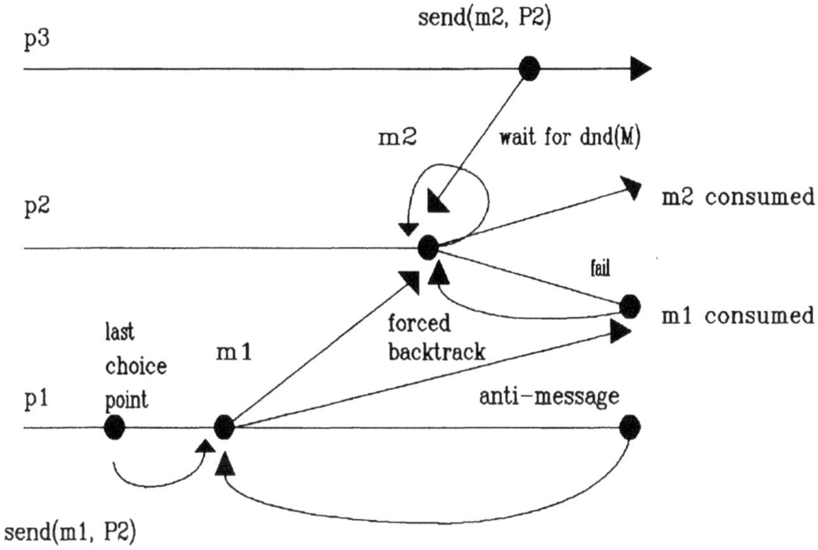

Figure A.4: Forced backtracking

- if during backtracking a process arrives at a communication choice point, then, if there are further matching messages for the process, the next message is selected, the process becomes running and the forward execution begins. Otherwise, the process becomes waiting on the communication choice point;
- all processes are in the waiting or finished state (deadlock situation) and there are no messages in transit. In this case, global control is required
  - to recognize the deadlock situation;
  - to select a process which can continue backtracking until it arrives at a new *wait_for_dnd* procedure call causing a new deadlock situation, and then continues,

  or it finds a new alternative path on which a new or send procedure call is executed, hopefully causing the reactivation of other processes. The original process continues in parallel with the other processes which were reactivated.

A.5 Distribution of Work

The first and most important design decisions in a distributed implementation of a process oriented language are

- how to map the processes into the processor space;
- how to distribute work between the host computer and the processor space;
- how to allocate data structures into the memory space.

In the following discussion a solution of these problems is given. Note that the allocation algorithm presented in Chapter 6 is also based on these fundamental characteristics of CS-Prolog.

A.5.1 Mapping of CS-Prolog Processes

CS-Prolog offers two basic solutions for mapping processes in a multiple processor environment:

- static mapping considering the execution of each process to be restricted to a specified transputer;
- dynamic mapping, where processes can be moved between transputers during their execution.

Though the second alternative insures more flexibility and letter load balancing OCCAM 2 and Parallel C realize the static mapping. In case of CS-Prolog moving a process from one transputer to another would require the movement of a large amount of data usually stored in three Prolog stacks (Environment, Copy, and Trail) representing the history of the process execution. Nevertheless, this progress would speed down the computation. Therefore, CS-Prolog also uses the static mapping technique.

Considering static mapping, the next question to be solved is how to choose transputers for processes. Again two possible alternatives arise:

- user controlled mapping, where the user should decide how to map the processes into the processor space. To control the mapping, language tools are available for him;
- run-time system controlled mapping, where the run-time system decides on the process allocation based on run-time information such as the current load balancing of the system.

The advantage of the first alternative is that the run-time system can be kept simple and fast. In many cases, the programmer designing the parallel algorithm is able to control the process allocation in a much more effective way than even an intelligent run-time system. Obviously, a drawback of this alternative is the burden of the (task) process allocation.

Both, OCCAM 2 and Parallel C apply this mapping strategy. In OCCAM 2, the *PLACED PAR*-construct serves for controlling the the process mapping, while in Parallel C a special configuration file is deployed for this purpose.

In CS-Prolog, processes are dynamically created by the *new*-built-in predicate. The optional third argument of this predicate is used for specifying the transputer where the new process should be executed. This argument can be a variable being unified during the execution. This way the CS-Prolog mapping solution is somewhere between both alternatives described above. When the third argument is missing, the new process is mapped on the parent's transputer. Like in OCCAM 2 and in Parallel C, the mapping of processes does not effect the logical behaviour of CS-Prolog programs but has a great influence on the overall system performance.

On each transputer any number of concurrent processes can be executed together, sharing the processor time. To dispatch the processes, a CS-Prolog scheduler is applied. Unlike in OCCAM 2 and in Parallel C, each Prolog process has the same priority in CS-Prolog. Processes are not distinguished since the initial goal of CS-Prolog is successfully resolved when all the created Prolog processes are successfully terminated.

A.5.2 Function Distribution between Host and Transputers

Since all the IO devices are connected to the host computer any operations concerned with IO activities should be executed by the host. According to this rule in the distributed CS-Prolog system, the host provides functions enabling the application of the user environment and the IO built-in predicates. The CS-Prolog system always works in one of the following modes:

- environment mode;
- execution mode.

The purpose of the environment mode is to prepare the system for execution of CS-Prolog programs. The subsequent main activities are included through this mode:

- program loading with syntactic checking;
- program editing;
- defining the initial goal statement;
- starting the execution of the initial goal.

In environment mode, the host is the active part of the host — multi-transputer system. The only task of the transputer network in this mode is to transmit the Prolog clauses packed into *DATABASE* messages in a broadcast way to each transputer of the system. The environment mode finishes when the initial goal statement is sent to the root transputer. The root is the only transputer connected to the host and initiates the broadcast messages for the other transputers.

The execution mode starts when the Prolog interpreter on the root receives the "start initial goal" message and begins the execution of the initial goal. The other transputers are activated by the *new*-built-in predicates of CS-Prolog generating Prolog processes on different transputers. Whenever a Prolog process on a transputer reaches an IO built-in predicate, it creates an "IO service" message being intended for the host. It is the responsibility and the only task of the host to execute the IO predicates.

A.5.3 Data Distribution

CS-Prolog deploys several main data structures such as:

- *Source Table* representing the CS-Prolog source code;
- *Prog Table* describing the clauses of the CS-Prolog program in term format;
- *Constant Table* containing Prolog names;
- *Operator Table* defining Prolog operators;
- *Environment Stack* presenting the history of a CS-Prolog process;
- *Copy Stack* storing the dynamically created compound terms;
- *Trail* including information to undo variable bindings in case of backtrack;
- *Scheduling Lists* for mapping the concurrent CS-Prolog processes.

Since the *Source Table* represents the source text of the program, it is only located in the host memory.

The *Prog* and *Constant Table* together present the inner format of a Prolog database consisting of static and dynamic clauses. Static clauses are defined by the original program text and are visible for each Prolog process. Therefore, a copy of them is stored in every transputer's memory. Since static clauses are commonly used by all of the transputers, they are not allowed to be moved through any Prolog process. Furthermore, one copy of these tables is also stored in the host memory in order to assist program editing in the environment mode and IO operations in the execution mode. Clauses of this type are broadcasted through the host during the program loading and editing phases of the environment mode.

Dynamic clauses are created by different processes during execution of the goal sequence. Dynamic clauses are local to the creator process. Thus, they are only stored in the local memory of the creator and can only be removed by their creator process. As a result, dynamic clause operations (*assert*, *retract*, etc.) do not require any intertransputer communication.

Additional operators can be added to the *Operator Table* either in environment or execution mode. In the latter case, the *add_operator* built-in predicate is responsible for generation of new operators by sending an *ADD_OP* message containing the operator definition. The host syntactically checks if the operator is acceptable. Subsequently, it is added to the *Operator Table* of the host and a broadcast message is generated by the host for the transputers causing the operator to be added to the *Operator Table* of the transputers. Deletion of operators are performed in the same way.

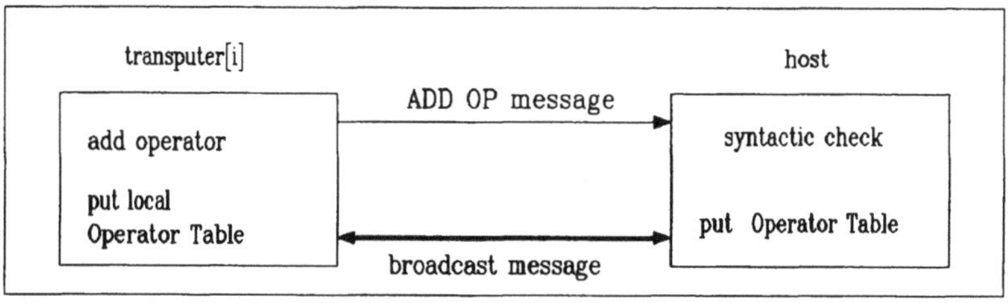

Figure A.5: Distributed execution of add_operator built-in predicate

The data structures *Environment Stack*, *Copy Stack*, *Trail*, and *Scheduling Lists* represent the dynamic behaviour of the Prolog processes in the execution mode. These data structures are stored on the transputers but not on the host since it is the task of the nodes to run CS-Prolog processes.

A.5.4 Communication Subsystem

CS-Prolog provides four basic types of messages in the multi-transputer system:

- user;
- broadcast;
- acknowledge;
- deadlock token.

The so-called user messages serve for passing information between two transputers or between a transputer and a host. Two subclasses of the user messages can be distinguished according to the progress direction of the sender interpreter. Positive messages are sent in the case of forward progress and negative messages during backtrack. Functionally, the user messages support the distributed implementation of the *send*, *new*, *io*, *database*, and *control* built-in predicates.

Broadcast messages are applied for transmitting information to all transputers of the multi-transputer system. Typically, broadcast messages appear in the program loading, process allocation, and *Operator Table* management. From the view of broadcast transmission, transputers are connected in a logical tree where the root of the tree is always the root transputer.

Acknowledge messages and deadlock token messages support the detection of the global deadlock situation, which is important in distributed backtrack. The system is in global deadlock when both the Prolog interpreters and the communication subsystem are without any work, i.e., there is no Prolog process to resume by any interpreter, no message searching its way to the destination transputer and there is at least one process waiting for a message.

The global deadlock detection algorithm is a distributed one where the transputers are organized in a logical ring. A so-called deadlock token is circulated in the ring. The deadlock token is passed by a transputer if its interpreter is in local deadlock and all the messages sent by this interpreter have arrived in their destination transputers. If the deadlock token can reach the emission transputer having passed through the ring finding all transputers in local deadlock means that the system is in global deadlock.

A.5.5 Implementation Layers on Transputers

The implementation of the CS-Prolog system is folded into four layers on each transputer:

- communication subsystem layer (CSL);
- communication control layer (CCL);
- Prolog control layer (PCL);
- Prolog interpreter layer (PIL).

The following view highlights the special features and tasks of every layer underlining the importance as functional component of CS-Prolog.

Communication Subsystem Layer

The CSL is the nearest layer to the physical hardware and responsible for hiding the physical topology of the transputer network. It realizes a logical network topology defined by the user and stored in the *Topology Description Table.*

CSL assures the following characteristics of the intertransputer communication:

- messages can be of unlimited size but should be composed from packages with maximum size of 256 bytes;

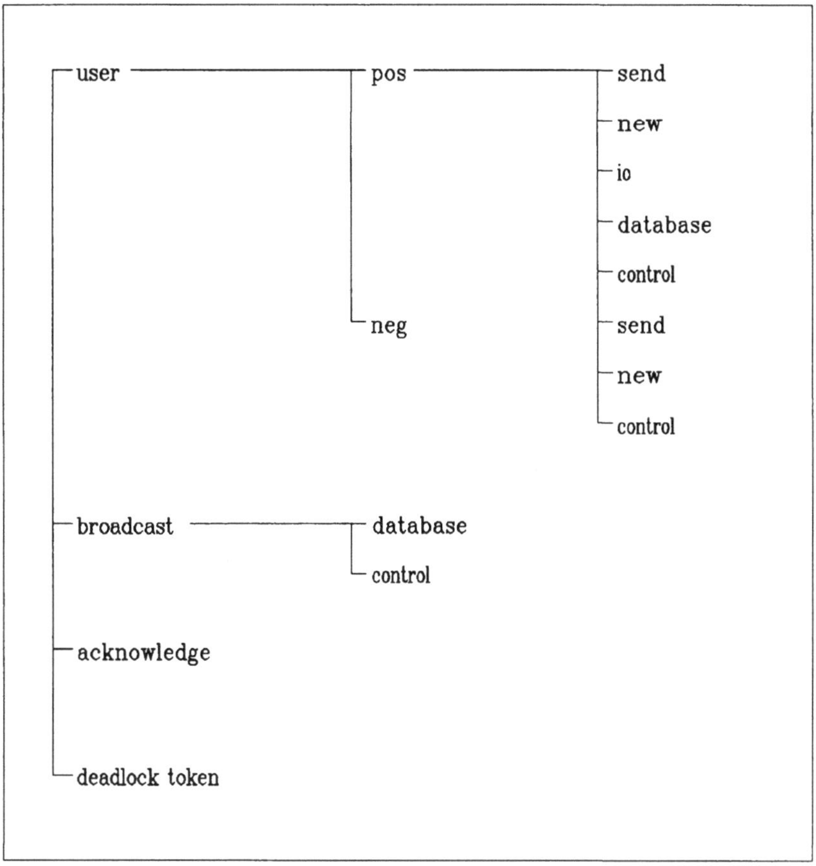

Figure A.6: Message types of the communication system

- the order of packages belonging to the same message does not change during communication;
- packages are guaranteed to arrive to the target transputer except for the case of hardware error;
- no communication deadlock can arise in the network.

Communication Control Layer

The tasks of the communication control layer CCL are as follows:

- receive of user and broadcast messages from the Prolog control layer, de-integration of them into packages shorter than 256 bytes and sending them to the CSL;
- receive and processing of messages from the CSL;
- generation and transmission of acknowledgement (*ACK*) messages for the user and broadcast messages;
- receive and handling of deadlock token messages;
- detection of local and global Prolog deadlocks.

The *ACK* and deadlock token messages are created and processed in the CCL. The main reason for introducing the CCL was to detect the global Prolog deadlock as it is described above. The basic system processes of CCL are shown in Figure A.7.

Outgoing messages are taken from the *Message Out Table* (*MOT*) of PCL. Incoming messages are put into the *Message In Table* (*MIT*) of PCL. In order to assist CCL in determining the local deadlock state of the node, the interpreter sets a *Deadlock State Flag* whenever it can not find any Prolog process to run.

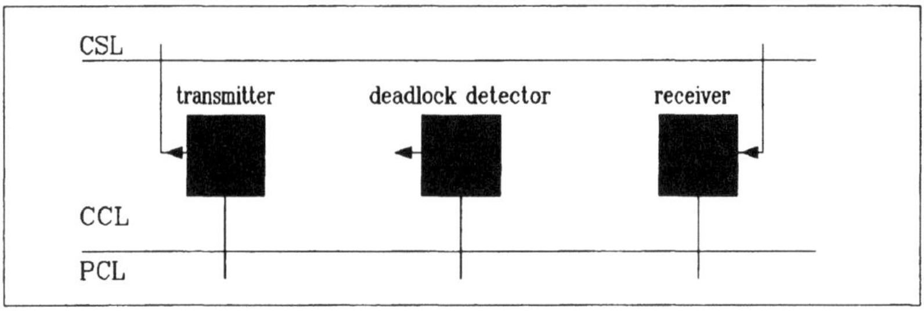

Figure A.7: Communication control layer of CS-Prolog

Prolog Control Layer

The tasks of PCL is to organize the work of the Prolog interpreters running on different processors into an integrated system resolving the initial goal statement of CS-Prolog. The simplified structure of PCL is shown by Figure A.8 where black boxes present system processes and white boxes the data structure.

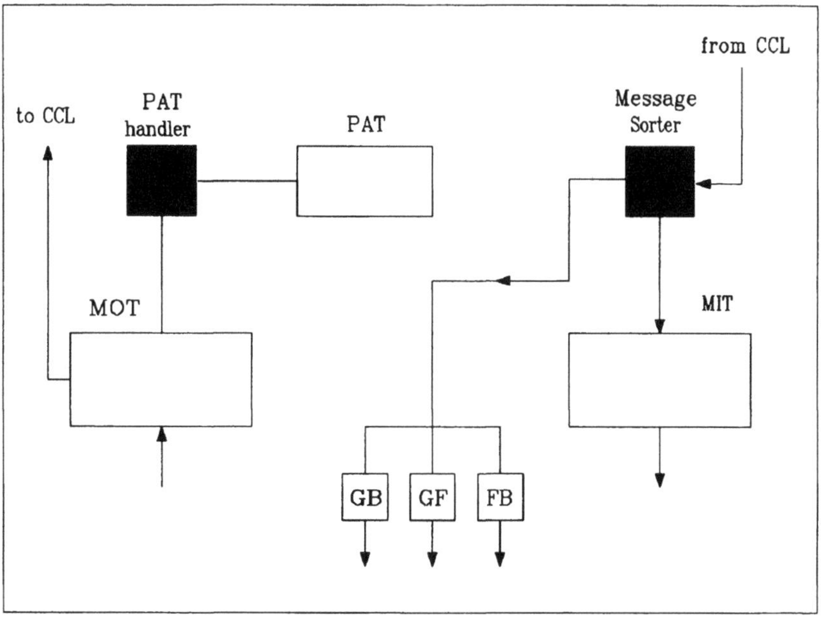

Figure A.8: Structure of the Prolog control layer

The main tasks of PCL are as follows:

- PCL has to administrate the process allocation on transputers. For this purpose, the so-called *Process Allocation Table* (*PAT*) contains pairs of process names and their associated transputers where they were created. Whenever a message is sent to a Prolog process running on a different transputer, it is the task of the *PAT* handler to determine the receiver of the message deploying the information of the *PAT*;
- based on the type of the incoming messages, *Message Sorter* places them in one of the *MIT* or sets one of the *State Vector Flags.*

The *MIT* holds the incoming user message and according to these messages it is classified into six groups:

- table of incoming *new* type messages (*NEW_MIT*);
- table of incoming *send* type messages (*SEND_MIT*);
- table of *IO* type message (*IO_MIT*);
- table of *DATABASE* type message (*DBASE_MIT*);
- table of *CONSUMED* type message (*CONS_MIT*);
- table of *RESUME* type message (*RESUME_MIT*);

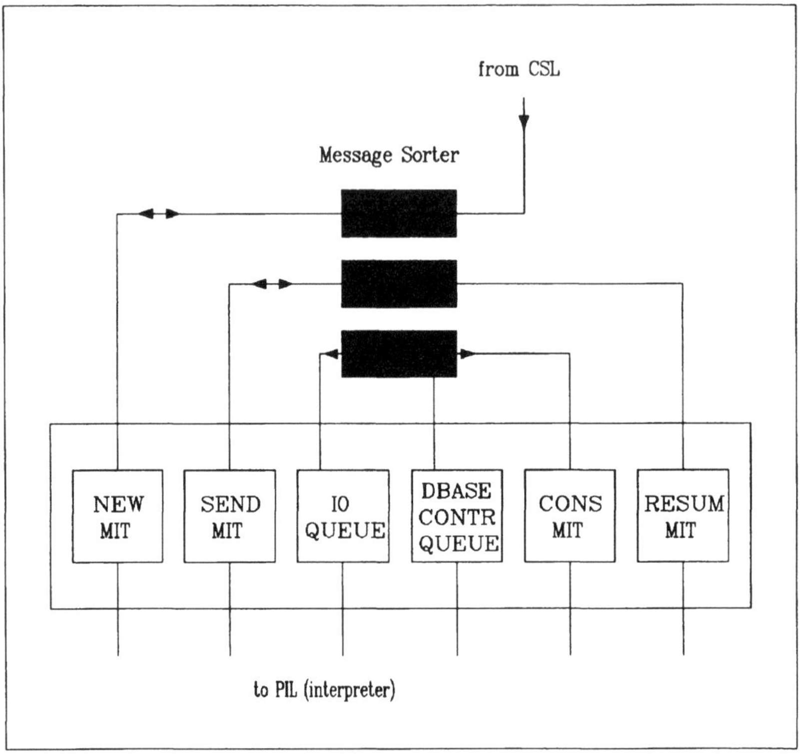

Figure A.9: Structure of the *Message Input Table*

Figure A.9 shows the structure of *MIT* and illustrates the functional relations. *CONS_MIT* and *RESUME_MIT* support the realization of the *TRANSIENT BACK* state. The *State Vector Flags* serve for realizing the state transition diagram of the schedulers distinguishing the *Global Backward Flag* (*GB*), the *Global Forward Flag* (*GF*), and the *Forced Backtrack Flag* (*FB*).

Prolog Interpreter Layer

The PIL contains the Prolog interpreter and the Prolog data structures described above. This layer also materializes the *Process Level* and *Mono-transputer Level Scheduling*. The interpreter and scheduler basically work within the *PIL* calling the underlying layers only in the following cases:

- creating a process by the *new* built-in predicate;
- sending a message to a process running on another transputer;

- executing IO built-in predicates;
- detecting local deadlock.

PIL always generates user messages and places them into the *Message Out Table* of the PCL.

A.5.6 Distributed Simulation

Distributed simulation means "independent" execution on different processors, the processes forming the simulation model. During the following discussion, it is supported that there are as many processors as processes.

It has been seen that a central problem of system simulation is the handling of time, which is used as the main synchronization mechanism. In a uni-processor implementation, time is global for all the processes, i.e., local times associated with the processes are always equal to global time, also called system time. Maintaining the same notion of global time with the same scheduling algorithm leads to inefficiency due to the use of centralized control in a decentralized multi-processor environment.

To avoid this inefficiency, a new decentralized control mechanism based on the "virtual time" concept was introduced [49]. The time warp mechanism is an algorithm based on this concept and can be roughly explained as follows. Each of the processes has a local clock which keeps virtual time. When a process sends a message to another process, it stamps the message with its virtual time called the "virtual send time". Virtual send time is the local time of the sender at the moment of sending the message. When receiving the message, the receiver process may be in two possible states:

- the local time of the receiver is less or equal to the send time of the message;
- the local time of the receiver is greater than the send time of the message.

In the first case, the receiver process continues its activities without any modification due to the new message. If this is the only available message then it proceeds with this message; if there are other messages available then the receiver takes one of the messages conforming to the message selection algorithm.

In the second case, however, the receiver process turns back its local time to the moment of the send time of the message and will continue its activities taking into account (if necessary) the new message. Obviously, if the receiver turns back past a communication point where it had sent a message to another process, an anti-message is sent to annihilate the message sent previously. This anti-message may in turn cause a further turn back at the receiver process. The mechanism described above proved to be more efficient in most cases but it supposes that time is not turned back frequently.

Some time warp implementations introduced recently do not send these anti-messages until they have checked that the local time of the process turned back does not reach the previous moment of communication. If at the moment to which the process is returned there is no message to send or the message is different from that previously sent, then an anti-message can be sent. It has been shown [26] that this method can be more efficient than all previous time warp implementations and traditional scheduling.

From the above discussion the requirement appears that the implementation of the rolling back mechanism is associated with the storage of the intermediate states of the processes (all or some, depending on the implementation). This need saving the states makes CS-Prolog a good candidate for distributed simulation. Due to its Prolog base all the necessary intermediate states in CS-Prolog are automatically saved to ensure, by means of backtracking, the complete traversal of alternative solutions. Efficient implementation methods are already available and are in constant development for Prolog-based languages to store the intermediate states.

Another advantage of CS-Prolog for distributed simulation is related with the possible theoretical gain in efficiency due to its non-determinism. Nondeterminism in CS-Prolog means that an interpreter finds all the possible solutions of a problem (in case of correct programming) if needed, but the order of these solutions is irrelevant. In case of distributed simulation, this nondeterminism may result in the following modification of the time warp mechanism: if the send time of a message is less than the receive time, it is not obligatory to turn time back.

The explanation of this phenomenon is connected with the termination of receiver process. If the receiver process can terminate successfully, together with all the other processes of the system, this means that for finding a solution the message (or the content of the message) was irrelevant.

The only thing that has to be ensured is that when enumerating all the possible solutions the solution given by the standard time warp mechanism must be among these solutions. Correct implementations of backtracking ensures this prediction.

A.6 Scheduling

Control of the CS-Prolog system is realized on three different levels:

- process level;
- mono-transputer level;
- multi-transputer level.

Below the scheduling strategies are presented in detail and their mechanisms are discussed each in a subsection.

A.6.1 Process Level Scheduling

Every Prolog process can be in one of the following states:

sleeping	the process is created and waiting to start;
running forward	the process is using the transputer and going ahead;
running backward	the process is using the transputer and backtracking;
waiting	the process is waiting for a message;
transient waiting	the process is waiting for *send* and *new*;
finished	the process has resolved its initial goal.

The state transition diagram of the processes is given through Figure A.10 presenting the functional relations between these states. Since a CS-Prolog program successfully terminates when all the processes have reached their *finish* state, any process can monopolize the processor. The scheduler tests

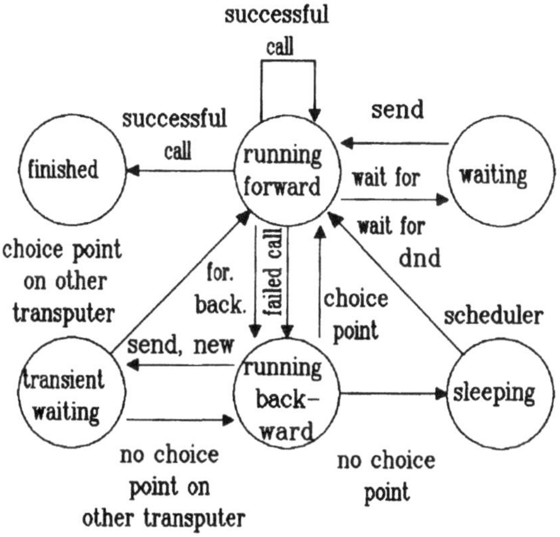

Figure A.10: State transition diagram of processes

the state of the current process before taking its next subgoal. This test is executed at the beginning of the main loop of the interpreter. If the state is *running forward* then the current process can use the processor further. If the state becomes *waiting* or *finished* then a new process is selected to run.

The execution of the running process is based on the sequential Prolog execution mechanism. It realizes the LRDF strategy. Control and database built-in predicates (*cut*, *assert*, etc.) are allowed which are applied in ordinary Prolog.

The process changes to the *waiting* state when a *wait_for_dnd* procedure was called and no message for the process has been sent. The *finished* state is reached when the process has resolved its initial goal. In case of a failed call or a backtrack, the process executes backtrack in the *running backward* state. If there is a choice point in the search tree of the process, then the process continues from this point in the *running forward* state. If no choice point is left, then the process changes to the *sleeping* state waiting for a new activation. The *transient waiting* state is explained in the further discussion below.

A.6.2 Mono-Transputer Scheduling

On each transputer more than one Prolog process can run in virtual parallel. A transputer can take one of the subsequent states of the processes allocated to it:

local forward — a process is on the transputer in the *running forward* state, and all the others are *waiting*, *finished*, or *sleeping*;

local backward — a process is assigned to a transputer and activated in the *running backward* state, and all the others are *waiting*, *finished*, or *sleeping*;

forced backward — a process is allocated to a transputer taking the *running backward* state, and all the others are *waiting*, *finished*, or *sleeping*;

local deadlock — all processes are in the *waiting* or *finished* state;

transient wait — one process is in the *transient waiting* state;

empty — a transputer without an assigned process.

The state transition diagram of the processes is shown by Figure A.11 including the mentioned states.

After loading a CS-Prolog program into the multi-transputer system, only the root transputer is working in *local forward*; the remaining ones are in *empty* state with no Prolog processes to be executed. The Prolog processes are allowed to the *empty* transputers by performing *new* built-in procedures on other transputers.

If transputer p_i is working in *local backward* and backtracks a *new* built-in procedure which is allocated as a process to transputer p_j, this transputer must change into the *forced backward* state if transputer p_i started a forced backtrack. If there was only one process on transputer p_j, then it takes the *empty* state, otherwise it returns to *local forward.*

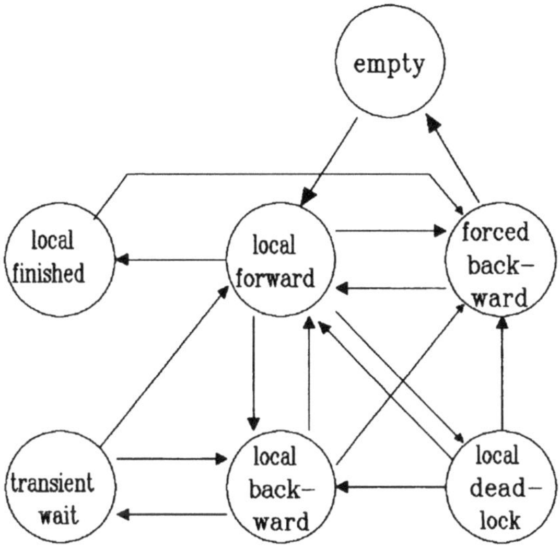

Figure A.11: State transition diagram of CS-Prolog on each transputer

In the *local deadlock* state, the transputer temporarily has no work to do because each process is either waiting for a message or has resolved its goal. When all transputers are in this state, the whole system is in *global deadlock*, where none of the processes are able to progress. In this case, a global scheduler is needed to choose for executing backtrack as was explained above. There exist two possibilities for exiting the *local deadlock* state:

- one of the *waiting* processes receives a message from another transputer. The new state will be *local forward*;
- in *global deadlock*, one of the transputer processes is selected for backtracking by the global scheduler, and the transputer changes into the *local backward* state.

A.6.3 Multi-Transputer Scheduling

The multi-transputer can take one of the following states depending on the states of the transputers:

local forward	all transputers in *local forward* or *local backward* or *forced backward*;
global backward	one transputer in *local backward* and all other in *local deadlock*;
global deadlock	all transputers in *local deadlock*;
global failed	all transputers in *empty*;
global finished	all transputers in *local finished.*

The state transition diagram is given in Figure A.12 containing the discussed states. The global scheduler performs a crucial and difficult job when *global deadlock* appears in the system. In this case, a process is selected for backtracking and the system changes into the *global backward* state. If the chosen process finds an alternative route in its search tree with a *new* or *send* built-in procedure, then the system changes into the *global forward* state. If the selected process has to undo a *new* or *send* built-in procedure, which effected another process, then the first process takes the *transient waiting* state, and the second process has to continue the backtrack. This is the *transient back* state of the system. If the chosen process cannot find any alternative route in its search tree, then the process changes into the *sleeping* state, and the global scheduler chooses another process for backtracking. If there is no further process to be chosen, then the system takes the *global failed* state, i.e., the CS-Prolog program has failed.

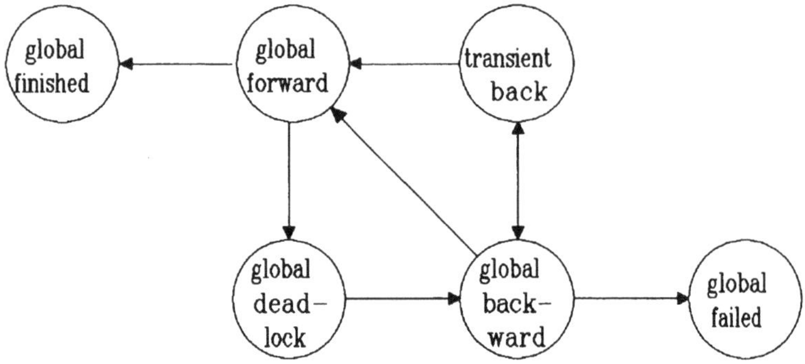

Figure A.12: State transition diagram of the multi-transputer

A.6.4 Distributed Implementation

The architecture of the underlying parallel computer to be deployed for implementing the CS-Prolog system should be provide following characteristics:

- the parallel computer system consists of a collection of transputers forming a processor network with point-to-point interconnection. The network topology is free-configurable by the user and may select topologies like trees, pipelines, cubes, etc;
- a separate memory space of at least 1 Mbyte should be provided by each transputer;
- each transputer can access only its local memory space disabling the multi-transputer supporting a shared memory system. Transputers communicate with each other by sending messages via the network.

The mono-transputer version of CS-Prolog has been written in C, so the multi-transputer version is developed in Parallel C. Subsequently, the tasks and thread concepts of Parallel C is used to describe the implementation of CS-Prolog on the underlying parallel architecture. For each transputer, an interpreter task is allocated containing:

- the whole static database of the CS-Prolog program;
- CS-Prolog interpreter thread responsible for running the CS-Prolog processes;
- stacks and registers of the CS-Prolog interpreter;
- scheduling lists;
- router thread executing the network topology-dependent tasks;
- *Message Out Table* and *Message In Table*;
- *Process Allocation Table*;
- *Topology Description Table*;
- four receiver threads;
- the message queue.

Figure A.13 illustrates the overall structure of an interpreter task representing threads through circles and data structures by rectangles. The arrows demonstrate the direction of data flow in the system. The first three elements of the interpreter task are deployed for any sequential Prolog interpreter. The scheduling lists are needed to realize the mono-transputer schedulers of CS-Prolog; they are applied even it the CS-Prolog system is implemented on mono-transputers, i.e., the same mono-transputer schedulers are used in the multi-transputer environment.

The latter six elements of the interpreter task support intertransputer communication of Prolog processes. The receiver threads place the arriving messages into the message queue. The task of the router is to check if the received messages are addressing a Prolog process on the actual transputer or if they have to be sent to another transputer.

Since the topology of the network can be changed, it is reasonable to separate the topology-dependent tasks from the others. This separation only enables the router thread to be modified in case of porting the CS-Prolog system between different multi-transputers. If a message queue is addressed to another transputer, then the *Topology Description Table* defines to which adjacent transputer the router should send the message. Similarly, the *Pro-*

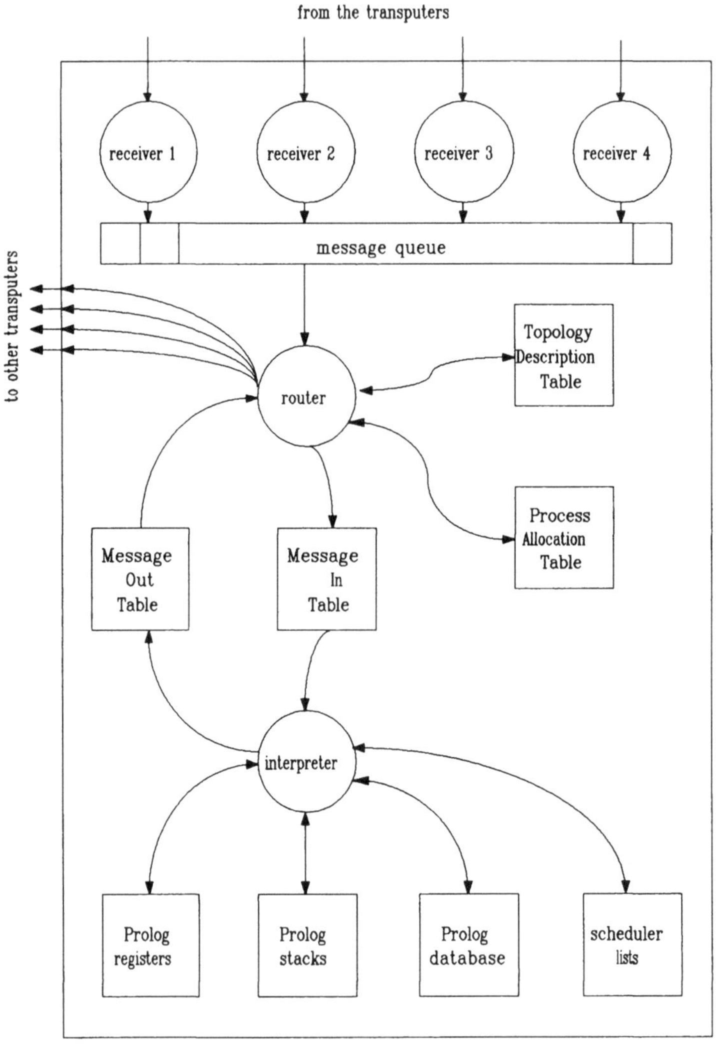

Figure A.13: Structure of the interpreter task on each transputer

cess Allocation Table supports the router to discover the destination transputers the different Prolog processes were allocated.

The transmission of a message is based on the *Message Out Table* containing the identifier of the target process which are placed there by the interpreter thread. The router composes an intertransputer message from the contents of this table and sends it to one of the adjacent transputers based on the *Process Allocation Table* and the *Topology Description Table*. The router of the target transputer the destination process is residing will place the received message of the transmitter transputer into the *Message In Table*, from where the interpreter process is able to pass to the target Prolog process.

Further information about all technical CS-Prolog features mentioned in this section can be found in [97] representing the overall system description of the CS-Prolog system also including numerous example applications with corresponding program comments.

Appendix B
The Overall Concept of the Experimental Robot Programming System

This appendix presents the concept of the logic/object-oriented robot programming environment including the present and future components which are not described in Chapter 5. The overall structure of the robot programming system is represented by means of a layered model and by Petri-nets whose theory and general principles are discussed first.

B.1 Theory of Petri-Nets

The components of the robot programming system are represented by Petri-nets, especially by predicate/transition nets [13]. Brief explanations introduce into the theory of Petri-nets describing their features and their functional behaviour. Detailed information about Petri-nets can be found in [113, 114].

B.1.1 The Characteristics of Petri-Nets

Petri-nets consist of transitions, places, and edges connecting transitions and places. Activities are represented in Petri-nets by a transition (marked with a T) and liabilities by a place (marked with a S). The places include token as pre- and postconditions. The graphical presentation of a transition is given by a rectangle and the depiction of a place by an arc. Transitions and places are numbered consecutively.

Petri-nets offer the possibility of refinement [114]. Refining means to replace a transition or a place by a complete net of transitions and places so that the original state of the complete net will not be changed. Such refinements are marked by a dotted line and denoted as a usual element of the net. Figure B.1 shows a typical example of a refinement.

The new refined net elements are also numbered consecutively ($T_i, S_i, i \in \mathbb{N}$). Using the expressions of the refinements in a documentation, the original terms are extended by the new transition or place expression separated by a dot, e.g. $(T1.T1)$ or $(T1.S1)$. Section B.3 of this chapter includes the Petri-net structure of the introduced experimental robot programming system depicting the methodology of refinement by means of a greater example.

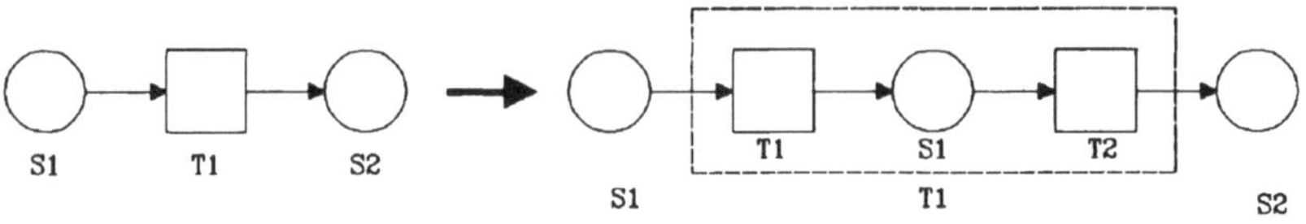

Figure B.1: Example of transition (T_1) refinement

B.1.2 The Functionality of Petri-Nets

The token of the places depict pre- and postconditions, i.e., if the precondition of a state transmission is met, the transition is activated (fired) and a new output state is created. Figure B.2 illustrates this process.

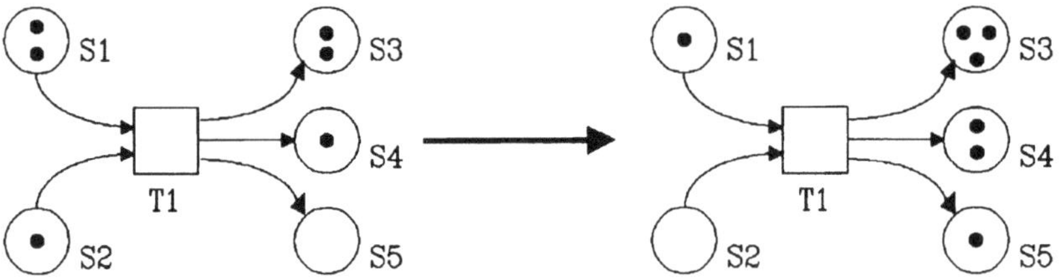

Figure B.2: Activating of transition (T_1)

The places $S1$ and $S2$ include tokens and meet the conditions for an activating of transition $T1$ changing the number of tokens. A further activating of the transition is impossible since the precondition is not met, i.e., the place $S2$ is token-free.

The further discussion about the robot programming system is based on representations using predicate/transition nets. The special properties of this net type are explained in the following.

B.1.3 Special Petri-Nets: Predicate/Transition Nets

Predicate/transition nets (PrT) are particular Petri-nets. In contrast to the general net features described above, predicate/transition nets use tokens as information-related objects, i.e., the places (or better called predicates and predicate places, respectively) include tokens representing different entities. After firing a transition, the output predicates contain tokens whose type is variable and specified by means of logical expressions. These expressions also define which and how many tokens flow from an input predicate to the output predicates. Figure B.3 illustrates this procedure.

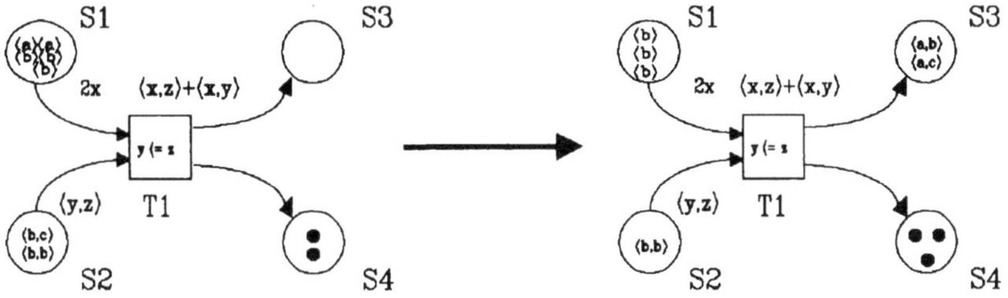

Figure B.3: Activating of (T_1) of a PrT

A PrT can be formally described as a triple $P = \langle S, T, F \rangle$ with:

- S limited set of input/output predicates;
- T limited set of transitions;
- F flow direction.

In consideration of these definitions, following rules are valid:

1. $S \cap T = \phi$
2. $S \cup T \neq \phi$
3. $F \subset S\ x\ T \cup T\ x\ S$
4. $dom(F) \cup ran(F) = S \cup T =: X$

- Rule 1 defines that the sets S and the sets T have no common element, i.e., a predicate cannot be a transition at the same time and vice versa;
- Rule 2 excludes that the union set of S and T is an empty set, i.e., at least, one predicate and one transition exists;
- Rule 3 ensures that edges only connect different elements, i.e. it is impossible that two transitions or two predicates are connected;
- Rule 4 ensures the vitality of the Petri-net and the exclusion of isolated elements.

Figure B.3 shows a predicate/transition net consisting of the predicates $(S1, S2, S3, S4)$. The predicate $(S1)$ includes tokens of the type a and b. $(S2)$ includes tuples of tokens of the elements b and c. The logical expression $y \leq z$ of the transition $(T1)$ specifies its firing condition. After its activation, the output predicate $(S3)$ contains the tuples $\langle a, b \rangle$ and $\langle a, c \rangle$ depending on the functions given on the edges. The output predicate $(S4)$ contains general, non-specified tokens. The firing of the transition increments the tokens by one.

B.2 The Hierarchical Structure of the Model

The robot programming environment with its various functions for robot controlling leads to a hierarchical architecture consisting of the function layer (FL) and the knowledge layer (KL). Figure B.4 shows the model of the programming system. In the following, the layers are briefly surveyed and the functions are represented by Petri-nets.

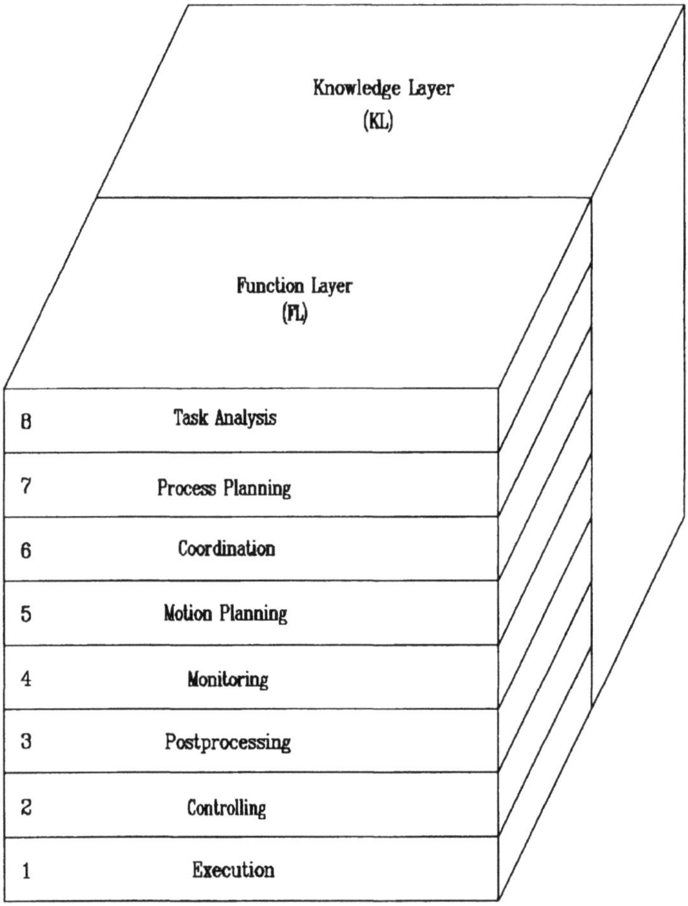

Figure B.4: Architecture of the programming model

B.2.1 The KL

The KL represents an object-oriented database and provides geometrical and machine-specific information about the robots, the working cell, and periphery equipments. These data are used by the routines of the FL. Further, the static data of the KL are deployed for modelling a dynamical environment, the dynamical world model. A dynamical world model describes the current state of the robot working cell and supports e.g. time-dependent manufacturing processes within this environment. The dynamical world model consists of:

- the robot model generation ($T1.T1$);
- the periphery model generation ($T1.T2$);
- the cell layout generation ($T1.T3$).

The data of these models support the creation of the world model ($T1.T4$).

B.2.2 The FL

The FL includes following routines for robot controlling:

- task analysis [83];
- process planning [40, 48];
- (multi-robot) coordination [3];
- motion planning [122];
- monitoring;
- preprocessing.

The lowest layers present hardware-oriented functions like the joint controlling and the robot instruction code interpreter (postprocessor). These functions are not realized by the programming system. They are given by the drive units of the robots. However, a bi-directional data transfer is possible between the drive units and the programming system.

The Task Analysis

The input of the task analysis ($T2$) [12] consists of an abstract task description of a final handling state (e.g. assemble the car) that is given by the user. In consideration of this input, the task analysis has to plan the task, i.e., to generate the necessary robot activities transferring the initial state into the final state. The created robot activities are similar to a robot program written by a programmer. To translate the abstract task descriptions, the task analysis needs information about form, size, and orientation of the involved objects. This information is provided by the environment model and the dynamical environment model.

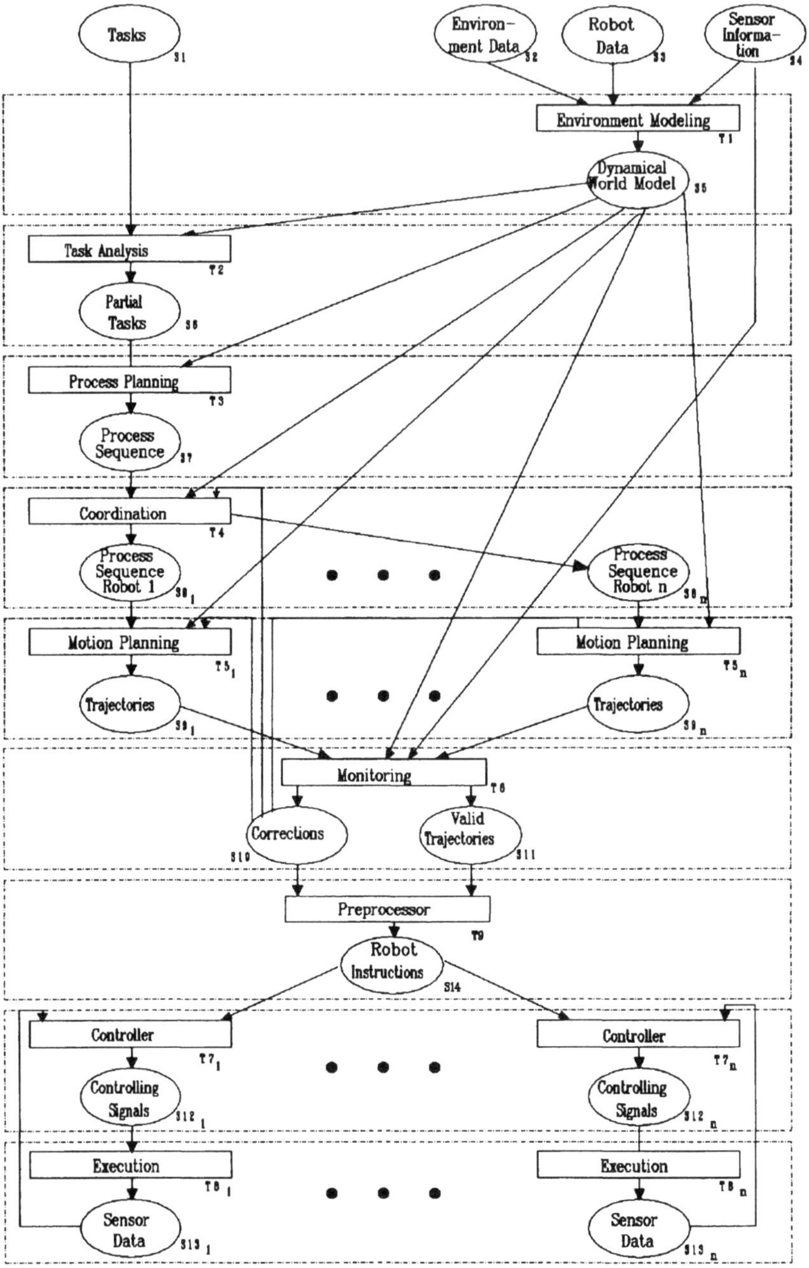

Figure B.5: Petri-net of the overall concept

Figure B.6 shows the Petri-net of the environment modelling component as a refinement of the transition (T1).

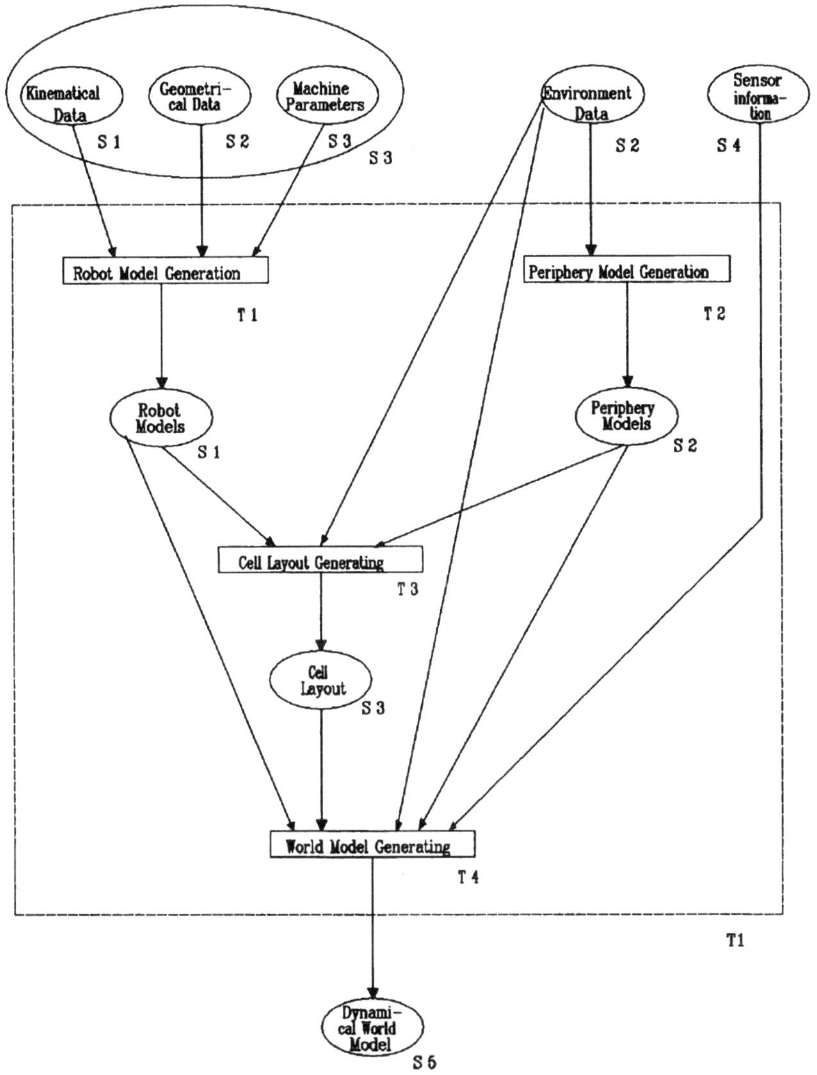

Figure B.6: Environment modelling

The Process Planning

After generating the partial tasks, the process sequence ($S7$) is planned, i.e., the process sequence of the partial tasks is determined in order to solve the given robot task by a meaningful sequence of robot operations considering dependencies and conditions like [48]:

- assembly restriction according to penetration. The assembly restrictions regarding penetrations mean that an assembly component is able to penetrate another assembly component. As a typical example, the assembly of a cover sheet can be considered. It has to be ensured that the cover sheet is being assembled after the component that should be covered;
- precedence constraints. Precedence constraints influence the execution of robot operations through precedence constraints, i.e., the proceeding robot operation must be finished before the following can be started;
- robustness requirements. An assembly process has to exclude side effects, i.e., an assembly step must not change or distroy a previous assembly step by slipping or overthrow of assembly components.

The Coordination

The coordinator ($T4$) distributes the process sequences onto -if existing- n manipulators of the robot system and organizes their speed and timing.

If only one robot exits ($n = 1$) or the execution of the robot operations can only be done by one robot, the assignment of the partial tasks and their process sequence is trivial. In case of more manipulators executing the operations concurrently, an assignment of these operations to the robots can be supported by different strategies (e.g. load balancing of the robots, maximal throughput, etc.). Detailed information can be found in [48].

The Motion Planning

The motion planning [122] is a part of the planning unit determining the trajectories of the robot arm. The motions planning distinguishes:

- free motions;
- monitored motions;
- fine motions;
- gripping planning.

The free motion is characterized by missing of any monitoring, i.e., it is guaranteed that neither the arm nor the gripped object collide with barriers in the working cell. Thus, no sensor operation is necessary during the execution of a free motion.

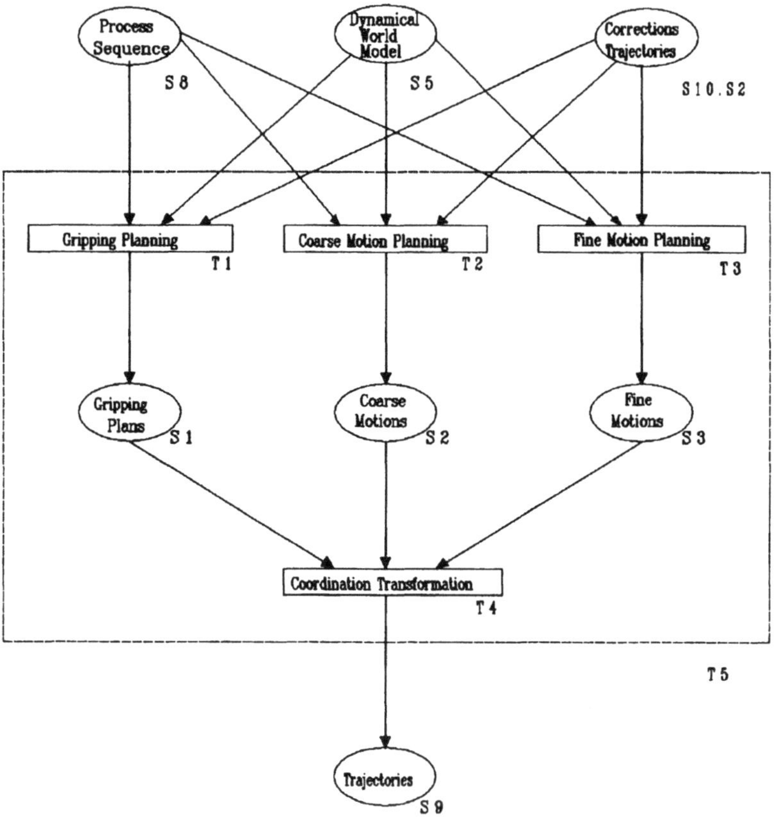

Figure B.7: Motion planning

While the realization of the first motion type is based on computations the monitored motion cannot be computed by a given geometrical model. It is controlled by sensors information of the robot working cell. To obtain this information, force and torque sensors assemblied in the robot's hand are mainly used. An important problem is the inaccuracy of the arm and the joints. For reaching a final position, frequently a strategy of monitored and fine motion is applied.

The fine motion is characterized by a constant contact between the manipulating object and other objects like workpieces, i.e., the robot arm is controlled by a guide-way representing a defined object contact.

The motion planning ($T5$) is executed after the robot coordination ($T4$), i.e., after assignment of the process sequences to several robots. This component includes functions for coarse motion planning ($T5.T2$) -this is a free motion-, for fine motion planning ($T5.T3$) and for gripping planning ($T5.T1$). The input of the motion and gripping planning consists of the process sequences, the data of the dynamical world model ($S5$), and the (off-line determined) trajectory corrections ($S10.S2$). These data determine the coarse motion and fine motion planning for each of the n robots. The output data of the three planning components (gripping plans ($T5.S1$), coarse motions ($T5.S2$), and fine motions ($T5.S3$)) are passed to the coordination transformation ($T5.T4$). The gripping planning ($T5.T4$) solves the problem how a stable grip between the workpiece and the robot's gripper can be realized. This problem is relatively complex because of some conditions which have to be met:

- the grip has to be determined in that way that no other object or workpiece in the working cell can be touched. Thus, the grip is dependent on the geometry of the gripper and the environment of the workpiece in the initial and final position.
- the grip has to be stable, i.e., the risk of slipping or release of the workpiece should be minimal. The risk is dependent on the type of the gripper spaces, on the gravity center of the workpiece, and on some physical factors like mass and rubbing between gripper space and workpiece. For realizing of a stable grip, the gripping force has to be determined in order to ensure that the force and torque the workpiece is setting out in a later action cannot affect its stability;
- special parts and workpieces have areas that need not be touched by a gripper. To guarantee this, the gripping planner has to consider the protected areas. The information about these areas is provided by the environment model.

The Monitoring

The monitoring includes online-monitoring routines ($T6.T1$) and offline-checking components ($T6.T2$).

The input of these routines are the trajectories ($S9$), the sensor information ($S4$), and the data of the dynamic world model ($S5$).

The output of the online-monitoring consists of the sensor data ($S10.S1$) and the online trajectory corrections ($S10.S2$). The output of the offline-checking component consists of the offline-trajectory corrections ($S10.S3$), the restrictions of robot coordination ($S10.S4$), and the valid trajectories ($S11$).

The refinements of the online-monitoring results in the sensor controlling ($T6.T1.T1$) and the collision detection ($T6.T1.T2$). The integration of sensors into the robot programming environment requires functions for sensor controlling and for reading and evaluating of sensor information. The sensor controlling component can be refined in the sensor data preprocessing ($T6.T1.T1.T1$), the sensor data analysis ($T6.T1.T1.T3$), and the sensor data diagnosis ($T6.T1.T1.T3$).

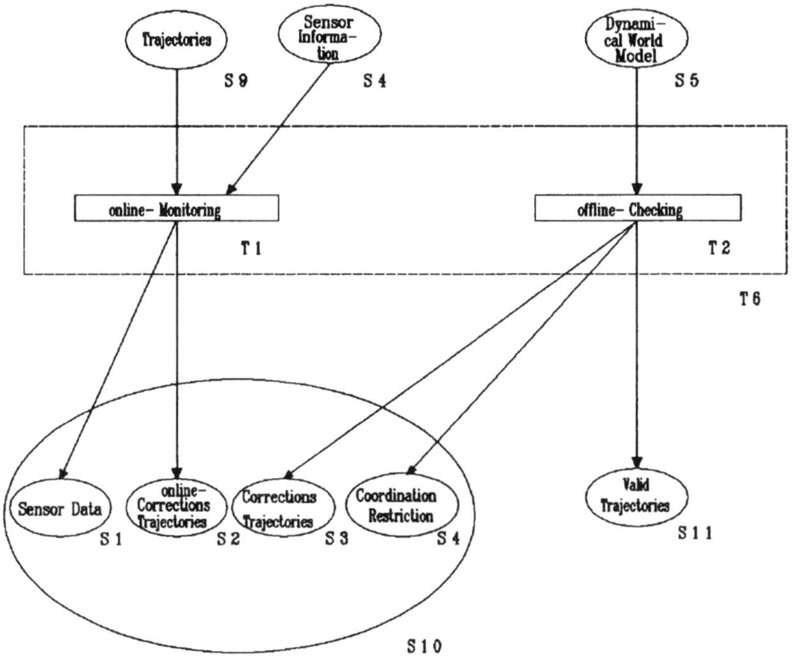

Figure B.8: The monitoring component

The sensor data preprocessing reads the sensor information generated by the sensor and executes the sensor data preprocessing. The preprocessed sensor data ($T6.T1.T1.S1$) are passed to the sensor data analysis ($T6.T1.T1.T2$) that validates the received data on errors.

At first, this component converts the preprocessed data into sensor patterns ($T6.T1.T1.S2$). The correctness of the sensor data is proved by a comparison of the sensor patterns with the sensor patterns of the world model. If the comparison fails, the error handling routine ($T6.T1.T1.T4$) is activated.

In case of non-object identifying sensors like light barriers or tactile sensors, the sensor information is assigned to the corresponding sensor, like *Light_Barrier_1*. In the next step, the sensor pattern are passed to the sensor data diagnosis ($T6.T1.T1.T3$). The diagnosis checks whether the expected object could be identified. If an unexpected object has been identified, a further error handling routine ($T6.T1.T1.T5$) is called.

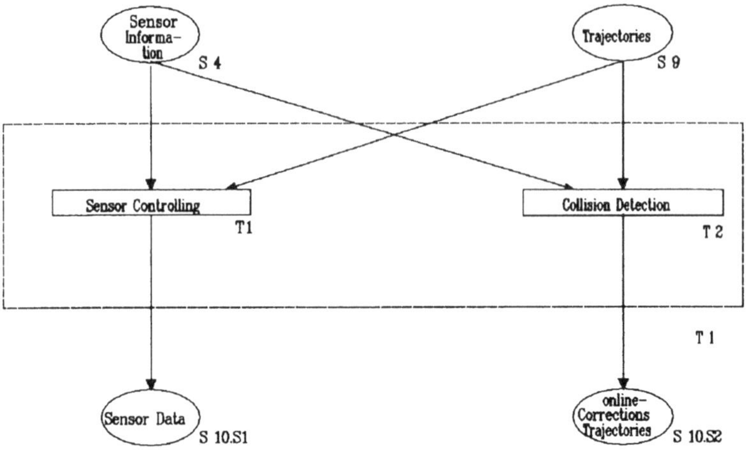

Figure B.9: Refinement of online-monitoring

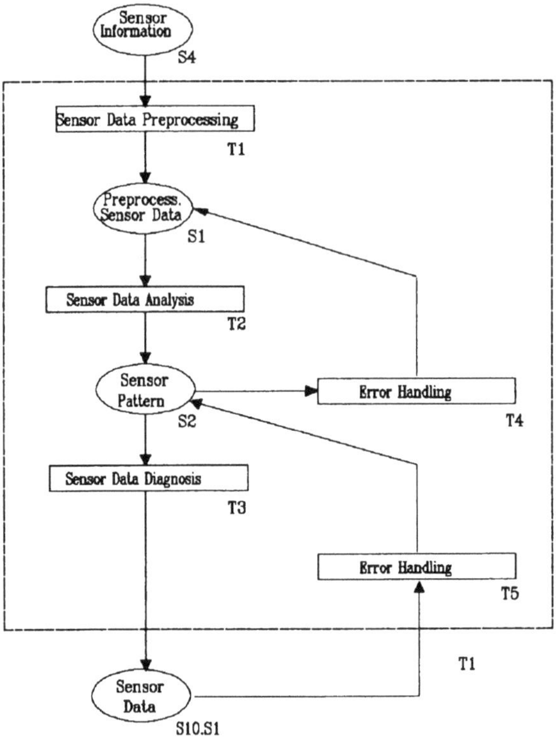

Figure B.10: Refinement of sensor controlling

The Postprocessor

The postprocessor ($T9$) translates the robot commands into the robot instruction language which is comparable with an assembler of a microprocessor. The translated robot instructions are sent to the drive units and interpreted by the robot instruction interface (postprocessor).

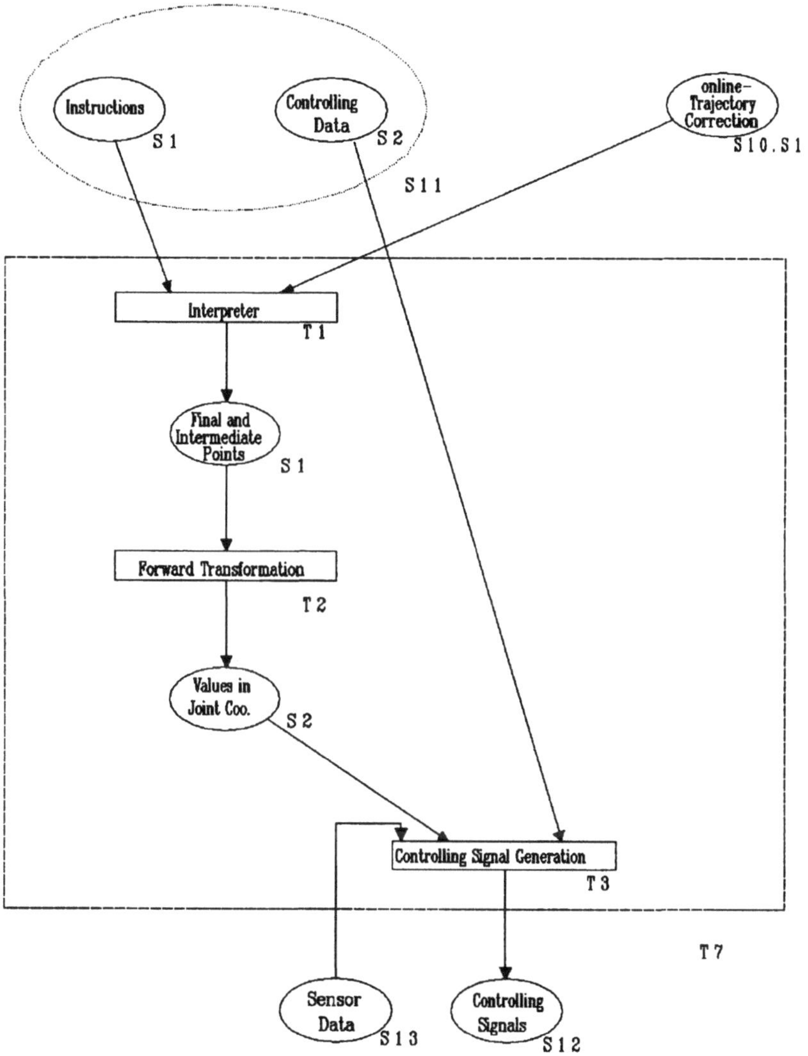

Figure B.11: Robot controlling

The Controlling Functions

The controlling layer includes components for robot controlling ($T7$). At present, the robot controlling is achieved by the drive unit of the manufacturer.

Each robot has its own drive unit. The drive unit interprets the instructions by means of the postprocessor. Typical inputs of the postprocessor for robot controlling are the trajectories and instructions like gripper or I/O-commands. The interpreter ($T7.T1$) generates intermediate and final points ($T7.S1$) of a path. The forward transformation ($T7.T2$) creates values in joint coordinates ($T7.S2$) for controlling the axes of the robots. This process is supported through the values of the internal sensors. These sensors are assembled closed to the joint motors of the axes.

The Execution Functions

The execution layer ($T8$) is also realized by the hardware of the robot system and generates the controlling signals ($S12$) for the joint motors. Further, the internal sensor signals ($S13$) are evaluated by corresponding hardware and returned to the controlling component. The data of these sensors are not accessible by the user.

B.3 The Petri-Net Structure of the Model

T1 Environmental modeling

T1.T1 Robot model generation
T1.T2 Periphery model generation
T1.T3 Cell layout generation
T1.T4 Generating of the world model
T1.S1 Robot models
T1.S2 Periphery models
T1.S3 Working cell layout

T2 Task analysis

T3 Process planning

T4 (Multi robot) coordination

T5 Motion planning

T5.T1 Gripping planning

T5.T2 Coarse motion planning
T5.T3 Fine motion planning
T5.T4 Coordinate transformation
T5.S1 Gripping plans
T5.S2 Coarse motions
T5.S3 Fine motions

T6 Monitoring

T6.T1 online-monitoring
T6.T2 offline-checking

T7 Controlling

T7.T1 Interpreter
T7.T2 Forward transformation
T7.T3 Controlling signal generation
T7.S1 Final and intermediate points
T7.S2 Values in joint coordinates

S1 Handling tasks

S2 Environmental data

S3 Robot data

S3.S1 Kinematical data
S3.S2 Geometrical data
S3.S3 Machine parameters

S4 Sensor information

S5 Dynamical world model

S6 Partial tasks

S7 Process sequence

S8 Process sequence of robot x

S9 Trajectories

S10 Corrections

S10.S1 Online trajectory corrections

S10.S2 Offline trajectory corrections
S10.S3 Coordination restrictions

S11 valid trajectories

S11.S1 Instructions
S11.S2 Controlling data

S12 Controlling signals

S13 Sensor data

Appendix C
A Formal Representation of the Experimental Programming Environment

C.1 Survey of Methods for Robot and Sensor Control

This section surveys the implemented methods for robot and sensor control. Note that the upper and lower bounds of the technical data of the robot system can be found in [95, 99]. The methods are classified in:

- universal methods;
- methods for general status checks and position manipulations;
- special position manipulations;
- basic robot operations;
- methods for setting tool options;
- methods for setting robot motion options;
- methods enabling different robot motions;
- methods realizing gripper operations;
- manipulation of internal register and counter;
- general sensor services;
- conversion of sensor data;
- list manipulation for sensor data processing;
- sensor data processing combined with robot manipulation;
- complex handling tasks;
- manipulation of external digital in- and outputs.

Universal methods of the root class are inherited to all subclasses realizing basic operations such as:

reset	resets the drive units and the warning lights
write_robot(< S >)	realizes the data transfer between the robot programming system and the connected equipment. The data S may be a string or an integer or a real
set_val(< S >)	unifies an instance variable with a specified value
get_val(< S >)	returns a value of an instance variable
read_robot	reads the coordinates of the current robot position
create(< $Ins, Port$ >)	creates an instance of an object and assigns a port for data transfer

The following methods enable general status checks and position manipulations:

test_pos_nr	tests the scope of the specified position number
test_grip_stat	checks the gripper status
save_pos(< P, C >)	saves a position P under the corresponding coordinates C
define_pos(< P, C >)	defines the absolute coordinates (position and angle) C of a specified position P
increment	moves the robot to a predefined position with a position number greater than the current one
decrement	moves the robot to a predefined position with a position number smaller than the current one

The methods below inherit all methods above and provide various arm motions:

clear_pos(< $P_1, \ldots, P_n$ >)

clears the position data of specified position number or numbers $P_1, \ldots, P_n$

transfer_pos($< P_1, P_2 >$)

assigns the coordinates of a given position P_1 to another specified position P_2

exchange_pos($< P_1, P_2 >$)

exchanges the coordinates of a given position P_1 with the coordinates of another specified position P_2

add_pos($< P_1, P_2 >$) shifts the coordinates of position P_1 in increments representing the coordinates of position P_2 and redefines the new coordinates

The methods below realize movements and definitions of a specified reference position in the Cartesian coordinate system:

define_home establishes the reference position in Cartesian coordinates

move_home moves the robot arm to the reference position

move_nest returns the robot arm to mechanical origin

The ensuing methods consider a gripped tool for the motions:

set_tool($< L >$) establishes the tool length L, i.e., the distance between the hand mounting surface and the end of the hand

move_tool($< P, L, G >$) moves the end of the hand from the current position to position P considering the tool length L and the gripper status G (open/closed)

The following methods influence the robot movements:

set_speed($< I, A >$) sets the operating velocity, acceleration, and deceleration time for a robot

set_timer($< I >$) interrupts the motion for a specified period of time

The different robot motions are materialized through the methods:

move moves the robot to a destination specified by the instance variable *pos_nr*

relativ($< X, Y, Z >$) moves the end of the gripper to a position away from the current one covering the distance given in x-, y-, and z-axis direction

$move\_approach(< P_1, P_2, G >)$

moves the gripper from the current position to position P_1 in increments as specified in position P_2 in increments considering the gripper status

$move\_to(< P, G >)$ moves the hand to position P in consideration of the gripper status

$move\_continuous(< P_1, P_2 >)$

moves the robot arm continuously through the predefined intermediate points between the two specified positions P_1 and P_2

$move\_joint(< C >)$ turns each joint the specified coordinates C (angles) from the current position

$move_absolute(< C >)$moves the end of the effector to a position whose coordinates (position and angle) are specified

$move\_straight(< P, N, G >)$

moves the robot to a specified position through the given number of intermediate points on a straight line

Gripper operations support following methods:

open opens the gripper

close closes the gripper

$pressure(< SF, RF, SFR >)$

defines the starting gripping force SF, retained gripping force RF, starting gripping force retention time SFR to be applied when the motor-operated hand is closed and opened

$flag(< F >)$ defines the open/close state of the grip of the hand

The manipulation of internal register and counter of the drive unit permit the methods:

$comp\_counter(< I >)$ loads the value $(1 \leq I \leq 99)$ of a specified counter into the internal comparison register *decr_counter*(< I >) subtracts 1 from the value in a specified counter

incr_counter(< I >) increments the value of a specified counter by 1

set_counter(< I, V >) loads a value $V, (-32768 \leq V \leq 32767)$ into a specified counter

The following methods provide more complex robot operations:

pallet(< N, Cl, R >) defines the number of grid points in the column and row directions for a specified pallet. The method additionally computes the coordinates of a grid point on the pallet and identifies the coordinates as the position number corresponding to the specified pallet. In order to execute this method, the grid points at four corners of the pallet must be properly defined (e.g. by teaching). The pallet counters for column and row must be properly set specifying a particular grid point on the pallet

transfer(< P_1, P_2, P_3 >)

transports a part or workpiece from the position P_1 through an intermediate position (reference position) P_2 to the destination position P_3 by means of an instance of the class "arm"

The sensor manipulations are based on methods reading and evaluating sensor data. The following methods provide general sensor services such as RS232 data transfer and the initialization and error detection.

write_to_sensor(< C >)

writes data to a sensor

get_data reads asynchronously sensor data returned by a sensor that is connected to a port and specified by the instance variable *interface*

test_error(< D >) checks the received sensor data D on errors

write_code(< Π, V >) transmits the value V to the specified port Π

read_code(< Π, V >) realizes the synchronous transfer of the value V which are received at port Π

$if\_code\_then(< L >)$ enables a predefined robot operation if the expected sensor data (treated as a label L) could received

$if\_not\_code\_then(< L >)$

causes the predefined robot operation if the expected sensor data (treated as a label L) could not be returned

$if\_not\_code\_then\_else(< L_1, L_2 >)$

executes the predefined robot activity marked by the label L_1 if the sensor data D_1 could be returned else the activity marked by the label L_2 will be performed

The methods below convert sensor data into object-describing expressions:

$convert\_code$ transforms the sensor data passed by the instance variable *term*

$convert\_part$ determine special characteristics of an object evaluating the received sensor data

List manipulations for sensor data evaluation is materialized through the methods:

$append\_l(< V >)$ appends a value V to the list *list* given as class variable

$delete(< V >)$ deletes the value V from the list *list*

$search\_for(< V, N >)$ searchs the *list* for the value V

$new\_element(< V, E >)$

creates a new element of a data base of the class "control_list". The entry E is assigned to the new instance

$save\_database$ saves the data base of "control_list" using the instance variable *file*

The following more complex sensor-based robot statements consist of methods for sensor data processing and methods for robot manipulation:

take_defined($< S, R, P_1, P_2, P_3 >$)

causes a robot to transport a programmer-specified object from position P_1 through the intermediate position P_2 to the destination P_3. This statement fails if the sensor S cannot identify the expected object

take_or_store($< S, R, P_1, P_R, P_A >$)

causes the same robot activities as in the previous statement only distinguishing the fail handling, i.e., if the expected object cannot be identified the robot transports the object through the reference position P_R to depot P_A to be manipulated in a later operation

The following instructions manipulate digital in- and outputs of the robot drive units as well as control a critical section within a common working area:

activate_output($< V >$) sets the output specified by value $V, 0 \leq V \leq 15$, to logical 1

desactivate_output($< V >$)

resets the output specified by value $V, 0 \leq V \leq 15$, to logical 0

critical_section($< N >$) specifies a common robot working area to be a critical section denoted by the name N

lock_sec($< N >$) locks a critical section denoted by N

unlock_sec($< N >$) unlocks a critical section denoted by N

C.2 Syntax Diagrams

In the following the syntax diagrams of the presented methods are given.

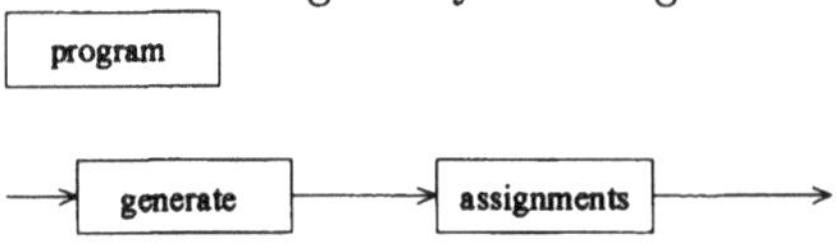

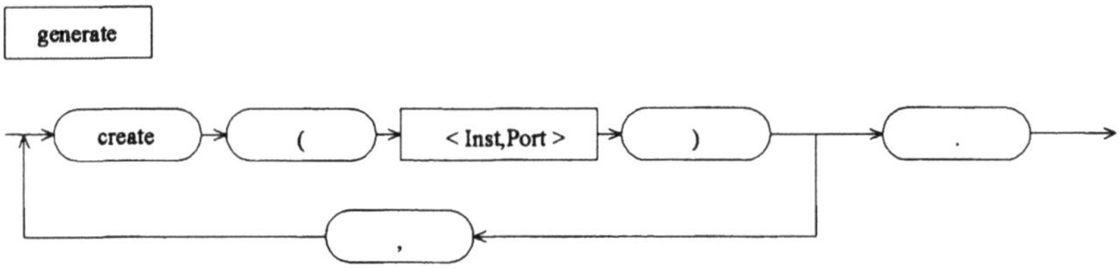

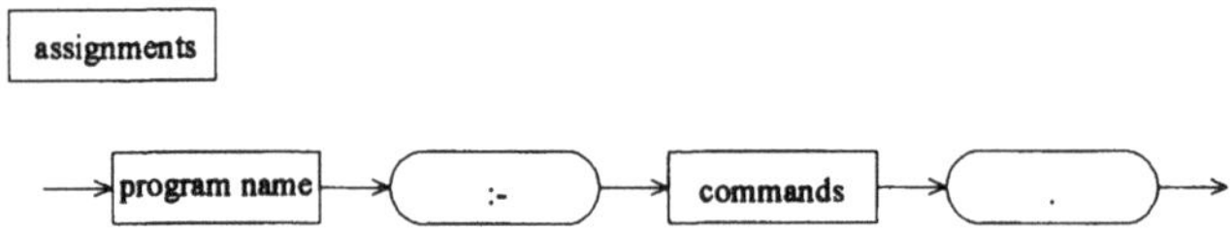

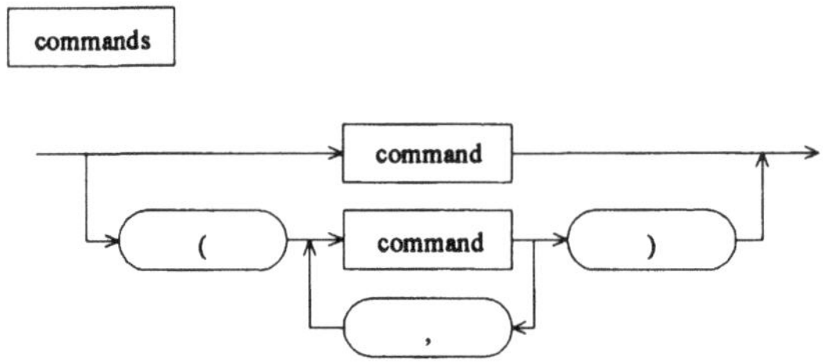

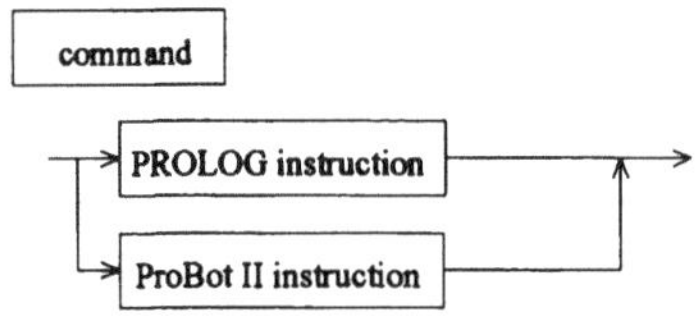

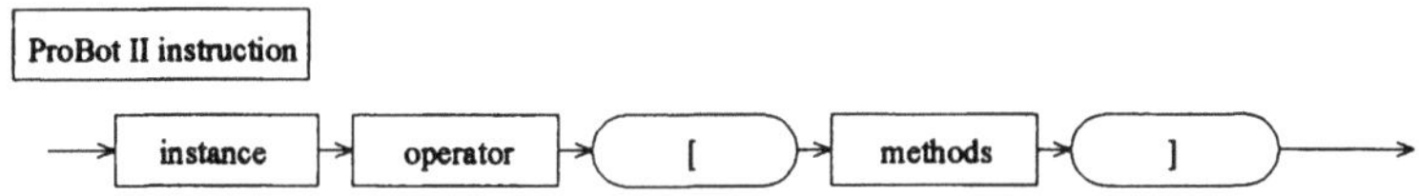

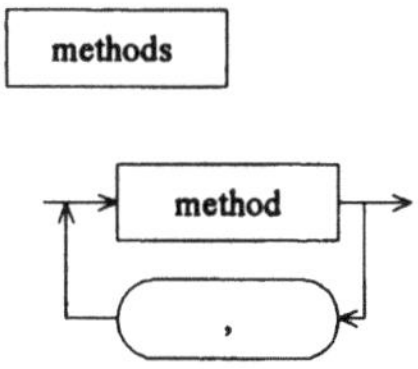

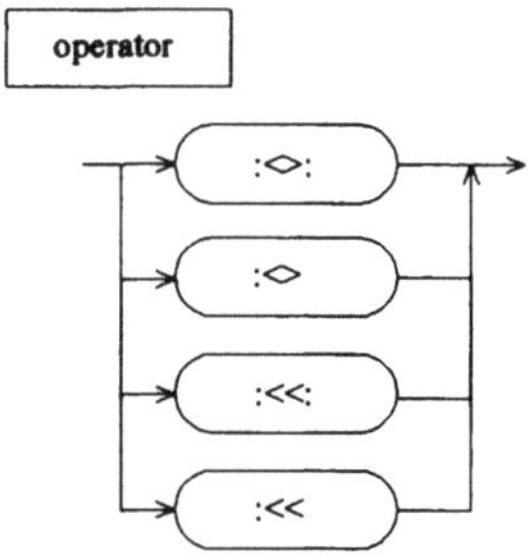

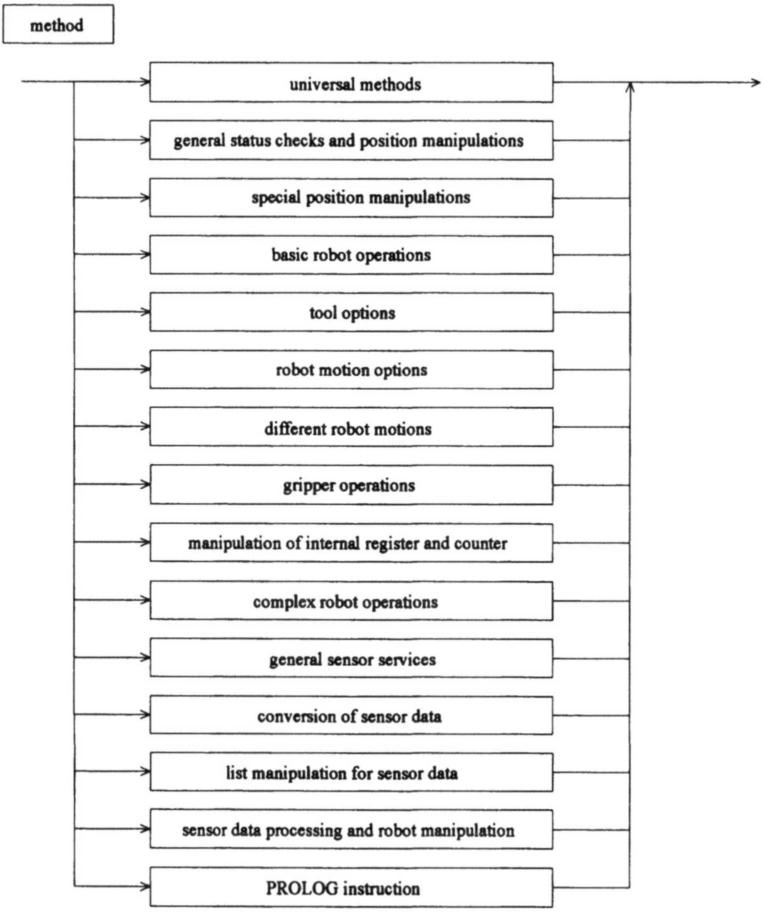

The representation concentrates on the object-oriented system; the syntax of Prolog is omitted and can be found in the referenced literature.

universal methods

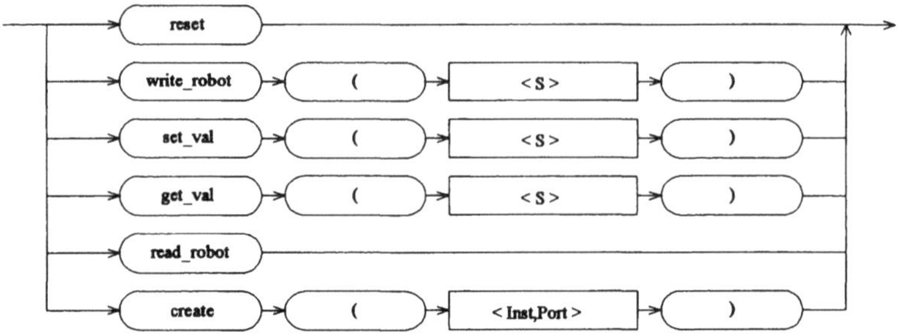

general status checks and position manipulations

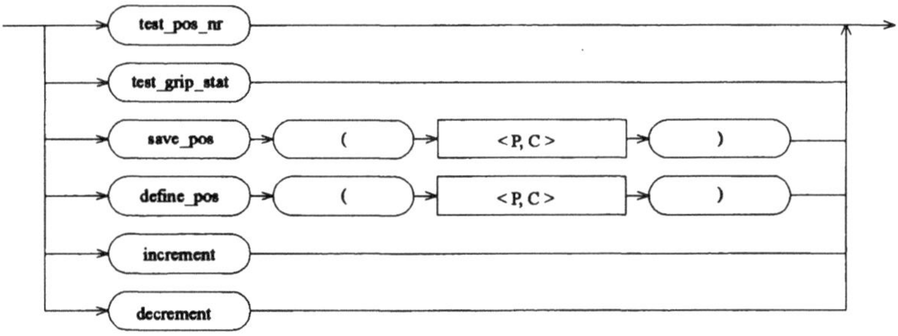

special position manipulations

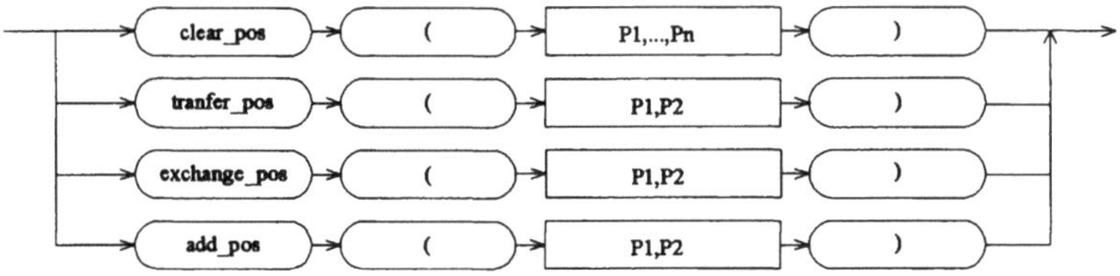

basic robot operations

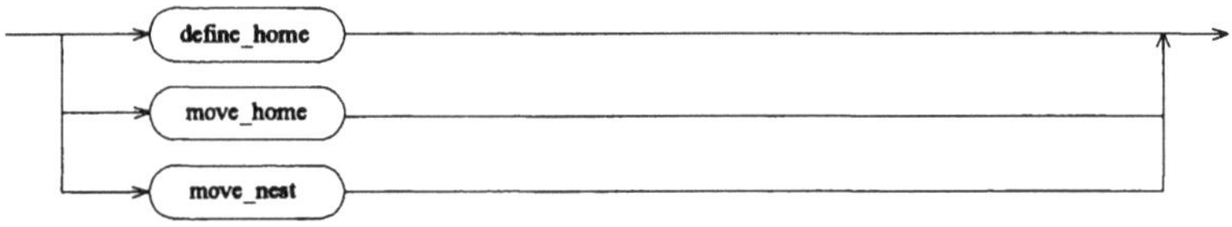

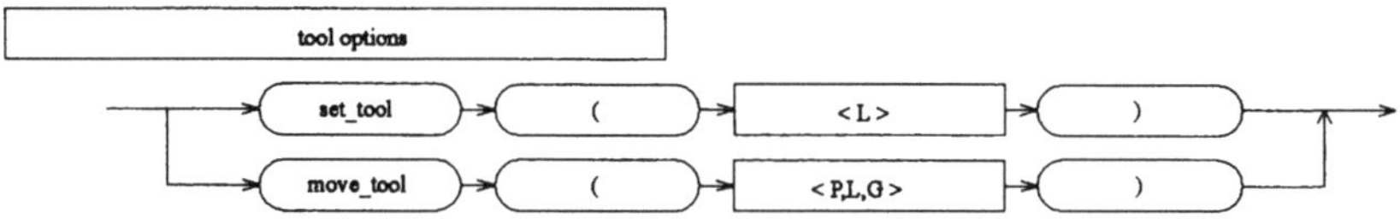
tool options
set_tool
(
< L >
)
move_tool
(
< P,L,G >
)

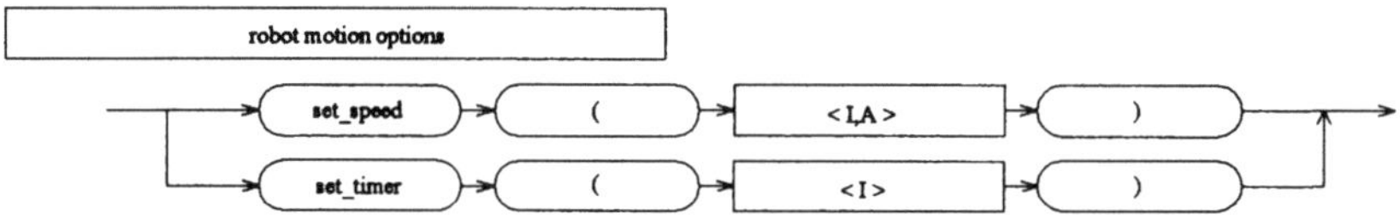
robot motion options
set_speed
(
< I,A >
)
set_timer
(
< I >
)

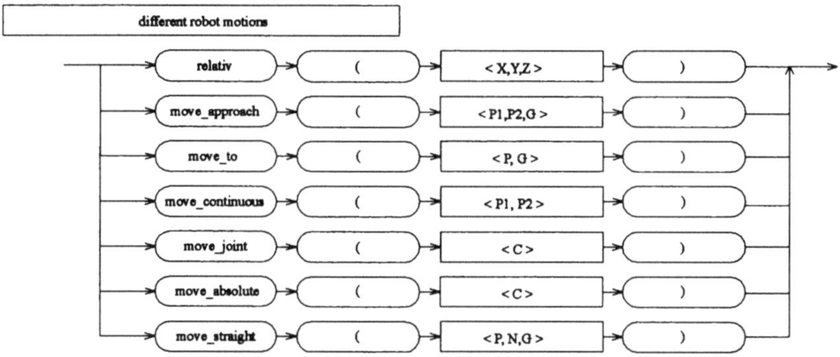
different robot motions
relativ
(
< X,Y,Z >
)
move_approach
(
< P1,P2,G >
)
move_to
(
< P, G >
)
move_continuous
(
< P1, P2 >
)
move_joint
(
< C >
)
move_absolute
(
< C >
)
move_straight
(
< P, N,G >
)

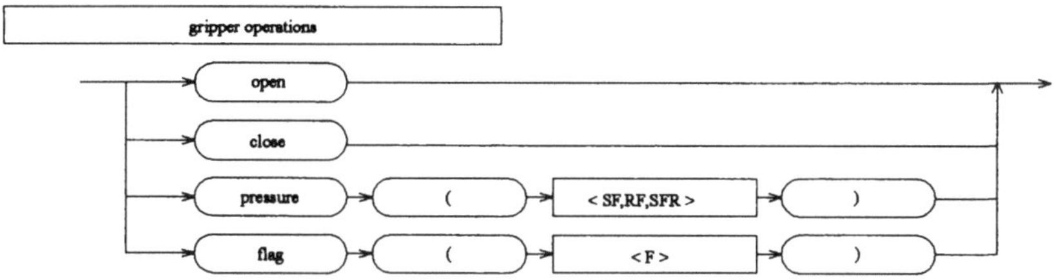
gripper operations
open
close
pressure
(
< SF,RF,SFR >
)
flag
(
< F >
)

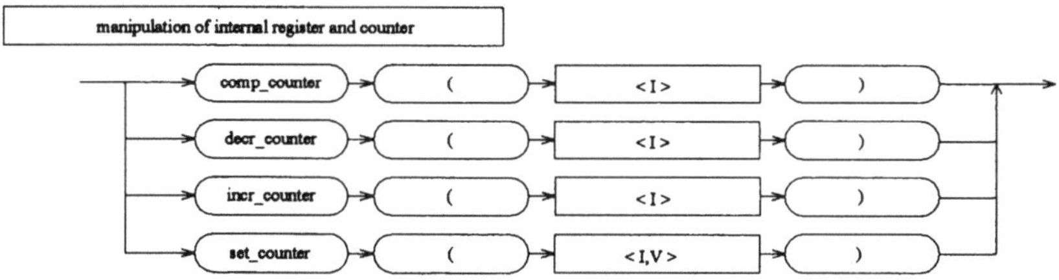
manipulation of internal register and counter
comp_counter
(
< I >
)
decr_counter
(
< I >
)
incr_counter
(
< I >
)
set_counter
(
< I,V >
)

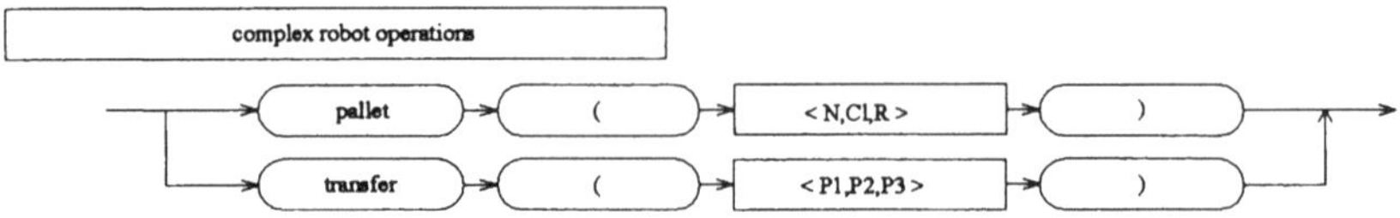
complex robot operations
pallet
(
< N,Cl,R >
)
transfer
(
< P1,P2,P3 >
)

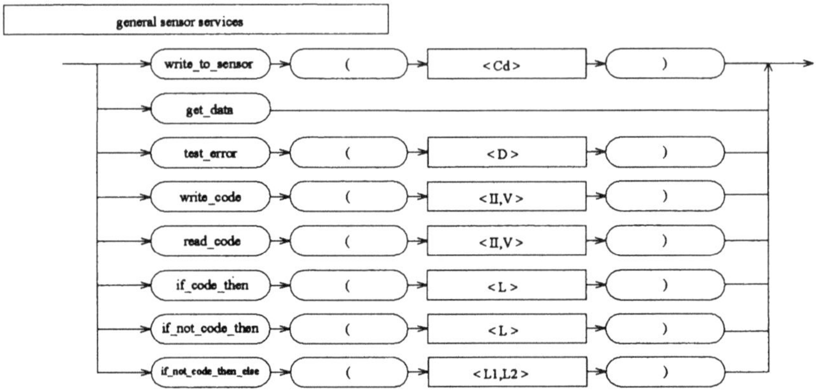
general sensor services
write_to_sensor
(
< Cd >
)
get_data
test_error
(
< D >
)
write_code
(
< II,V >
)
read_code
(
< II,V >
)
if_code_then
(
< L >
)
if_not_code_then
(
< L >
)
if_not_code_then_else
(
< L1,L2 >
)

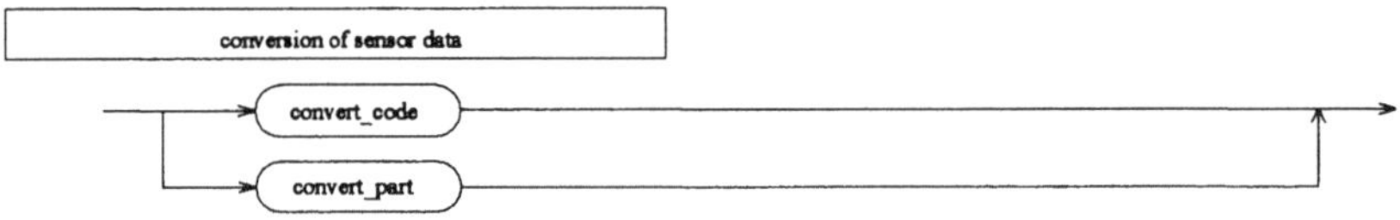
conversion of sensor data
convert_code
convert_part

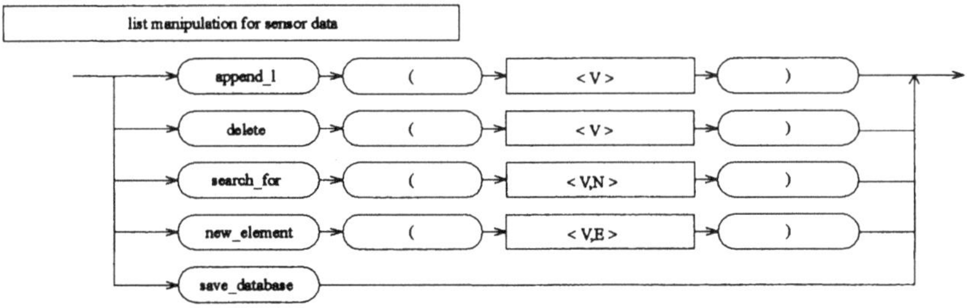
list manipulation for sensor data
append_l
(
< V >
)
delete
(
< V >
)
search_for
(
< V,N >
)
new_element
(
< V,E >
)
save_database

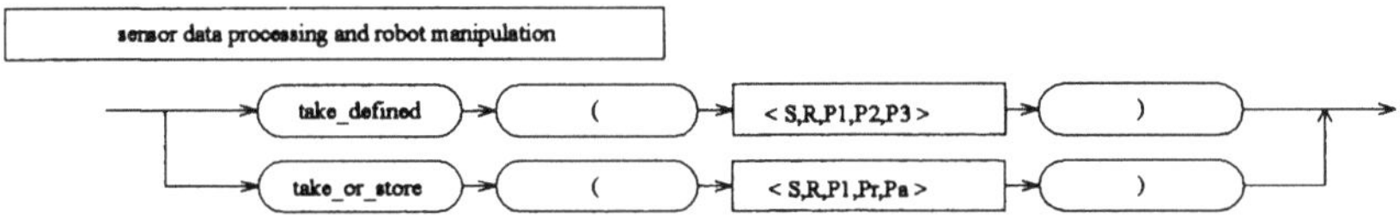
sensor data processing and robot manipulation
take_defined
(
< S,R,P1,P2,P3 >
)
take_or_store
(
< S,R,P1,Pr,Pa >
)

Index